Global Emissions Trading

NEW HORIZONS IN ENVIRONMENTAL ECONOMICS

General Editors: Wallace E. Oates, *Professor of Economics, University of Maryland, USA* and Henk Folmer, *Professor of General Economics, Wageningen University and Professor of Environmental Economics, Tilburg University, The Netherlands*

This important series is designed to make a significant contribution to the development of the principles and practices of environmental economics. It includes both theoretical and empirical work. International in scope, it addresses issues of current and future concern in both East and West and in developed and developing countries.

The main purpose of the series is to create a forum for the publication of high quality work and to show how economic analysis can make a contribution to understanding and resolving the environmental problems confronting the world in the twenty-first century.

Recent titles in the series include:

Principles of Environmental and Resource Economics
A Guide for Students and Decision-Makers
Second Edition
Edited by Henk Folmer and H. Landis Gabel

Designing International Environmental Agreements
Incentive Compatible Strategies for Cost-Effective Cooperation
Carsten Schmidt

Spatial Environmental and Resource Economics
The Selected Essays of Charles D. Kolstad
Charles D. Kolstad

Economic Theories of International Environmental Cooperation
Carsten Helm

Negotiating Environmental Quality
Policy Implementation in Germany and the United States
Markus A. Lehmann

Game Theory and International Environmental Cooperation
Michael Finus

Sustainable Small-scale Forestry
Socio-economic Analysis and Policy
Edited by S.R. Harrison, J.L. Herbohn and K.F. Herbohn

Environmental Economics and Public Policy
Selected Papers of Robert N. Stavins, 1988-1999
Robert N. Stavins

International Environmental Externalities and the Double Dividend
Sebastian Killinger

Global Emissions Trading
Key Issues for Industrialized Countries
Edited by Suzi Kerr

The Choice Modelling Approach to Environmental Valuation
Edited by Jeff Bennett and Russell Blamey

Global Emissions Trading

Key Issues for Industrialized Countries

Edited by

Suzi Kerr

Director, Motu: Economic and Public Policy Research, Wellington, New Zealand

In collaboration with the
Center for Clean Air Policy, Washington DC, USA

NEW HORIZONS IN ENVIRONMENTAL ECONOMICS

Edward Elgar
Cheltenham, UK • Northampton, MA, USA

Published by
Edward Elgar Publishing Limited
Glensanda House
Montpellier Parade
Cheltenham
Glos GL50 1UA
UK

Edward Elgar Publishing, Inc.
136 West Street
Suite 202
Northampton
Massachusetts 01060
USA

A catalog record for this book
is available from the British Library

Library of Congress Cataloging in Publication Data

Global emissions trading : key issues for industrialized countries / edited
  by Suzi Kerr
    (New horizons in environmental economics)
    Includes bibliographical references and index.
    1. Emissions Trading. I. Kerr, Suzi, 1966– II. Series.

  HC79.P55 G56 2001
  363.738'745—dc21   00–064690

ISBN 1 84064 415 X

Printed and bound in Great Britain by Bookcraft (Bath) Ltd.

Contents

Figures

Tables

Contributors

Tim Denne

Tim Denne graduated with a PhD from the University of London in 1988. He was coordinator of climate change policy in the New Zealand Environment Ministry and subsequently head of environmental economics at UK-based consultants, Environmental Resources Management, and a Director of the UK Climate Impacts Programme. He was Deputy Director of the Center for Clean Air Policy in 1999–2000 and is now Senior Managing Consultant at Oxford Economic Research Associates.

Tim Hargrave

Tim Hargrave, a Senior Policy Analyst at the Center for Clean Air Policy, has worked on global climate change policy for over five years. During that time he has participated as an observer in the UNFCCC negotiations and has carried out projects for the US Environmental Agency, the European Commission, the Dutch Ministry of Housing, Spatial Planning and the Environment, and others. He has authored papers on international and domestic greenhouse gas emissions trading, joint implementation, compliance and other international climate policy issues. Mr Hargrave has also worked as a financial analyst and financial accountant. He holds a Master's degree in Energy and Resources, an MBA and a BS in Business Administration, all from the University of California at Berkeley, and is also a Certified Public Accountant. Mr Hargrave lives in St Paul, Minnesota, USA with his wife and daughter.

Edward A. (Ned) Helme

Mr Helme, Executive Director of the Center for Clean Air Policy, has over 20 years' experience working in the energy and environment field, specializing in air quality issues including acid rain, air toxics, ozone and global climate change. He has been heavily involved in climate change negotiations from the beginning, in particular working on the European Commission's proposed carbon emissions trading system, facilitating discussions on international emissions trading, the Clean Development Mechanism and worked on the capacity building efforts on the CDM and Joint Implementation in Mexico,

Brazil, the Caribbean, and Eastern Europe. In the US he was involved in the development of the US Climate Change Action Plan (1993), and efforts resulting in the establishment of the US Initiative on Joint Implementation (USIJI). Mr Helme holds a BA in Psychology and Political Science from Haverford College and a Masters degree in Public Policy from UC Berkeley with a focus on energy economics. He has written and lectured extensively on domestic and international environmental and energy issues. Prior to establishing the Center, Mr Helme served as the Director of the Natural Resources Division of the National Governors' Association and as Legislative Director to a member of Congress.

Cathleen Kelly

Cathleen Kelly is a Senior Policy Analyst at the Center for Clean Air Policy. Cathleen oversees the Center's work in assisting Mexico, the Caribbean, Brazil, Poland, Slovakia, and Ukraine to establish climate change mitigation policies and programs and to build the technical and institutional capacity to participate in the Kyoto Protocol. Before joining the Center for Clean Air Policy, Ms Kelly was a Senior Associate at ICF Incorporated, where she examined a wide range of international climate change policy questions including options for designing the market-based mechanisms under the Kyoto Protocol and developing country perspectives on the Clean Development Mechanism. Cathleen holds a Bachelor of Arts from the University of Wisconsin-Madison, and a Master of Arts in International Environmental and Energy Policy from the Johns Hopkins University, Paul H. Nitze School of Advanced International Studies.

Suzi Kerr

Suzi Kerr graduated from Harvard University in 1995 with a PhD in Economics. She was an Assistant Professor at the University of Maryland from 1995 through 1998. She has been a visiting scholar at Resources for the Future and Victoria University. She is now Director of Motu: Economic and Public Policy Research in New Zealand. Her research work empirically and theoretically investigates domestic and international emissions trading issues with special emphasis on tropical carbon sequestration, domestic carbon permit market design, the New Zealand Fisheries Individual Transferable Quota system, and transaction costs and technology change during the United States Lead Phase-down.

Catherine Leining

Catherine R. Leining is a Senior Policy Analyst at the Center for Clean Air Policy, where she co-manages the Center's State Roundtable on Global Climate Change, conducts research on state-level greenhouse gas mitigation options, and contributes to the Center's analytical and educational outreach work on the Kyoto Protocol. In her prior position as an Associate at ICF Consulting, Ms Leining specialized in the analysis of inventory and project-based greenhouse gas accounting methods, provided technical support on a broad range of climate change issues to the US Environmental Protection Agency, the US Initiative on Joint Implementation, the US Country Studies Program, the World Bank, and Canada's National Climate Change Process. She also spent two years working with local governments on environmental issues through the International City/County Management Association. Ms Leining has a BS in biology and French from Duke University.

Center for Clean Air Policy

The Center for Clean Air Policy

The Center for Clean Air Policy is a non-profit public policy research organization based in Washington, DC, which was created in 1985 by Mr Helme and a number of current and former state governors. The Center's purpose is to develop and promote innovative policy approaches to major state, federal and international energy and environmental problems. Its work is guided by the belief that sound energy and environmental policy solutions serve both economic and environmental interests. The Center's programs include policy research and analysis, policy mediation, advocacy and international technical assistance and exchanges. For a full sampling of policy papers, publications and for more information on current projects, please visit the Center's website at http://www.ccap.org.

Motu: Economic and Public Policy Research

Motu is a non-profit research institute in New Zealand. We promote well-informed debate on public policy issues, with special emphasis on issues relevant to New Zealand policy. We do this primarily by carrying out objective academic research. We are committed to disseminating our work and facilitating discussion with others through workshops, dialogue groups, teaching, publications and sponsorship of overseas visitors. For information about our research programs and access to our publications see http://www.motu.org.nz.

Acknowledgements

This book brings together years of thinking, learning and discussion of issues relating to international agreements and international emissions trading. The chapters I was directly responsible for have their roots in my PhD thesis work at Harvard. For their insights and support during that period I would like to thank my advisors Robert Stavins, Jerry Green, David Cutler and Ed Glaeser. My understanding of international politics benefited enormously from being based for two years at the Center for International Affairs as a Graduate Research Associate. In particular I would like to thank Robert Keohane for his extreme generosity toward a non-government student and for his constructive criticism. Thanks also to Barbara Connolly, David Fairman, Dan Thomas, Miranda Schreurs and Michael Ross for many stimulating discussions.

My work and understanding of international emissions trading developed during my time at the University of Maryland and I would like to thank my students there as well as participants in the Microeconomics seminars in the Economics Department for bearing with me in discussions of evolving ideas. Mike Toman at Resources for the Future helped me to develop this work further by hosting me, providing intellectual and moral support and helping me to find funding both through Resources for the Future and the US Environmental Protection Agency to continue this work.

This research was brought together into its current form through the opportunity to write a series of papers for the Center for Clean Air Policy as part of its International Emissions Trading Dialogue, funded by the Netherlands Ministry of Housing, Spatial Planning and the Environment. Yvo de Boer, the Netherlands principal climate negotiator, and Ned Helme of the Center ably co-chaired the meetings. The papers in this volume were first written as background papers by myself and the Center staff for these meetings and were honed as a result of the discussions. Ned coordinated the choices of topics for discussion with the participants and contributed in valuable ways to the discussions and ideas behind many of the papers. We are indebted to the meeting participants for their thoughtful discussion and insights. Christine Denuel, James Earl, Clara Jones, and Ona Bunce provided logistical support that helped make the meetings productive and harmonious.

I would particularly like to thank Tim Hargrave, Ned Helme, Tim Denne, Cathleen Kelly and Catherine Leining for their work under pressure to revise the papers after the meetings and bring them to the quality you see in this volume. Maxine Watene, Jason Timmins and William Power have done an excellent job with the formatting and editing under acute deadlines and with problematic software. The staff of the Brass Monkey Café on the south coast of Wellington have unwittingly played a major role in the editing of the volume by providing endless cups of coffee to fuel revisions. Finally throughout the final stages of the project Norman Meehan has provided steady support and encouragement.

Suzi Kerr
Director, Motu: Economic and Public Policy Research
Wellington, New Zealand, June 2000

Foreword

In 1995, the Intergovernmental Panel on Climate Change (IPCC), a body of over 2,000 leading scientists from around the world, concluded that 'the balance of evidence ... suggests a discernible human influence on global climate'.[1] This influence is the result of emissions of greenhouse gases, mainly carbon dioxide. The human activities that produce greenhouse gas emissions are many and diverse, but are primarily the burning of coal, oil and natural gas, land-use change and agriculture. The IPCC has predicted that average global surface air temperatures are likely to rise by between 1 and 3°C in the next 100 years. While this may not sound like a great change, it should be kept in mind that the planet was about 5°C colder during the last Ice Age. The change that is expected to occur would be greater than any experienced since modern civilization began to develop.

The impacts of human climate interference are expected to be dramatic. The IPCC has said that the projected changes in temperature, precipitation, soil moisture and sea level have the potential to increase 'extreme high-temperature events, floods and droughts, with resultant consequences for fires, pest outbreaks and ecosystem composition structure and functioning'.[2]

The need to respond to these problems becomes more urgent as scientific evidence on the reality and seriousness of the impacts of global warming mounts. Since the IPCC reached its conclusion in 1995, there have been numerous indications that the climate is already changing and is doing so faster than was originally predicted. US National Oceanic and Atmospheric Administration researchers have found evidence that the rate of global warming is accelerating and that in the past 25 years it achieved the rate of 2°C per century.

The nations of the world took the first major step in response to the problem of climate change in 1992, when they agreed to the United Nations Framework Convention on Climate Change. The 'ultimate objective' of the UNFCCC is 'to achieve stabilization of greenhouse gas concentrations in the atmosphere at a level that would prevent dangerous anthropogenic

---

[1] Intergovernmental Panel on Climate Change. *IPCC Second Assessment: Climate Change 1995. A Report of the Intergovernmental Panel on Climate Change.* United Nations Environment Programme, World Meteorological Association, 1995.
[2] Ibid.

interference with the climate system'. In 1997, the Parties to the Framework Convention agreed to the Kyoto Protocol, which requires industrialized countries to reduce their combined annual average emissions during the period 2008 to 2012 to five percent below 1990 levels.

The Kyoto Protocol marks a major departure in international environmental law, as it is the first international environmental agreement to rely significantly on market-based mechanisms such as emissions trading. Since the meeting in Kyoto, the Parties have been busy filling in the structure established under the Protocol. This work has included developing rules and guidelines in the areas of international emissions trading, project-based emissions reductions (Joint Implementation and the Clean Development Mechanism), national greenhouse gas emissions accounting and reporting, and the compliance and enforcement regime.

Against this backdrop, in September 1998 the Center for Clean Air Policy began to facilitate meetings of its 'International Emissions Trading Dialogue.' The Center is a Washington, DC-based environmental policy organization that specializes in designing and promoting market-based solutions to environmental problems. The organization played a key role in the development of the sulfur dioxide control cap and trade program now in place in the US Clean Air Act, one of the world's first emissions trading systems. In the area of climate change, the Center has been involved in the international negotiations since before Rio. Among other accomplishments, the organization brokered the world's first energy sector 'joint implementation' project, a fuel switching project in the Czech Republic, helped the European Commission design a plan for emissions trading within the European Union, and provided capacity building assistance to Eastern European and developing country Parties.

The trading dialogue group's meetings brought together high-level climate negotiators and select private sector representatives from fourteen industrialized nations under the co-chairmanship of Yvo de Boer of the Netherlands Ministry of Housing, Spatial Planning and the Environment (VROM) and me. Participants included Christian Albrecht (Switz), Jean-Jacques Becker (FR), Dan Chartier (Emissions Mktg Assoc – US), Jos Delbeke (EC), David Doniger (USA), Harald Dovland (NOR), John Drexhage (CAN), Kathy Garden (Fletcher Challenge, NZ), Niels Gram (Danish Industry Assoc), Hayo Haanstra (Neth), David Harrison (Australia), Enno Harders (Ger), Joachim Hein (Assoc. of German Industry), Geir Hoeibye (Confederation of Norwegian Business), Eugeniusz Jedrysik (Pol), Naoki Matsuo (IGES – Japan), Ole Plougmann (Dk), Oleg Ploujnikov (Russia), Maria Robertson (Comalco Aluminum – Australia), Miel Rumpol (Shell), Franz Josef Schaffhausen (Ger), Jo Simons (UK), Peter Vis (EC),

Murray Ward (NZ), Richard Williams (West Coast Energy – Can), Simon Worthington (BP), and Nicolai Zarganis (Dk).

The process, which was financed by the Netherlands Ministry, gave participants a chance to discuss different approaches to the design of an international greenhouse gas trading system and related issues in a relaxed and off-the-record way. The goal was to build mutual understanding on the key issues that divided the Parties in the negotiating process. The Center for Clean Air Policy's staff and consultants prepared background papers and gave presentations to guide the discussions. The papers were 'living documents' which evolved to reflect the insights drawn from the process.

The chapters in this book grew out of the papers developed for the International Emissions Trading Dialogue. They have been presented in various forms to dialogue group participants; in addition, they have been presented in special events at the international negotiations, in UNFCCC-sponsored expert workshops from Bonn to Tokyo, and in numerous other fora. They are developed here in a more systematic fashion with the goal of providing greater background and context for the lay reader.

The authors are grateful for having had the opportunity to serve the negotiating process and are thankful to the dialogue participants for the commitment they showed to the process and for their substantive input, which ranged from suggestions about which trading-related topics were most important to specific recommendations about policy conclusions. Input from such a diverse and knowledgeable group of negotiators and leading industry experts was invaluable to the authors. The blend of pragmatism and real-world workability with sound economic and political theory has helped us produce what we hope are compelling recommendations and conclusions about the structure of an effective international emission trading regime. The conclusions presented in this book should not be construed as reflecting any consensus opinion of the dialogue members. The Center for Clean Air Policy and the authors take full responsibility for all of the information and conclusions presented here.

Developing a solid foundation and infrastructure for international emissions trading is one of the keys to achieving progress in reducing the threat of global warming. Emissions trading offers the potential of a least cost path to needed emission reductions, and lower costs translate directly into a higher likelihood of compliance by both Parties and legal entities. We are at a stage in the implementation of the UNFCCC where building confidence in our ability to make the tough decisions to reduce emissions is critical. Getting the emissions trading and compliance structure right will go a long way to inducing the proverbial camel to put his 'nose in the tent'.

For those of you involved in the UNFCCC process, we hope that the book will help you to clarify your own thoughts on Kyoto Protocol design and implementation issues. For those of you just learning about global climate change and the Kyoto Protocol, we hope that the book stimulates you to look even more deeply into these important topics.

Ned Helme
Executive Director, Center for Clean Air Policy
Washington, DC, June, 2000

1 Introduction: Trading Toward a Stable Climate

Suzi Kerr

November [2000], . . . It gets hot and exciting at a UN climate control conference. The follow-up to the 1997 Kyoto conference asks how to trade surplus emissions quotas. Phew. The Economist.[1]

Quiet but significant steps have been taken towards controlling climate change. The UN Framework Convention on Climate Change, agreed in 1992 in Rio de Janeiro, set overall goals.

The ultimate objective of this Convention . . . is to achieve, . . . stabilization of greenhouse gas concentrations in the atmosphere at a level that would prevent dangerous anthropogenic interference with the climate system. Such a level should be achieved within a time-frame sufficient to allow ecosystems to adapt naturally to climate change, to ensure that food production is not threatened and to enable economic development to proceed in a sustainable manner.[2]

Since 1992 negotiators have refined the institutions for implementing these goals. The Intergovernmental Panel on Climate Change has provided considerable academic and technical input on the costs and benefits of climate change, on policies for mitigation and adaptation and methodologies for measurement of emissions. In Kyoto in 1997 the nascent architecture of these institutions was formalized and binding short-term emission control targets were agreed by developed countries. The Kyoto Protocol outlines institutions for monitoring emissions, sets targets and outlines trading or 'flexibility' mechanisms to ease the implementation of these targets. National governments have assessed their own emissions sources and trends, have created some policies to begin to control emissions and have put considerable effort into investigating their future domestic and international

---

[1] Calendar of Events for 2000, Jan 8–14, 2000, p. 7.
[2] Article 2 UN Framework Convention on Climate Change.

interests and roles in the climate change effort. On the negative side, the Framework Convention also set targets for carbon dioxide stabilization at 1990 emission levels by the year 2000 in developed countries. Despite this target, emissions have continued to grow rapidly so the atmospheric accumulation of greenhouse gases is accelerating. Few states and no key states have ratified Kyoto. The details of the trading mechanisms still need to be fleshed out and the effort to create inventories of emissions across all sources and countries continues.

Many aspects of the climate change effort will be in evolution for many years as we resolve scientific uncertainty about the scale and nature of climate change and economic uncertainty about costs of mitigating it and adapting to it, learn how to operate effective international institutions, develop domestic policies, take advantage of existing technologies and develop new ones. Critically, we need to develop trust among nations that the commitments made by states are credible and will be backed up by real, effective action.

This book addresses one part of this overarching problem – how to design institutions for trading of emission commitments among developed or 'Annex B' states. 'Annex I' states are also formally known as 'Annex B' states. For a list of Annex B states see Appendix 1. In addressing this component, many of the complex issues that bedevil the agreement as a whole arise in a more restrictive well-defined context. Clarifying these issues in a simpler context and finding solutions may facilitate a more constructive dialogue on the same basic issues in the wider, more fraught global negotiations.

Many concerns are raised about trading greenhouse gas emissions. Concerns about maintaining environmental integrity are foremost. Maximizing administrative and private sector feasibility by making rules simple and practical is a concern of both government officials and business. Less well articulated, but no less important, are concerns about fairness. These range from fear that some countries will exploit others through trading or that some countries or companies will cheat and hence gain advantage over others, to fundamental unease with the idea that countries can meet environmental commitments with money rather than through direct domestic action. Countries are also resistant to the idea of paying large amounts to other countries for a global good. This problem is unavoidable in a world where the opportunities for emissions abatement are differently located from the concern and resources to take advantage of those opportunities. Trading may ease this problem by making the transfers less transparent than with direct side payments among nations. Finally any discussion of trading is implicitly confronted by skepticism that climate is a problem or that, even if it is, the international community will really be able to create an agreement with bite.

A clear understanding of how to design an Annex B trading market is a critical building block for addressing climate effectively in the long run. For those concerned about the potentially devastating effects of climate change, a strong core of effective developed country institutions that demonstrates the economic feasibility of emissions reductions and a credible commitment by the 'North' would be a fundamental building block for intensification of the global effort. Implementing effective institutions would also provide a stimulus to develop workable domestic policies and commercially applicable technologies that could be used anywhere.

For the climate skeptics, designing effective institutions is just as critical. Poorly designed regulations would be very costly and intrusive with few side benefits for technology or other environmental benefits such as local air pollution or biodiversity. If we take serious action to curb greenhouse gas emissions and it turns out not to have been necessary, we will want to have minimized the cost and maximized the associated benefits. Poorly designed institutions would not necessarily curb the climate effort but they would certainly make it more expensive. The design of trading is not an appropriate issue to use to resist any action.

Designing an international market is not a trivial exercise. Although a number of successful domestic markets have operated for many years we have no significant international examples.[3] The international context is different from the domestic context for several reasons. The key difference is that an international market involves a cooperative agreement and trading among sovereign states. While the academic and policy literature has begun to investigate these issues, we have a long way to go. This book aims to present and extend our current understanding and empirical knowledge in a consistent, coherent way that is accessible to the interested lay person. While striving to be grounded in the realities of international and domestic regulation, we also try to be optimistic about the possibility that the international process is capable of designing efficient effective institutions. We concentrate not on what we think will happen but what could happen and what we can strive for.

The rest of this introductory chapter will provide some background to readers who are new to climate change or trading and provide an introduction to the issues discussed in the later chapters. The Glossary also will be useful to readers unfamiliar with the many acronyms and technical terms used in

---

[3] Key domestic examples are the US Acid Rain program for limiting sulphur-dioxide emissions from electric utilities, the US Lead Phasedown program that reduced the use of lead in gasoline, and a plethora of Individual Transferable Quota systems for fisheries management.

this debate. We begin by looking at some existing literature on international emissions trading; literature related to specific chapters will be discussed there. We briefly present key points on the science and economics of climate change and discuss the theory of international agreements. We present some of the background to the Framework Convention on Climate Change and the Kyoto Protocol to give some context to the narrower range of issues discussed in this volume. We also include a basic primer on the function and purpose of tradable permit markets. None of these sections is intended to be a definitive literature survey or presentation of issues. For those who are interested, we provide some references to facilitate deeper exploration. Finally we outline the issues discussed in each chapter to provide an overview of the volume.

1   EXISTING LITERATURE ON INTERNATIONAL TRADING

The first important work on international greenhouse gas trading came out in the mid 1990s. UNCTAD funded two reports that covered many of the basic institutional issues and framed the debate (Tietenberg and Victor, 1994 and Sandor et al. 1994). Hahn and Stavins (1995) wrote a more concise paper pulling out the key issues and the key differences between international and domestic trading. The IPCC also reported on policies that could be used to address climate change (IPCC, 1996c). More recently, a number of reports have been produced on different aspects of international trading. Key reports are the more recent UNCTAD report (Tietenberg et al. 1998) and a series of OECD/IEA reports by authors including Mullins, Corfee-Morlot and Baron. Some of these were produced through the Annex B Experts group process.[4] The European Commission has recently produced a Green Paper on trade within the Community, which addresses many issues that arise at an Annex B level (European Commission, 2000). This was heavily based on input from Hargrave et al. (1999a) and Yamin and Lefevere (2000).

The academic literature on permit trading is extensive although relatively little is directly applied to climate change. Mostly it has tried to take lessons from domestic tradable permit systems and apply these to international markets. Some key pieces include Schmalensee (1998), and a variety of issues briefs produced by Resources for the Future through their 'Weathervane' site http://www.weathervane.rff.org. Weyant and Hill (1999)

---

[4] The Annex B Experts group is a group of people nominated by their governments that gives advice on policy issues to the Secretariat.

provide an excellent summary of key empirical evidence on the effects of trading and limitations on trading on costs. Other literature is discussed in the relevant sections. The contribution this book makes is to focus on trading only among developed countries and to provide an accessible, less bureaucratic, overview of the range of relevant issues. We link the academic and policy literature and provide an integrated discussion of different elements of design. For example, the effects of national sovereignty and international constraints on compliance mechanisms affect all aspects of trading design. By going into more depth in some of the options and issues raised by others we are able to identify design decisions that will have pervasive effects across a range of concerns, environmental and economic. We also identify which characteristics of a trading system are essential and which would be helpful but not key.

2   THE SCIENCE AND ECONOMICS OF CLIMATE CHANGE

A tradable permit market is created to support the effort to control emissions. Why do we want to control these emissions, what gases should we control and how stringently should we control them over what time period? These questions have a scientific and an economic angle. The science can inform us about the causes of climate change, the relative contributions of different gases and the likely physical effects of increasing atmospheric concentrations of gases. The science is still however very uncertain. On an issue such as this where the costs are extremely high, uncertainty tends to lead to controversy and it is critical that scientific advice on the expectations and the associated uncertainty is given in what is seen to be an objective way. The Intergovernmental Panel on Climate Change was created by the World Meteorological Organization in 1988. Their charge is to provide high-quality, unbiased, and policy-relevant syntheses of knowledge concerning the science of climate change and its potential impacts and also the socioeconomic consequences of climate change and greenhouse gas limitation policies.[5] The credibility of the IPCC, which is created through its own processes, limits the extent of politically or economically motivated scientific controversy and facilitates free and informed discussion of what we do and do not know.

The 1996 Intergovernmental Panel on Climate Change (IPCC) report cautiously states that human activities have influenced the world's climate

---

[5] Toman, in Nordhaus (1998).

(IPCC, 1996a). 'Based on the range of sensitivities of climate to increases in greenhouse gas concentrations reported by IPCC Working Group I and plausible ranges of emissions . . . climate models, . . . project an increase in global mean surface temperature of about 1–3.5°C by 2100, and an associated increase in sea level of about 15–95cm. The reliability of regional-scale predictions is still low, and the degree to which climate variability may change is uncertain. However potentially serious changes have been identified, including an increase in some regions in the incidence of extreme high-temperature events, floods, and droughts' (IPCC, 1996b). [6]

The economic angle first needs to assess the magnitude of damage to human welfare from the likely change in climate and sea level. This is extremely difficult to do with any degree of certainty, especially when regional effects are highly uncertain but some attempts have been made. The IPCC carried out an assessment of evidence on likely damage (IPCC, 1996b). See also the critical discussion of current evidence in Mendelsohn (1998). He points out that damage estimates not only require understanding the ecological impacts but also the human responses to those impacts and social values.

To carry out any (even rough) form of cost–benefit analysis we also need estimates of the costs of abating emissions. The economic analysis on this is more advanced than that on damages, particularly for developed countries. The estimates still vary by more than an order of magnitude, however. One excellent summary of evidence from current models is given in Weyant (1999), which resulted from the Energy Modeling Forum run at Stanford University.[7] Many different modelers ran identical scenarios through their models to allow direct comparison of results. Despite the coordination of scenarios, the models produce a wide range of estimates of marginal costs and total costs in terms of GDP. As Weyant and Hill point out, this is not a reflection of hapless ignorance on the part of the modelers but an inherent reflection of future uncertainty.

The causes of economic uncertainty include potential new technologies, uncertainty about paths of economic development, and the timing and extent of human behavioral responses to regulation. Many new technologies are being developed to provide energy with fewer emissions. Alternative energy sources include solar, wind, hydrogen and biomass.[8] Energy efficiency options are also important, as well as fuel switching, such as coal to gas

---

[6] This statement of the scientific evidence is accepted by the US government despite some criticisms of the IPCC in the popular press. 'We are not swayed by and strongly object to the recent allegations about the integrity of the IPCC's conclusions.' Senator Tim Wirth speaking on behalf of the US government at COP2, Geneva, July 17, 1996.

[7] This updates the evidence available for IPCC (1996c).

[8] For discussion of these alternatives see Brower (1992).

conversions, which reduce emissions for a given amount of energy produced. Some new possibilities for sequestering carbon using technical methods could potentially reduce net emissions significantly (Parson and Keith, 1998); however, technical and commercial issues related to these are unresolved and some may pose new environmental risks. Biological sequestration through changes in agricultural practices, reforestation or preventing deforestation could have a large, especially short term, impact. The measurement of carbon stocks and dynamics are still highly uncertain. Moulton and Richards (1990) and Stavins (1998) offer two different approaches to estimating the costs of biological sequestration using data from the United States. Vincent and Strukova (1998) consider the costs in Russia.

Future economic growth and development is always hard to predict as macroeconomists can attest. Yet emissions are critically related to economic activity so this is a major driving force. The response of individuals to changes in technology and energy prices also is hard to predict. Some research finds that humans are irrationally slow in adopting new technologies or take inadequate account of energy efficiency in purchase decisions.[9] Some explanations for this seeming irrationality are high discount rates, capital constraints, slow information dissemination, aversion to the risk of new technologies and transaction costs between landlords who make investments and tenants who bear running costs.

Two key issues challenge anyone making decisions on the appropriate level of abatement in response to the threat of climate change. The first issue that makes comparison on costs and damages difficult is that costs and benefits occur at very different times. The people who bear the costs of abatement may not be those who would have borne the damages from climate change. This introduces not only discounting issues but also intertemporal equity issues. Similar problems arise across space. Some regions may actually benefit from climate change (though we are not sure which). They may still bear costs of abatement although the benefits of their efforts will go to those who are vulnerable to climate change. Such interpersonal comparisons of costs and benefits pose a challenge for analysts. For a recent discussion of these issues and comments on the IPCC approach to them see Lind and Schuler (1998).

The second issue is one of decision-making under uncertainty. If there were uncertainty about only costs or only benefits, the direction of effect on appropriate current measures would be relatively easy to predict. Uncertainty about damages, and the potential risks of catastrophic events, might suggest making greater efforts to abate emissions as a form of insurance against

---

[9] For discussion of these issues see the 1994 special edition of *Energy Policy* on Markets for Energy Efficiency.

damages. It would also suggest serious efforts for adaptation to climate change. In contrast, uncertainty in costs, that might be resolved through learning and technology development, would tend to suggest holding off abatement effort until we have learned more. The problem of irreversibility, potentially in environmental damage and certainly in large investments, makes the uncertainty issues harder to address. The combination of uncertainty in science, damages and costs both now and in the future makes careful modeling of uncertainty critical for decision-making. Simple policy conclusions are not possible.

A number of efforts have combined damage and abatement cost estimates to carry out cost–benefit analysis. In particular, key early works were by Cline (1992) and Nordhaus (1994). The 1996 IPCC report (IPCC 1996c) attempts to pull together the range of evidence to carry out a cost–benefit analysis. Portney (1998) discusses the strengths and weaknesses of their attempt as well as outlining issues associated with any attempt to carry out cost–benefit analysis on such a complex uncertain issue. He also stresses that despite the difficulties, policy-makers must and will make decisions. Any attempts to improve the information they can incorporate in their decisions and the structure they put on this information are extremely valuable.

The economics can tell us, with more certainty, the relative costs of different approaches to abatement. For example it is more expensive to try to cut emissions quickly than slowly; the more countries and gases can be included in the emission abatement effort, the lower will be the cost; the more countries are able to trade among themselves and across time the lower will be the cost. These are true in all models regardless of their point estimates of the cost of abatement. Models are also reasonably consistent in their estimates of relative costs across countries. Thus in many ways this book focuses on the most certain aspect of the problem. However the uncertainties relating to science and technologies of abatement are resolved, trading will reduce the costs of achieving our goals.

It will be many years, if ever, before we can determine the optimal level of emissions and hence emissions reduction from a cost–benefit analysis. It is almost certain, however, that the optimal level of reductions is positive and highly likely that it is higher than the level that will be achieved with no agreement, i.e. complete free riding. Therefore designing an effective international agreement will almost certainly be valuable whatever happens. We cannot create an effective agreement overnight. It requires experimentation, learning, and building trust. We can with relatively little cost enhance the learning process in motion by designing architecture for compliance and trading. This will put us in an excellent situation to respond quickly to future environmental challenges.

3 THE DESIGN OF INTERNATIONAL ENVIRONMENTAL AGREEMENTS

An international agreement is necessary to address climate change because the stability of the climate is a global public good. Every person can benefit from any abatement or mitigation activities undertaken anywhere in the world.[10] Because greenhouse gases are uniformly distributed (their effects are not localized), and the global climate system is one interrelated system, the source of emissions does not matter. This provides the benefit of enormous flexibility in addressing the problem, but also leads to serious potential free riding. All countries would probably be willing to make costly reductions to reduce climate risk, but they would prefer even more to benefit from others' actions and not bear costs themselves. The extra environmental benefits to them from their own actions are probably not worth the cost to them even though globally they are beneficial.

Forming an agreement requires finding an agreed level of global reductions and a cost allocation across countries that means that all countries benefit from the agreement. This must be done in the face, not only of uncertainty, but also lack of information about different countries' preferences and interests.[11] Countries are uncertain about their own interests but also want other countries to think they are less concerned than they really are in order to reduce their share of costs. The negotiation process is further complicated by the fact that states are not unitary (indivisible) actors. Negotiators represent the combined interests of different domestic groups. This means that a 'state's' interests can be volatile and that negotiators are unable to make firm commitments.

A final issue relates to the dynamics of forming an agreement. Because of the complexity of the process and the large number of actors it is often very difficult to get all parties involved in an agreement at the same time. However, having some parties move earlier can influence the terms on which later entrants choose to participate. A tension arises between early action with some institution building and trust creation relative to starting at a later date but achieving fair and meaningful participation by all actors. Sometimes it is possible to get all parties to agree to a broad but weak agreement. The

---

[10]In fact, some regions may benefit from climate change. However, we do not know which areas these will be or what the effects of change in the rest of the world will have on them indirectly. Given the uncertainty, they would probably be better off without the potential change.

[11]This 'veil of ignorance' could help the negotiations because they would be seeking an agreement fair to parties in all possible situations because they would not know their own situation (similar to Rawls' (1971) device). If countries did not believe they could discover their interests this might work. In the current context, however, it often simply leads to delay while countries do research and backtracking as countries learn more.

advantage of this is that all parties feel involved in the effort and the institutions they develop are responsive to a range of needs. The alternative is to find a small committed group that will take serious action. The advantage of this approach is speed and the ability to learn during institution building by building relatively simple institutions for the simpler, small group problem and then adapting them as new actors participate. The disadvantage is that the later entrants may free-ride on the first group or may feel disenfranchised.

The climate change effort is a combination of these two approaches. The Framework Convention on Climate Change was signed by most countries. In contrast, the binding commitments in the Kyoto Protocol only apply to a relatively small group of countries, those in Annex B.

4   THE FRAMEWORK CONVENTION AND KYOTO

The Framework Convention on Climate Change was adopted in Rio de Janeiro in May 1992. It entered into force in March 1994. 176 countries have now ratified it. The Convention set up the international process for attempts to mitigate and adapt to climate change. It set a target for stabilizing emissions at 1990 levels by 2000 for a group of developed countries now known as Annex B but did not set binding targets or create a compliance mechanism. Annex B predominantly includes the OECD, Eastern Europe and the Former Soviet Union (see Appendix 1).

The first form of international trading of emission obligations was created at the first Conference of the Parties in Berlin in 1995. The pilot phase of 'Joint Implementation' (also known as AIJ or 'Activities Implemented Jointly') created a process for developed countries to finance emission abatement projects in other countries in order to partly meet their own stabilization targets. These targets were not binding; neither did the Joint Implementation process provide any formal credit for these projects. AIJ has however been a useful process for learning and experimentation in international trade.[12]

In December 1997, the Kyoto Protocol was adopted. By January 13, 2000, 84 countries had signed and 22 had ratified. It will not come into force until the ninetieth day after at least 55 countries, incorporating Annex B parties that cover 55% of 1990 emissions from that group, have ratified. For the purposes of this book, it has four key features. First, binding emission targets are defined for Annex B countries for the commitment period 2008

[12]For information about Activities Implemented Jointly see the *Joint Implementation Quarterly*, ed. Catrinus Jepma.

2012. Second, these targets are differentiated substantially across countries with some required to make deep cuts in emissions relative to 1990 while others are allowed considerable growth and even gain 'hot air' (are allowed to emit more than they are likely to under business as usual) (see Appendix 1). Third, these targets apply to a basket of six gases and also include sinks. The gases are carbon dioxide (CO_2), methane (CH_4), nitrous oxide (N_2O), hydrofluorocarbons (HFCs), perfluorocarbons (PFCs) and sulfur hexafluoride (SF_6). Sinks are allowed for CO_2 sequestered through afforestation, reforestation and deforestation relative to levels in 1990. Agricultural soils may later be included. The exact rules are not yet defined. The IPCC is reporting on the appropriate way to measure this carbon. These gases are combined in a basket using greenhouse warming potentials developed by the IPCC to compare gases in terms of their carbon equivalent (see Appendix 2). Carbon dioxide is the most important gas; it currently leads to over half of the increase in current radioactive forcing. However it is not the most potent, and the importance of different gases varies across countries and time.

Fourth, the Kyoto Protocol defined three processes for international trade in emissions. The key form that this book deals with is international emissions trade among Annex B parties based on their defined commitments.[13] The second form is Joint Implementation among Annex B parties.[14] This form involves project-based trades where each trade must have the approval of both host (seller) and investor (buyer) country. The different roles of Joint Implementation and international emissions trading are discussed in Chapter 9. This form of trading must be distinguished from the earlier form of Joint Implementation that could also involve non-Annex B parties. The earlier form has evolved into the Clean Development Mechanism (CDM).[15] None of these 'flexibility mechanisms' is very clearly defined yet. The rules for their operation will be a key focus of future negotiations.

The other key outstanding issue, that permeates all negotiations, is the role of developing countries. Many developing countries have ratified the Framework Convention and even Kyoto and are monitoring their emissions. Provisions for technology transfer and scientific cooperation and provisions to help vulnerable countries adapt involve them directly but they currently have no emission control obligations. Important and difficult equity issues between North and South and intertemporally need to be resolved to the satisfaction of major actors both in Annex B (e.g. the US) and outside (e.g.

[13]This is defined in Article 17 of the Kyoto Protocol.
[14]This is defined in Article 6 of the Kyoto Protocol.
[15]The basic form of the Clean Development Mechanism is defined in Article 12 of the Kyoto Protocol.

China and India) before the agreement can be truly global. Although Annex B parties have historically produced the vast majority of emissions that have currently accumulated, in a relatively short time developing countries will be the major emitters. Their full participation is essential in any effective agreement.

Understandably, climate is low priority in many nations that face serious poverty and health issues as well as critical local environmental issues. Developing countries may be very vulnerable to climate change because of their often tropical climates and their emphasis on agriculture, but involving them may, at least in the short run, require considerable inducement and facilitation from Annex B. The CDM is one mechanism to begin this process of 'southern' participation and learning. If we can create an effective Annex B trading system we might help facilitate the effective development of the Clean Development Mechanism. At the same time, a trading system that facilitates Annex B compliance with their commitments will help to build confidence among developing country actors that the 'North' is serious about this effort and will bear their share of the overall costs.

5   INTRODUCTION TO TRADING

The basic elements of any trading program are binding caps on emissions, a clearly defined trading unit and a trading period. The actors that are responsible for achieving the caps must be clearly identified. In the case of climate change, these are states that comprise Annex B. Their caps are defined in terms of percentage reductions from 1990 levels of emissions or 'assigned amounts'. For example Canada's cap is 94% of their 1990 emissions annually. The unit of trade in this case will be one ton of CO_2 equivalent greenhouse gas (where the equivalences are defined by greenhouse warming potentials). For this book we call this an 'assigned amount unit' or AAU.[16]

Governments can devolve their responsibilities to actors within their states if they choose.[17] In this case they would break up their cap and assign emission limits to legal-entities within the state, so that including those AAUs they retain at governmental level, the limits sum to this cap. The entities that trade, government or legal-entities, must be well defined, liable for compliance to either the state or the international community and monitorable. Annex B states meet these requirements and whether they feel there are sub-state actors within their countries that meet these requirements

---

[16]Some people prefer the term 'part of assigned amount' or PAA. They are equivalent.
[17]This is explicit for Joint Implementation but not stated either way in Article 17 for IET.

is left to their own discretion. The state is still ultimately responsible for the actions of their legal-entities.

The trading period is a five year commitment period with an allowance for banking for use in the next commitment period. Within each period, the only units that can be used to show compliance are those available for use in the current commitment period. In the first period these are simply first commitment period units. In future periods, if banking is utilized, first commitment units that have not been used up will be effectively equivalent to second period units; both will be available for current compliance so they will have equal value. Banking will only be utilized if second period targets are more stringent than the first or costs of abatement are rising and if compliance penalties are credible for the second period.

These are international rules. Domestic trading systems will have to mirror these rules if their legal-entities are directly involved in the international market. If not, states could define different rules. A key reference on the design and benefits of trading is Tietenberg (1985). Stavins (2000) summarizes current experience with the use of emissions trading and other economic instruments.

5.1 Static Gains from Trading

The basic idea of emissions trading is that it allows one agent that finds compliance very expensive to reduce its compliance effort by paying another agent that finds additional compliance relatively easy to increase its compliance. The overall environmental impact is zero if there are no concerns about the location of the emissions. The buyer increases emissions but the seller decreases. The total cost of achieving the environmental goal falls and both parties to the trade benefit. Buyers can reduce their domestic costs of compliance while sellers profit from selling Assigned Amount Units (AAUs) for more than the cost of reducing emissions. Part of this profit may come in access to new technology, as foreign exchange or with improved access to international capital markets. Under perfect market conditions, trading can achieve the environmental goal at the lowest possible cost with no central coordination.[18] In any case, trading can always lower costs by moving towards equalizing the marginal costs of abatement.

If the international community had perfect information about each state's abatement opportunities and their costs, it could set targets to equalize marginal costs up front and trading would not be valuable. The international community does not have this information; even the individual states do not

---

[18]For seminal references on trading see Montgomery (1972) and Dales (1968). For good general discussions see Tietenberg (1985) and Hahn and Stavins (1992).

really know their true situation, but they and their private sector actors do
have better information. This private information about their abatement
opportunities leads to an important benefit of trading. An outsider cannot
observe these opportunities and hence cannot force the country or actor to use
them. Trading provides direct incentives for efficient use of private
information.

Several chapters in Weyant (1999) study the effects of trading on the cost
of Kyoto. Overall, moving from no trading to trading among Annex B
parties could lower the marginal costs in 2010 by a factor of two in the US,
EU, Japan, Canada, Australia and New Zealand. The fall in GDP costs are
similar. Part of this gain results from the release of 'hot air' (or AAUs that
countries in transition were allocated that are excess to their baseline needs)
but much also results from differences in abatement costs. Global trading
could yield much greater gains still but these are much more uncertain.

5.2   Dynamic Gains

Trading can affect dynamic efficiency in three broad ways. First, trading can
improve flows and patterns of investment and the level and effectiveness of
spending on research and development. Second, banking allows flexibility
across time that may lower costs significantly with little or no environmental
effect. Third, trading will affect the level of commitment of states but also
the credibility of future commitments.

Trading can provide a strong incentive for research and development,
investment in plant and equipment and adoption of new technology. An
innovator gains the benefits of their own reduced abatement costs and profits
either from buying fewer AAUs or selling more. They could also potentially
benefit from the dissemination of their technology. Economic theory
suggests that economic instruments are superior to other forms of regulation
in encouraging the private sector to carry out R&D and disseminate and use
the results.[19] Trading between the more developed states in Annex B and the
countries in transition, such as Russia, will improve the dynamic efficiency
of the agreement by providing an effective mechanism to transfer skills and
technology.

'Banking' is a specific form of trading where emissions today can be
reduced so that emissions in a future commitment period can be increased. If
the marginal cost of compliance rises with time, this can lead to significant
dynamic cost saving. For example if rapid economic growth were expected
to raise emissions over the next decade at a faster rate than technological

---

[19]For the theory see Fischer et al. (1998b) and Jaffe and Stavins (1995). For some empirical
    evidence see Newell et al. (1999) and Kerr and Newell (2000).

development can offset, banking in the early years when emissions are relatively low and hence may be easier to constrain will free up AAUs to cover later emissions growth. 'Borrowing' could offer significant gains if the commitment problem (will they ever really pay back) could be solved. Several empirical models suggest that current Kyoto targets are too strict if we want to achieve climate stabilization by the most efficient path.[20] This would argue for borrowing. Trading with maximum spatial and dynamic flexibility can, in theory, lead to efficient climate stabilization.[21]

In the context of an international agreement that currently only lasts until 2012, however, and more generally for environmental regulation controlled by sovereign governments that cannot commit future governments, we have to consider the strategic relationship between emissions reductions and future commitments.[22] The first problem is simply one of time inconsistency. The government may agree now to increase future abatement in return for less current abatement but when the future arrives they may not want to carry out this promise.

Even without 'borrowing', dynamic inefficiency can arise if countries are not committed in the long term. Abatement can be achieved in two fundamentally different ways. Some abatement involves long-term investments and changes in production patterns, processes and lifestyles. Even if no formal commitments are agreed after 2012, these investments will continue to generate emission reductions. Other abatement can be achieved through short term, easily reversible changes such as turning off lights and appliances, or reducing driving but not changing transport infrastructure or vehicle technology. A key short-term domestic strategy is simply purchasing permits. Current purchases of permits do not commit the purchaser to future abatement or lower the cost of future abatement. Of course they do imply that the seller has made abatement investments. With certainty about future commitments, the short or long run nature of abatement strategies does not matter. However, when long-term commitments are uncertain, the nature of abatement strategies can affect future negotiations; hence the anticipation of future negotiations can affect the nature of current abatement activities. This is dynamically inefficient.

First, if future commitments are uncertain it is sensible for investors to require higher returns on their investments. This will mean less investment in abatement technologies and in R&D and a bias toward short-term

---

[20]See papers by Nordhaus, Boyer, Manne, Richels, Tol, Peck and Teisberg, all in Weyant (1999).
[21]Some work argues that taxes would be more efficient than tradeable permits. Most of these models put unrealistic restrictions on trading that make it less responsive to shocks (such as ignoring banking and the ability to change targets over time) and in any case taxes are not a politically acceptable international instrument.
[22]These issues are discussed in Fischer et al. (1998a).

approaches. The earlier agreement can be reached and the more credible is enforcement and continuation of the agreement the less unnecessary uncertainty investors will face. They will always face unavoidable uncertainty because of the uncertainty in the science and because of ordinary economic uncertainties.

Second, countries that are strategic may choose to invest less, or less visibly, in long-run abatement in order more credibly to be able to claim high costs in the second round of commitment negotiations. This may allow them to negotiate less stringent targets relative to their competitors. This benefits them but raises global costs for a given environmental target.

Some countries, in the EU particularly, have suggested that this problem be addressed using 'supplementarity' that would require that countries do most abatement domestically, using only a small percentage of trading. This would likely force some more long-term investment to achieve stringent targets but at a high cost. High cost domestic options would be used. Some of these would include the long-term investments that would be efficient in a certain world with perfect commitment. Many good long-term investments, however, would not be affected because their payoffs will not be seen in domestic reductions in the first commitment period in any case. It would not avoid short-term domestic options and would force the adoption of some very high cost ones. We would argue that the benefits of trading: information revelation, clear incentives, and 'where' and 'when' flexibility, outweigh any possible negative effects on strategic behavior. Long run certainty should be sought through early agreement on future commitment periods and through cooperative research.

5.3   Benefits of Trading for the Agreement

Trading has several benefits that go beyond the efficiency improvements discussed above that lead to lower compliance costs in the short and long run. From a political standpoint, trading is attractive because it allows a separation between the negotiations of emissions reductions targets across countries and the efficient way to achieve those targets. The places with the greatest abatement opportunities may not be those with the greatest concern or ability to fund abatement. Direct side payments are very difficult to achieve for political reasons. Experience with their use for environmental goals has been largely negative.[23] This allows negotiations to focus on equity and political feasibility in what is essentially a distributional debate. Estimates of the cost

---

[23]For discussion of a number of case studies of transfers for environmental protection see Keohane and Levy (1996). For discussion of the potential benefits of tradable permit markets for this purpose see Kerr (1995).

of abatement in each country will inform this negotiation by clarifying the distributional impacts of different targets but the decisions will not affect efficiency.

Efficient trade also has the advantage that it reduces any impacts of the agreement on fair competition in goods. If all sectors in all countries trade competitively (i.e. do not have limits on trade or exploit market power) marginal costs of emission reduction are equalized and the increased marginal costs of production of goods truly reflect the cost of greenhouse emissions involved in production. No sector in any Annex B country gains an artificial cost advantage. Using trading avoids the need to try to harmonize regulatory instruments across different countries. This harmonization effort is not only technically extremely complex but also becomes quite intrusive into the domestic affairs of individual countries. Trading achieves the same goal with less intrusion.

Finally, using trading, especially at a legal-entity level, broadens the base of actors directly engaged in the climate effort. This increases the amount of information and innovative, entrepreneurial energy applied to the problem and also develops vested interests that will continue to support the effort and will contribute to the oversight of enforcement on their competitors within their state and in others. Increased volumes of trade by more atomistic actors (i.e. actors that cannot affect the price) will reduce price volatility, increase liquidity and reduce the risk of involvement in the market. They will reduce the ability of large players to exert market power.

5.4   The Role of National Governments

Governments have two basic roles in trading. First, they can trade in their own right. Not only do governments create emissions directly and influence them through their infrastructure decisions, but also they may trade on behalf of the private sector if they choose a form of regulation that does not allow legal-entities to engage in international trade.

Second, they can set up domestic regulatory infrastructure that devolves the right to internationally trade AAUs to their legal-entities while simultaneously requiring them to control their emissions within a defined cap. They are then responsible for allocating caps across entities and enforcing their legal-entities' behavior both domestically and internationally. This essentially requires ensuring that at the end of the commitment period all entities will have sufficient AAUs to cover their cumulative emissions. National governments may also have a role in overseeing trading exchanges that operate in their countries. This would be equivalent to their role in any stock market. Their role is to protect the investing public and, if necessary, avoid undue market power by any agent.

5.5 Private Sector Roles

The private sector is the main source of emissions in Annex B countries and hence controls the main opportunities for emissions abatement. Individuals, firms and corporations can change emissions by changing consumption, input and production patterns, changing processes, investing in technology that lowers emissions, and carrying out research and development that can lead to lower emission activities in the future. Ultimately, the main purpose of the international agreement is to induce them to do these things and facilitate the process so they can be done efficiently.

The private sector also controls much of the capability for emissions reduction. They have private information about their preferences and the potential to reduce emissions in their processes; they own the technology and often the intellectual property rights such as patents. They have the technical and commercial expertise to develop and disseminate new technologies.

The private sector role in trading will vary from country to country and will depend on the form of regulation each government chooses for different sources and sectors. If a private sector entity is covered by a domestic tradable allowance system they have an obligation to meet their domestic targets but may also have the right to trade any excess emissions allowances internationally. If they are covered by regulation that does not allow them to trade they will not participate through their role as emitters. Major actors could still be involved as speculators. Most financial markets limit the direct involvement of the unsophisticated public to protect them from undue exposure to risk. The same approach may be taken here.

The private sector has the capability to create and run efficient effective trading mechanisms. If the international community and national governments can strictly enforce compliance with emissions caps, the private sector can enforce trading behavior. Trading is likely to occur in a number of ways. Bilateral trades involve customized contracts and frequently long-term complex legal agreements. Over-the-counter markets involve third party intermediaries and standard contract terms. Ultimately, the most efficient form of trade is a commodity exchange with standard contracts; transactional certainty and clearly defined mechanisms, which mitigate counter party risk (i.e. risk of non-payment or non-delivery).[24]

The private sector will determine how different trades will best occur and will gradually develop the institutions to allow a commodity exchange if AAUs are defined in a homogeneous and certain way. These institutions include review and limitations on who can participate in the exchange, impositions of credit requirements on participants and use of clearing

[24]Williams (1999).

facilities to manage the transfer of title and payment. These latter would interact with the official registries discussed in the following chapter. Governments can use these private sector mechanisms to trade or can use bilateral trading. The private brokering and exchanges will provide clear price signals if AAUs are homogeneous and will provide a liquid market that facilitates compliance by making AAUs available quickly at all times.

The final role of the private sector is a less direct one that relates to overall treaty compliance. In previous international agreements the private sector has played a key role in providing information to assess compliance and in pressuring governments to enforce compliance on competing firms. If one firm faces strict compliance rules while another competing firm is facing lax enforcement or lenient regulation the first firm loses. In a classic case, Dupont, which faced strong ozone related regulation in the US, played a key role in forcing governments to come to an agreement so that their European competitors faced equivalent regulation.[25]

The private sector is already beginning to participate in the international climate change effort in a number of ways. For example, BP/Amoco have an international carbon trading system within their company that puts a real cap on emissions from their own activities: exploration, refining etc.[26] Many companies have been involved in Joint Implementation pilot projects (see discussion below). Private domestic actions have involved voluntary agreements as well as investment in research and development of alternative fuel technologies, energy efficiency and many other abatement options. Private sector actors are actively monitoring and participating in the international process.

5.6   Non-governmental Organization Roles

Non-governmental organizations (NGOs) such as environmental groups have become important players in international agreements both in the effort to create agreements and during enforcement and implementation. Some groups, such as Greenpeace and the World Wide Fund for Nature are now very sophisticated and international in scope. NGOs can collate, analyze and disseminate information on emissions abatement opportunities and on observed compliance.[27] They can put pressure on those who domestically or internationally are found to be out of compliance. They have played an active role in certifying projects under 'Activities Implemented Jointly' and

---

[25]Benedick (1991), pp. 30–31.
[26]For details see http://www.bpamoco.com/climatechange.
[27]For a discussion of the emerging role of non-governmental organizations in international environmental affairs see Princen and Finger (1994).

will probably continue this role under the CDM and maybe JI. They can provide analysis to help develop domestic or international policy in an effective way. They apply continuous pressure at all levels to maintain the environmental goals of the agreement.

5.7   Previous Experience with Emissions Trading Worldwide

While there are many domestic trading programs worldwide, only one international emission-trading program has been of any significance. This is the 'industrial rationalization program' under the Montreal Protocol on Substances that Deplete the Ozone Layer.[28]   The Montreal Protocol set country-specific targets for consumption and production for two groups of ozone depleting substances. Different chemicals could be used to meet each target in a fungible way within groups. Ozone Depleting Potentials defined the rate of exchange among chemicals. Only the production targets were tradable.

Trading was designed to allow one plant to close and another operate at capacity rather than requiring two plants in different countries to run uneconomically at half capacity during the phaseout of the chemicals. Initially, in 1987, in a parallel to the 'supplementarity' debate in Kyoto, a limit of 15 percent of production was placed on trading; this limit was removed in 1990. Trading was primarily done at the legal-entity level with major players, the US and the EU, devolving their caps to individual entities. Enforcement was primarily at the domestic level although trades were required to be registered with the UNEP Ozone Secretariat. When trades were not registered, the UNEP did not worry if the countries concerned were in compliance, which they were. Because of the low level of trades, a formal registry was not developed and buyer states checked that the seller state had approved the sale before they credited their entities with the additional permits to produce ODS.

Many trades occurred, more domestically than internationally. There were few players, which limited the need to trade. Initially, only 17 producers of ODS existed. EU producers, in 1992–93, traded 20–40 thousand tons. Many of these trades were between EU countries. This is relative to world production of around 800 thousand tons in 1987.[29]   US producers traded internationally 20 times in the period 1992–1995, aggregating to 36 thousand tons traded. In contrast, in the same period, 494 domestic trades were recorded in the US with total trading of 238 thousand tons.

---

[28]For a more detailed discussion of this program see Mullins (1998).
[29]See Benedick (1991), p. 27.

There are many strong parallels between ozone depleting substance production trading and greenhouse gas trading. In terms of compliance the ozone trading offers a positive precedent. However, the ozone issue was different in some key ways and some elements of its trading might be seen as warnings in the current context.

The key differences between Montreal and Kyoto were that the overall costs of controlling ozone depleting substances was relatively low and the key producers were in the US and the EU, states that were strongly committed to controlling ozone depletion. The context for the trading program was a strong level of commitment to compliance. Another difference was that a small number of producers needed to be monitored and could take advantage of trading. These were large, publicly visible companies with extensive experience dealing with their potential trading partners. The limited number of actors limited the liquidity of trading. Their small number and existing relationships meant that a bilateral market was probably sufficient to achieve most gains from trading.[30] In contrast, greenhouse gas trading will operate in a much less certain compliance atmosphere and will involve states that are less committed and less experienced with environmental regulation, such as Russia and Ukraine. The overall costs of Kyoto will be significant and the number of regulated entities even in an upstream system will be in the thousands – not less than one hundred.

A second, directly relevant example is the Joint Implementation Pilot Program.[31] This program is entirely experimental and offers no credit for emission reductions achieved. It is a project-based program and each trade requires host and investor country approval. A number of projects have been carried out successfully in Eastern Europe including the Decin Project in the Czech Republic.[32] This was the world's first energy sector joint implementation project, a coal-to-gas fuel switch and cogeneration project with investment from three US utilities. It was brokered by the Center for Clean Air Policy. By September 1999, 133 projects had been approved by host and investor countries; many of these projects, however, involve developing countries and are comparable to CDM projects rather than Annex B trading.[33] Although this has been a useful program for gaining experience with abating emissions in different countries and learning the basic mechanisms of trade, it is not easily comparable with a comprehensive

[30]For analysis of trading efficiency in a similar trading system, the US lead trading program, see Kerr and Maré (1999).
[31]This is also known as Activities Implemented Jointly or AIJ and is not to be confused with Joint Implementation under Kyoto that will involve only Annex B party project-based trades.
[32]Dudek and Wiener (1996).
[33]Jepma (1999).

trading program based on national level emissions caps.[34] Transaction costs are extremely high and the key issues have been defining project level baselines and inducing investment when returns are undefined. The limitations of this program make direct comparison or lessons for Annex B trading limited.

Domestic trading programs have now been used in many countries including New Zealand,[35] Canada,[36] Singapore,[37] Chile,[38] the US,[39] and Europe.[40] Four key lessons emerge for climate change. First, trading programs can facilitate significant environmental progress. By lowering costs and providing a mechanism for compensating key players (grandfathering) more stringent targets can be made acceptable to industry. The US Acid Rain program and the US Lead Phasedown both led to dramatic reductions in emissions.

Second, compliance with the overall environmental regulation is key to the operation of a permit market. Stringent compliance gives permits value and provides incentives to trade rather than simply go out of compliance. An adequate registry to track compliance is critical. The Chilean total-suspended-particulates market is an example where insufficient enforcement removed the incentive to trade. Trading can improve compliance by encouraging the private sector to be actively involved in compliance. Cheating is not only an environmental problem but creates a competitive advantage for the firm that cheats. Competitors will watch each other's behavior to avoid suffering economic disadvantage.[41]

[34]For discussion of the relationship between the new version of Annex B Joint Implementation and emissions trading see Chapter 9 in this Book.

[35]The New Zealand Individual Transferable Quota System has been used since 1986 to manage fisheries. See Annala (1996).

[36]Canada has two pilot programs for controlling greenhouse gas emissions. See Stavins (2000) p.19.

[37]Singapore has used a tradeable permit system to control ozone-depleting substances since 1991. See Mullins (1998).

[38]Chile has a tradeable permit system for controlling total suspended particulate emissions from stationary sources in Santiago. It has largely been unsuccessful mainly because of inadequate enforcements and high transaction costs. See Montero and Sánchez (1999).

[39]Three key programs in chronological order are the EPA emissions trading program (see Tietenberg, 1985 or Hahn and Stavins, 1992), the US Lead Phasedown (see Hahn and Hester (1989), Kerr and Maré (1999), and Kerr and Newell (2000)) and the US Acid Rain program that controls SO_2 emissions from electric utilities (see Joskow and Schmalensee (1998), Stavins (1998), and Schmalensee et al. (1998)).

[40]European trading experience, outside of fisheries, is very limited. Germany has had a limited program for air pollutants since 1974 (see Klaasen and Nentjes (1997), Klaasen (1999) and Shärer (1994) cited in Stavins (2000)). Poland has a very limited program in Chorzów (Zylicz (1999) cited in Stavins (2000)).

[41]For an example of this from the Montreal Protocol see Parson and Greene (1995).

Third, introducing unnecessary complexity in the program raises the transaction costs of trading, makes compliance harder to assess and reduces liquidity in the market thus reducing the benefits from trading. The US chose to treat SO_2 as a uniformly distributed pollutant (one that mixes in the atmosphere so that the origin does not matter) in the Acid Rain program. Although this was not strictly true, this assumption has not led to serious pollution hot spots and the simplicity of the program has been key to its success. In contrast, the New Zealand individual transferable quota program for fisheries has very complex banking and trading provisions that many fishermen cannot understand and that make compliance assessment difficult.[42] These are now being simplified.

Finally, in a complex problem such as climate and with a very new instrument we are unlikely to set the rules perfectly in the first place. Scientific and economic uncertainties persist about the appropriate level of targets, the different contributions of different gases, and the best methods for monitoring different gases and sources. The New Zealand ITQ system contains a system for updating total catches based on current information and has also been altered so that fishermen, not the government, bear the risk of these changes. The Lead Phasedown was updated with the addition of banking in 1985 when trading was found to be successful and more rapid phaseout was sought. We will inevitably learn with time and need to adjust the targets and rules accordingly. The initial system should not be set in stone.

5.8   Experimental Evidence

Laboratory experiments have been used in an attempt to test the likely outcomes of different permit market structures. We will not discuss the results here because they require subtle interpretation. For the interested reader we suggest they look at the following sources. At the laboratory level, there are probably few differences between domestic and international markets. For general discussion of experimental evidence in tradable permit markets see Muller and Mestelman (1998), Ledyard and Szakaly-Moore (1994), a collection of articles in Isaac and Holt (1999), and Ben-David et al. (1999). Godby (1997 and 1999) and Godby et al. (1999) consider issues of market power in permit markets. For work specifically relating to international greenhouse gas trading see Bohm (1998), Carlén (1998) and Hizen and Saijo (1998).

---

[42]Hahn (1989) discusses some similar problems with early US implementation of tradable permits.

5.9   Requirements for an Effective Trading System

An effective international trading system depends at the most basic level on good enforcement of overall commitments at the national and international level. It requires clearly defined property rights, i.e. definition of units that can be traded and their ownership. The more homogeneous these units are and the more actors are involved in trading them, the more liquid will be the market. A more liquid market reduces uncertainty, enhances price discovery, reduces the likelihood of market power and enhances efficiency. Restrictions on trading or the institutions on trade should be avoided as much as possible to allow experimentation and the development of sophisticated private mechanisms. The simpler are the international rules relating to trading the more transparent will be the process and the easier both trading and monitoring of trading will be.

6   OUTLINE OF CHAPTERS AND KEY ISSUES

This introduction has provided a broad overview of climate issues to put the discussion of Annex B trading in the context of the larger climate problem. The second chapter moves to the opposite extreme by talking about the specific administrative structures to track AAUs as they are traded and surrendered. The tracking system is the backbone of the trading system. The design proposed is simple and based on a familiar institution that tracks money, a banking network.

In Chapter 3, Tim Hargrave, Ned Helme and Tim Denne join with Suzi Kerr to present the issues relating to enforcing compliance with binding emission limitations. Although this is necessary regardless of trading, compliance is essential for an effective market. This chapter stresses the importance of good information, low costs and credible, fair institutions to assess compliance. Chapter 4 follows this with a discussion of compliance issues that arise only in the presence of trading. On the positive side, trading lowers costs for buyers so non-compliance is less attractive, and suspension or limitation of trading is a credible punishment for sellers; on the negative side, sellers are able to non-comply in ways not previously available. This chapter particularly emphasizes arguments for and against the use of 'buyer liability' for invalid AAU sales (i.e. AAU sales not backed by real reductions).

In Chapter 5 Tim Denne looks at the specific issues that are raised by the inclusion of gases other than CO_2 and carbon sinks. These gases and sinks offer additional opportunities for abatement but are more difficult to measure which creates potential compliance difficulties.

Chapter 6 steps down from international issues to the domestic level to examine the domestic instruments available, the arguments in favor of each and how international trading by governments and legal-entities might occur despite a range of non-economic domestic instruments. Chapter 7 picks up some of the 'competitiveness' implications of the treaty as a whole but also of the use of diverse domestic instruments. We conclude that the best way to ensure fairness in goods trade is to encourage as many countries as possible to implement legal-entity international trading.

We consider another issue of fairness, but also efficiency in Chapter 8 where we look at the sources, likelihood and appropriate responses to market power in the AAU market. Empirical evidence suggests it could be a problem with respect to Eastern Europe and the Former Soviet Union but we suspect that the problem will not be so great in reality. Market power requires government control of trading; an excellent response is to encourage the use of legal-entity trading.

In Chapter 9 Cathleen Kelly and Catherine Leining consider the appropriate design of additionality rules for Annex B Joint Implementation in the context of the binding caps. They conclude that for states with good inventories there should be no additionality requirements, while for states with inadequate inventories the emissions additionality rules should be the same as those for the CDM.

We offer some broad observations and conclusions in Chapter 10. International agreements are not simple and the institutions and their evolution will be complex. We must be open to learning and focus on building trust and strong institutions rather than fighting for short-term gains at the expense of long run sustainability of the agreement. In contrast, we find that overall, introducing effective trading among industrialized countries is quite simple from an international administrative point of view – few rules are required. The complexity is in domestic and private responses to these simple rules. This is not a facile conclusion, however, the reasons why simple rules are the best are often complex. The book provides clear arguments and some empirical support for why rules for trading can and should be simple.

2 An International Tracking System for Greenhouse Gas Trading

Suzi Kerr[1]

---

1 INTRODUCTION

The ability to assess compliance is basic to any effective international agreement. The Kyoto Protocol includes three 'flexibility mechanisms', which aim to improve efficiency in the achievement of our environmental goals: Annex B trading, Joint Implementation and the Clean Development Mechanism (CDM).[2] These make assessment a little more complex. In the Kyoto Protocol compliance is defined as net emissions over the commitment period not exceeding the total holdings of assigned amount units (AAUs allocated through Annex B commitments), emission reduction units (ERUs created from AAUs through Joint Implementation) and certified emissions reductions (CERs created through the Clean Development Mechanism) at the end of the commitment period. When parties trade through any of these mechanisms the international community needs to be able to track the units traded to ensure that two countries do not claim the same unit toward their compliance. Effective tracking allows, when combined with emissions inventories, determination of developed country (Annex B) national compliance at the end of the commitment period.

This chapter considers the design of a tracking system that provides accounting integrity for the three flexibility mechanisms, henceforth 'trading system', with minimum administrative cost. It considers the purpose of tracking and discusses common misperceptions of that purpose. It proposes

---

[1] An earlier version of this paper was prepared for the International Emissions Trading Workshop sponsored by the Dutch Ministry of Housing, Spatial Planning and the Environment. It benefited from discussions at the meeting and particularly input from Murray Ward and David Doniger. Thank you also Peter Zapfel for useful comments. Responsibility for all opinions, errors and omissions is however our own.

[2] The Clean Development Mechanism is defined in Article 12 of the Protocol. Article 17 defines Annex I trading. Article 6 defines Joint Implementation. AAUs are sometimes referred to as parts of assigned amounts, PAAs or allowances. These terms are equivalent.

one sufficient and familiar form of international tracking institution. It discusses the interaction between national compliance systems and the international tracking system. Finally it discusses variants on the institution proposed and the advantages and disadvantages of these. We conclude that a system of multiple registries that operate and are regulated in a similar way to the private banking system is optimal for reasons of national sovereignty and efficiency.

The basic design of a tracking system is primarily a technical issue, not dependent on the many other difficult decisions about the three flexibility mechanisms. It is possible that it could be resolved fairly quickly. Resolving the tracking issue would reduce the number of issues facing negotiators, provide a clearer framework for future discussions of trading and provide another critical element for effective early reductions and trading.

2   FUNCTIONS OF A TRACKING SYSTEM

2.1   Necessary Functions

A tracking system must provide sufficient information on trading to the international agency so that, when combined with reported national inventories, the Secretariat can determine national compliance at the end of the 'commitment period' e.g. 2008–2012.[3] The tracking system alone cannot show compliance. If national government net trading is self-reported to the Secretariat, the tracking system provides an assurance of accuracy in the actual accounting of trades and the information necessary for an audit of reports.

The tracking system also provides assurance to buyers that the AAUs they are purchasing are in the legal possession of the seller. Thus buyers can be assured of the existence of the product they are buying even if the seller's compliance is uncertain.[4]

2.2   Additional Functions

2.2.1   Provide information on interim progress toward compliance
Observing AAU holdings of national governments during the compliance period does not allow assessment of the nation's progress toward compliance even when combined with interim emissions inventory information. The national government could have devolved its AAUs to sub-national legal-

---

[3] Policy Options for improving compliance generally are discussed in Chapter 3.
[4] For an extensive discussion of the issues of 'buyer liability' see Kerr (1998a) and Chapter 4.

entities, it could plan to purchase AAUs later in the period (and even have private forward contracts to do so), and it could hold AAUs in private accounts separate from the formal national account. No tracking system will provide accurate information on interim progress toward compliance.

The tracking system can, however, when combined with annual inventories and surrender (see discussion in Chapter 3), provide valuable information on international progress toward compliance. It can also indicate which countries are likely to need to purchase AAUs later in the commitment period and which are likely to be sellers.

2.2.2 Provide more detailed information on trading/compliance to facilitate informal enforcement pressures

Public information about trading would facilitate informal compliance pressure by companies, individual nations and non-governmental organizations, that is pressure applied other than through legally defined treaty compliance mechanisms. Experience has taught us that in the enforcement of international agreements, informal pressure plays a key role because of the weakness of international law.[5] Actors could identify countries that are taking compliance risks by going into 'debt' and relying heavily on future purchases.[6] They could seek reassurance that these countries have a compliance plan and a source for their future purchases and pressure or help them if they do not. They could also put pressure on actors that are buying AAUs from countries that are taking large risks. These informal systems could also offer support to assist countries with compliance.[7]

2.2.3 Facilitate trading

The tracking system, particularly when combined with interim inventory information, can provide some information on which actors are likely to be able to sell or be interested in buying AAUs. This information is not accurate because the tracking system does not record private contracts or regulatory obligations of legal-entities to national governments. Tracking information combined with inventories also gives an indication of the total supply of AAUs because it traces additional AAUs created through CDM as well as those retired during 'annual surrender' to match interim net emission estimates.

---

[5] Keohane and Levy (1996) and Raustiala, Skolnikoff and Victor (1998).
[6] We define 'debt' as national emissions-to-date–(current government AAU holdings + AAUs expected to be surrendered by legal-entities).
[7] Many political science and legal scholars argue that positive inducements to comply and assistance are frequently as important as sanctions. See Chayes and Chayes (1993).

3   PROPOSED SIMPLE SUFFICIENT TRACKING SYSTEM

We first outline the simplest system that would be sufficient and then discuss the interrelationship between that system and different national regulatory systems.

3.1   Basic Institutional Structure

Think of the tracking system as a bank with a series of accounts, the International Assigned Amount Bank.[8]   AAUs are the currency.   Each account is represented by a heavily outlined box in Figure 2.1.   At the beginning of the first commitment period each country has an account with a balance equal to its assigned amount.   Non-Annex 1 countries initially have zero balances.

AAUs could be traded through Annex B emissions trading or Joint Implementation.   If they are traded through joint implementation an AAU from the country of the project is first translated into an ERU that is associated with the particular project.   The total number of AAUs plus ERUs does not increase.   When any unit is first sold, it is withdrawn from the national government's bank account and deposited in another account. National governments could also buy AAUs. AAUs and ERUs never leave the tracking system or bank.   At the end of the commitment period, Annex B countries must surrender AAUs equal to their emissions.   With 'annual surrender' they would surrender AAUs equal to estimated emissions each year.   Surrender could be formalized by depositing them in a 'compliance account' from which AAUs cannot be withdrawn.[9]

Non-Annex 1 countries can create 'certified emission reductions', CERs, through the Clean Development Mechanism.   If they pass the standards of the mechanism, these are converted into AAUs and deposited in an account. Thus a developing country could create a CER and deposit it in its bank account.[10]   The country could then trade this AAU directly or through a

---

[8] This must be clearly distinguished from an idea advanced by Chichilnisky (1997) for an International Bank for Environmental Settlements.   The Bank proposed here simply tracks ownership, it cannot lend or borrow.   The term Bank is primarily used to provide a clear analogy to a familiar institution.   Although the Bank may provide some information that facilitates trade, that is not its primary function.

[9] This is the approach taken in the US Acid Rain Program.

[10] If the Clean Development Mechanism were defined as a multilateral organization, the country would not be free to sell this CER except through an international agency.   It could not be translated into an AAU until sold by the agency.

broker who represents its interests. Alternatively the buyer of the CER could take responsibility for certification and pay the developing country in advance. Then it would go into the buyer's account when certified.

Figure 2.1 National banking accounts, trading and surrender

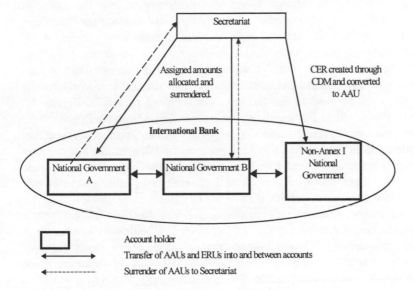

3.2   Interaction Between National Systems and International Tracking System

Countries will choose different approaches to domestic compliance, tradable allowances, taxes, and a range of policies and measures. The tracking system need not affect this choice in any way. Different countries should be free to choose different compliance approaches as long as all international AAUs are tracked.

A country that chose to comply with a domestic system other than a tradable allowance system also would probably retain control over all its international permit holdings. If the national government allowed legal-entities to sell international AAUs with no compensating domestic obligation it would risk non-compliance.[11]

---

[11]If a country knew it had 'hot air', or more AAUs than business-as-usual emissions, it could give or sell these excess AAUs to private actors and allow them to be sold internationally with no compliance risk.

A national government could allocate international AAUs at the beginning of the commitment period to domestic actors.[12]   At the end of the commitment period, and possibly at interim points, such legal-entities would surrender to their national government AAUs equal to their emissions. If these AAUs were freely tradable domestically, this would be a domestic trading market.[13] The national government would regain, over the course of the commitment period, a number of AAUs sufficient to make the balance in the national government account equal to national emissions. At the end of the commitment period only AAUs in the national government account would be surrendered internationally to establish compliance to the secretariat. Any positive balances in national or private accounts after the true up could be banked for the next commitment period.[14] Figure 2.2 illustrates this option. For simplicity we exclude CERs from the figure.

National governments also could sell AAUs without associated obligations to private traders that have their own bank accounts and to other national governments. Similarly, legal-entities within Country A could trade AAUs with other countries as well as legal-entities in other countries that have chosen the same approach, such as country B.

A national government may choose to create a domestic trading system but not disburse international AAUs. In Figure 2.3, National Government A chooses this option. It could instead create a domestic allowance currency that is used solely to establish company compliance at the domestic level. These AAUs could not be put into AAU bank accounts. No AAUs would be withdrawn from the national AAU bank account for the domestic system. The national government would still sell or buy AAUs if the emissions cap in its domestic system was not set equal to its assigned amount.

A national government that chooses to use Joint Implementation (JI) rather than emissions trading for its legal-entities may also maintain ownership of AAUs until the JI trades are approved. Then they could transfer the ERUs created to the legal-entity or transfer them internationally on behalf of their legal-entity.

---

[12]A government may choose to use a domestic trading system for some sources and gases and policies and measures for others. In that case they devolve only some AAUs to legal-entities.

[13]For discussion of the basic design of a domestic CO_2 allowance market, see Fischer et al. (1998a).

[14]An environmental group that purchased AAUs could choose to retire them 'for the earth'.

Figure 2.2 Domestic trading systems with legal-entity international trading

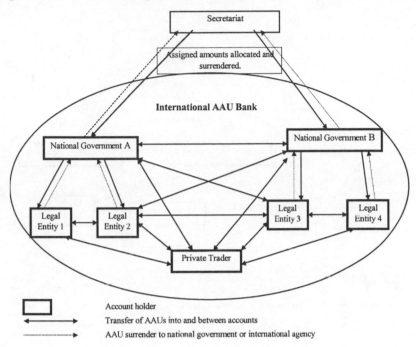

3.3   **Who Holds Accounts and Initiates Trades between Accounts?**

Every trader of AAUs would need to maintain a bank account and could only consummate a trade by transferring AAUs from one account to another. It would be sufficient for the seller to report the trade to the registry, and hence initiate the transfer.

Anyone could hold an account. Holding an account does not give any ability to carry out derivative transactions or give any right to trade any national government's allowances. Derivative traders/brokers could be separately regulated in the way that other financial instruments are regulated and monitored by private and public institutions. National governments can put whatever restrictions they choose on their own AAUs. If accounts can never be in 'overdraft', allowing an additional account creates no risk for the bank or international community. The bank would charge account fees to cover the administrative cost of operating accounts.

Figure 2.3 Domestic trading systems with no legal-entity international trading

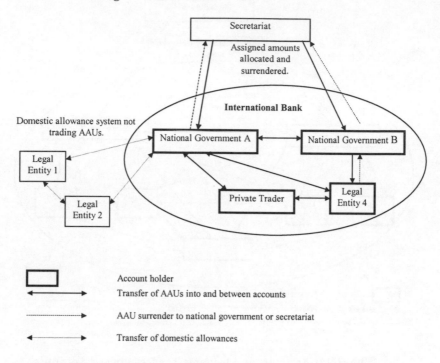

Account holder

Transfer of AAUs into and between accounts

AAU surrender to national government or secretariat

Transfer of domestic allowances

3.4 What Does the Bank Record?

Only three pieces of information are essential: the identity of the seller and buyer, the quantity of assigned amount – denominated in tons of carbon equivalent – bought or sold, and the commitment period the AAU relates to, if AAUs have been created for future commitment periods. If the AAU is banked from a previous commitment period it is unnecessary to distinguish it from current allocations. Other information could be collected depending on other potential functions of the Bank and other rules of the trading system. Unique serial numbers on all units would be useful to facilitate auditing and resolve disputes.

3.5 When and How Would Transfers be made between Accounts?

Two types of transaction will occur within the market. The first, here defined as 'transfers', is the obvious transfer of AAUs between account holders. The second is a private 'contract' which may ultimately lead to a transfer of

AAUs but in the short run does not involve any reporting or formal transfer. For example, a 2008 'contract' to sell AAUs in 2010 for a given price does not lead to an actual 'transfer' until 2010. Forward contracts, options, and other derivatives will hopefully thrive in the market but will occur privately, they are not the concern of the bank. The players and trades involved in the 'market' will include but not be limited to actors with accounts and transfers within the bank.

Transfers would be made on a real-time basis when the seller initiates the transfer.[15] The only AAUs that can be used for interim or final reported compliance are those actually in the national account; contractually promised AAUs would not count. Buyers would be liable for ensuring that their purchase involved a real transfer of AAUs so they would have an incentive to consummate contracts through registry transfers earlier to reduce their risk. Private contracts would not be recognized as legally binding on the international community even if there was no buyer liability system.

The bank would be an electronic database and transfers would occur electronically. This is administratively more convenient, more secure, and faster than paper records. The United States Environmental Protection Agency software used for the US Acid Rain program, or for that matter the software used by any private bank, could be used as a basis for the system.[16] Electronic records also allow easier collation of data for compliance purposes, crosschecking and easy public release of information in real time through the Internet. Trades could be initiated by any of the means available for financial transfers: fax, phone, Internet/email, writing.

3.6   Who Runs the Bank?

Whoever actually administers the bank must have certain characteristics. Account holders and the international community must be able to hold them liable for any errors. They would ideally have experience running similar electronic databases. They must be competent and incorruptible.

The Secretariat itself could carry out this function or they could give it to a private institution and strictly supervise it. The entire function need not be carried out by one single organization. If there are multiple banks the banks must readily be able to link all account information and must have consistent rules for transfer. If multiple AAU banks exist, rules of liability across banks must be determined. They must also all have reporting systems that allow

---

[15]Or at least as close to real time as bank transfers – 2 or 3 days.
[16]The United States EPA has adapted the software used for their Acid Rain program to be able to use it as the basis of an international greenhouse gas tracking system.

real time collation of international data to make overall holdings and flows of AAUs transparent. The issues of multiple banks are discussed further below under 'Variations on the Basic System'.

3.7   What Information Would the Bank Give to the Secretariat and What Would they Release Publicly?

3.7.1   Secretariat
National compliance account holdings are all that it is necessary for the secretariat to know. Other information that could be valuable would be the net pattern of trade as a possible indicator of misuse of market or political power. The volume of total trade would be valuable as an indicator of market liquidity and efficiency. Trade specific detail could be valuable for research purposes to assist in future improvements to the trading system.

3.7.2   Public
An important tradeoff exists between potential compliance gains from transparency and higher transaction costs. The AAU bank could release some information with little cost and high benefit whereas they should probably withhold other information.

As discussed above under 'Functions', transparency of reports could improve compliance. It would allow countries, companies and environmental non-governmental organizations to apply direct compliance pressure on each other during and at the end of the period. It would allow them to report to the international agency if they thought a country was likely to be out of compliance. If buyers were liable for the sellers' compliance, transparency would be more valuable because it would reduce the uncontrollable risk buyers would face.

Transparency also has costs. Transparency at the company level can raise transaction costs and hence raise compliance costs significantly.[17] Trading may reveal something about their current and future commercial plans. Companies may choose not to trade to avoid revealing this information. Companies also could create 'dummy' accounts to hide their identity but this raises their administrative costs as well as the complexity of auditing the tracking system. Alternatively governments could agree to trade on behalf of their legal-entities so that accounts will only show aggregate transfers. This would avoid revealing company information but would also create higher domestic administration costs and reduce the secretariat's information. We would not want a company or country's desire to avoid public release of

---

[17]For empirical evidence on this in the US lead phasedown, see Kerr and Maré (1996).

information to compromise the accuracy and comprehensibility of tracking reports. A useful analogy is to tax information, which is not publicly revealed in order to maximize tax revenue. In the US even much illegal income is reported to the Inland Revenue Service.

Many proposals exist to utilize the tracking system to provide information to facilitate trading. Many discussions confuse the two functions of providing information to the international agency to help determine compliance, and providing information to facilitate trade. The same agency might not do both. We must force traders to report information for tracking purposes. Traders will volunteer information to facilitate trade because it is in their interests to be identified by potential trading partners. Thus private agencies can easily offer brokerage information and services.

The tracking agency could release information in real time through the Internet. Publicly releasing AAU account balances would be valuable for compliance and would have no obvious cost. Releasing any more information would have some costs and these would have to be weighed against the benefits.

4   VARIATIONS ON THE BASIC SYSTEM

4.1   Multiple Banks

Above we outlined the simplest possible tracking institution, which involves one bank. For several reasons it may be preferable to have one integrated system with multiple, linked but separate banks. National sovereignty may create resistance to being forced to hold AAUs in one international bank. Some nations may want to limit legal-entities' ability to trade AAUs but not prohibit it.[18] This may most easily be done through restrictions on transfers from their accounts. An international bank may not be willing to administer this system.

Two other reasons relate to the efficiency of the bank. One key reason for multiple banks would be to induce competition in order to encourage reduced administrative costs, high quality service, and innovation in transfer technology. If we have multiple banks we would not need to fund them directly for performing this function, they could, without regulation, charge account and transfer fees to cover their costs. These costs would be held down by competition.

---

[18]This could be thought of as analogous to capital export/import constraints.

If we allowed multiple banks, we would need some overall regulation and qualification criteria for becoming a bank. Banks would need to satisfy a capital requirement to ensure that they could be held liable for extra AAUs that are mistakenly created, or transfers that go astray. On an ongoing basis, they would need to be observed to ensure they comply with rules standardized across banks. This would be similar to the regulatory systems for financial banks without the concern about prudential supervision – AAU banks would not take risks by lending AAUs or dealing in derivatives. Their AAU accounts would be backed one hundred percent by real AAUs.

With multiple banks, reporting protocols would have to be clearly defined so that aggregate holdings of AAUs, and possibly aggregate holdings by national governments, could be assessed on a real time basis. This is of increased importance with annual surrender of AAUs and the creation of CERs that are added to the system. Without these the total number of AAUs does not change although their ownership and location will.

4.2   Additional Recording Needs to Support Buyer Liability

If buyers were made liable for the compliance of the seller with whom the AAU originated, information other than the quantity of AAU would need to be tracked. The information required would depend on the form of buyer liability chosen. The most likely form is 'last-in-first-out' where AAUs from a given country are invalidated in reverse order until the seller's net emission match net valid sales. In this system the registry would have to record the origin of each AAU and the date at which it was first sold out of the country of origin.

4.3   Additional Information that Could be Required to Aid
         Monitoring

Reporting the gas that was reduced to create the surplus AAU that could be traded may provide a form of cross check against national inventories. For example a permit sold from the agricultural sector may be identified as a methane reduction whereas one from the electric utility sector would probably be identified as a CO_2 reduction. Although all gases are formally fungible under the treaty, if a country sold a large amount of a difficult-to-measure gas and could not justify that by pointing to any policies or economic changes that would have created the reduction other countries may reasonably be skeptical about the quality of the emissions inventory. This information could not necessarily be used for formal compliance purposes but it may allow informal interim pressure not to base trade on estimated surpluses of poorly measured gases and to improve inventories of such gases. Even if the gases traded are not recorded during the commitment period they will be implicitly observable after inventories are complete is established. By matching inventories before and during the commitment period we can identify where reductions were achieved.

4.4 Additional Information that Could be Collected to Facilitate Trade

Requiring traders to report price could provide some information for the market as a whole. The cost of requiring price, particularly if it is publicly released, is that countries and/or legal-entities may be concerned about the confidentiality of their deal. It is not necessary for determining compliance. Those who report will have an incentive to misrepresent price so the information will probably be unreliable in any case. Price information provided for a specific trade frequently cannot be verified. In any case, price information will be available through brokers.

5 PREVIOUS EXPERIENCES WITH TRACKING SYSTEMS

The tracking system was one of the weakest features of the US lead phase-down trading market. A poor computer system and large delays in detecting and following up on mistakes and cheating led to vocal congressional concern and much media attention.[19] Legal cases continued for years after the market ended. Despite this, compliance was extremely high – fewer permits were used in aggregate than were allocated, and the market was active and reasonably efficient.[20] Non-compliance was concentrated among very small entities and those not intrinsically related to the industry.

In the US Acid Rain Program, which controls sulfur-dioxide emissions from electric utilities, the US learned from the lead phase-down experience and EPA developed a relatively sophisticated tracking system.[21] Each utility and trader has at least one account. Any actor can hold 'General' accounts, while compliance or 'unit' accounts are held by utilities to show end of year compliance. Allowances are not paper certificates; account holders simply

---

[19] US Government Accounting Office (1986).
[20] For detailed discussion of these issues see Kerr and Maré (1999).
[21] They have recently adapted this system to deal with international trading of greenhouse gas emissions allowances.

receive balance statements. All transfers are recorded electronically. Each allowance has a serial number. When a transfer is requested, the transfer form must identify the serial numbers of the units traded. The account holder from which the allowances are being withdrawn must approve the transfer. The system successfully handles thousands of transactions each year. It provides a public record of ownership and date of transfer, and the ability to track each individual allowance at all times.[22]

6   CONCLUSION

We conclude that a tracking system for international greenhouse trading should be as simple as possible. Its design should focus on providing accurate, timely compliance data and low-administration-cost transfers of AAUs. The analogy of a Bank allows us to see how the underlying system would work, with a series of accounts and transfer rules. The bank should electronically record account balances at each point in time. Account balance information should be available in real time to both the Secretariat and the public.

The bank also could record the complete path of transfers throughout the commitment period to enable auditing. If each AAU, ERU and CER has a unique serial number and the bank maintains a record of holding at each point in time the secretariat could track the complete path of transfers. This would allow evaluation of the efficiency of the system and would provide information to address disputes and any market or political power concerns. This information could be kept confidential, to avoid confidentiality concerns and high transaction costs, but be made available for analysis. Additional information would need to be made publicly available and given to the secretariat if buyer liability is chosen. In a last-in-first-out system the country of origin and date and first international transfer would be recorded against the unique serial number.

The 'bank' could, and probably should, not be a multilateral institution. It has a purely technical role and should be non-political. A more complex system with multiple 'banks' or 'registries' linked in a consistent overall system has the same basic structure. Multiple 'banks' have advantages for sovereignty and for encouraging efficiency through competition among banks. With multiple banks, the tracking system could be funded through

---

[22]For more information see United States Environmental Protection Agency (1994 a and b) or contact the US EPA Acid Rain Program, Att: Allowance Tracking System, 401 M Street, SW. Washington DC 20460.

account and transfer fees with no concern about monopoly pricing. If multiple banks are used some basic regulation will be required to ensure that banks can be held liable for any 'errors' they make in transfers or account balances.

Creating a tracking system is a relatively simple familiar problem. The technical details should be resolved with the assistance of those familiar with international banking procedures. If the infrastructure can be created rapidly, future negotiations on trading may be more focused. Forward trading among Annex B countries and the creation of ERUs could begin in a more certain environment. We recommend a system of multiple banks with well defined and audited transfer protocols. These could be run by national governments or the role could be delegated to regulated private entities.

3 Treaty Compliance as Background for an Effective Trading Program

Tim Hargrave, Suzi Kerr, Ned Helme and Tim Denne[1]

1 INTRODUCTION

A strong credible compliance regime is the cornerstone of any effective environmental regulation, and the Kyoto Protocol will be no exception. No international compliance regime can be successful if signatories do not strongly support the treaty; Parties ratify only when they are willing to bear the costs imposed, if they perceive the relative contributions of different Parties to be equitable, and if they trust that others will comply. Experience suggests that this trust is achieved through a variety of different types of tools, including strong accounting and reporting infrastructure, measures to prevent non-compliance, efforts to facilitate compliance, incentives and deterrents, and moral pressure.

Many papers have been written about compliance with international agreements and compliance with the climate change agreement in particular. In particular see Mitchell and Chayes (1995), Corfee-Morlot (1998a) and Werksman (1999). This chapter summarizes the key insights from these papers but its key contribution is to discuss in more detail some of the very practical methodological and institutional issues associated with implementing the Kyoto Protocol. We draw on the theoretical literature and on previous experience with international environmental compliance in our search for solutions to key institutional design issues. A major emphasis is on the logistics of assessing compliance: who assesses it and how. While this is a book about Annex B Emissions Trading, we find that we cannot discuss the compliance issues relating to trading in the absence of the broader compliance context.

[1] The authors are grateful to all the members of the Center's International Emissions Trading Dialogue group for their comments on earlier drafts.

The goals of the climate convention are long term. They need to be achieved and sustained over the next one hundred years and beyond. Small differences in emissions over the next twenty years will be swamped by any changes in long-term emission trends. The key objective for implementing Kyoto needs to be to build strong institutions that will endure and produce benefits equitably and at low cost. We need to build trust and confidence. We need to encourage dynamic changes in technology, human behaviour and institutions. We need to encourage, facilitate and sustain participation in the global effort by all countries and peoples. The direct emission reduction impact of compliance by Annex B countries in the first commitment period will be relatively insignificant in the long run. That said, however, achieving compliance with short run targets is a critical step toward establishing confidence among both developed and developing countries, giving credibility to the commitments of the major players, and providing credible incentives for research and development and major changes in technology and infrastructure. The compliance structure needs to balance a desire for short-term compliance with the long-term needs.

The compliance problem we are ultimately concerned with in this book is compliance within the tradable permit market. This problem is embedded, however, in a wider problem of compliance with the international agreement the market is used to implement. If all countries comply with the agreement, they will automatically be in compliance with any of their trading. The Framework Convention and the Kyoto Protocol contain a combination of commitments aimed at short and long run environmental effectiveness. Commitments to emissions reductions between 2008 and 2012, commitments to inventory development and information dissemination, commitments to cooperate in research and facilitate the transfer of technology, as well as general short run goals, such as demonstrable progress in policy development and implementation, all have different roles in improving effectiveness. Efforts to improve compliance with these need to proceed regardless of the development of a tradable permit market.

The tradable permit market is simply a tool to implement the international agreement more effectively. It cannot compensate for any shortcomings in the ability of the Kyoto targets to actually lead to effective and efficient long-term control of greenhouse gas emissions.[2] Inappropriate targets cannot be corrected through market design. Measures within the trading system to enhance compliance cannot compensate for poor general compliance design. Good compliance is a precursor to an effective trading system. It gives value

[2] See Young (1994) for a discussion of alternative ways of defining the 'effectiveness' of an environmental regime.

to permits that they won't have otherwise. Trading is meaningless if states do not achieve a meaningful level of compliance.

A tradable permit market can improve compliance or goal achievement by allowing us to achieve our goals at the lowest economic and social cost possible.[3] It can also threaten compliance, however, by making behavior less transparent and hence perceived compliance more manipulable. A poorly designed market can also put the ultimate responsibility for compliance in the hands of actors with less concern and capacity to comply. A well-designed market will maximize the cost savings while ensuring that the required behavioral changes occur to stabilize greenhouse gas concentrations. These issues are discussed in detail in the next chapter.

The international community is concerned about short-run compliance for four main reasons. The first is that we want to achieve the short term overall objectives of the Framework Convention. These goals have direct implications for environmental effectiveness. Second, we are concerned about fairness in the implementation of the Convention. If some countries are able to avoid their obligations, this is not fair to those who comply. There would be competitiveness impacts on those who do comply if others don't.[4] Third, in the medium to long term, if many people cheat or are perceived to cheat it will be harder to maintain and build cooperation.[5] If some cheat, others will feel like 'suckers' and the treaty could unravel. Fourth, strong credible compliance mechanisms will actually lower the cost of compliance by providing investor security for long-term abatement-related investments and assuring buyers of AAUs that their purchases will have value.[6] Ensuring that AAUs have real value, because both buyer and seller states will face real consequences if they do not hold enough, will encourage potential buyers to provide capital for abatement investments in seller states.

In the international context, limits are placed on the design of a compliance system. Agreements are entered into by sovereign states that can choose not to participate or to withdraw.[7] Thus penalties are severely limited. Any compliance regime must therefore not only consider

---

[3] Mitchell refers to this as reducing the 'preference' for non-compliance. Chapter 2 Mitchell (1994b).

[4] See Chapter 7.

[5] Ostrom (1990) pp. 94–100.

[6] This observation is not dependent on their being buyer liability. Even with seller-only liability AAUs will only have value to the extent that compliance is achieved with the agreement as a whole. If the price of AAUs falls because of widespread non-compliance all AAU holders, including buyers, will lose.

[7] We regard sovereignty as a constraint on the power of international enforcement. It raises the cost of rewarding, punishing and monitoring by the international agency. For a full discussion of this topic see Susskind (1994).

international compliance institutions but also encourage parties to strengthen domestic regimes that could support the international institutions. The compliance regime also needs to reduce the risk faced by participants not only for abstract reasons of justice (which apply also in a domestic justice system) but also for the practical reason that countries may choose not to participate if they perceive the risks of facing non-compliance penalties as too severe.[8]

In this chapter we focus on compliance with the emissions limitation and reduction commitments made by Annex B countries under the Kyoto Protocol. We consider other commitments through their impact on compliance with these binding targets. We begin with a brief survey of three literatures relevant to compliance. We also specify what states agreed to comply with under Kyoto. We then consider how compliance may be measured. We focus on the processes and institutions needed at the national and international levels to create credible emissions inventories. Following that we look at how, during the commitment period, we can facilitate compliance and avoid non-compliance. At the end of the commitment period a state's compliance may be ambiguous because of the uncertainties and possible incompleteness associated with emission inventories. The international community may decide to allow a small margin of error in compliance before imposing penalties. We consider what sort of body and process should determine official compliance (or non-compliance). The possibilities range from automatic triggers to a politically representative compliance authority. When a country has been found to be out of compliance, several consequences could occur. The punitive aspects of these consequences should deter states from being out of compliance. We discuss the penalties available for addressing non-compliance and how they might be used most effectively. Finally we conclude.

2 CONCEPTUAL APPROACHES TO COMPLIANCE

Several academic literatures consider compliance from different conceptual backgrounds; each offers different insights. These literatures include the economics literature on crime and enforcement, monitoring and contract/mechanism design and cooperative game theory literature, and the political science and legal literature on verification and compliance.

---

[8] For further discussion of this issue see Downs (1998).

2.1 Economics Literature

Non-compliance could stem from two basic sources. First it could be a deliberate act by government. The government could deliberately flaunt the agreement though this is unlikely given that they voluntarily signed. They could, however, find that it is much more expensive than they anticipated when they signed or believe that others are not going to comply so not try to comply themselves. This could be argued to have happened with the FCCC goal of returning to 1990 emissions by the year 2000 which few countries are set to achieve; those that will achieve it will do so largely by chance and good fortune (or bad economic fortune).

2.1.2 Deterrence

In the economics literature, Becker (1968) formalized the analysis of optimal monitoring and punishment, modeling non-compliance as a rationally chosen action.[9] Put simply, an agent will comply if the probability of being caught times the fine is greater than the value of non-compliance.[10] A compliance regime needs to increase the probability that countries that deliberately non-comply are observed and punished and increase the intensity of the consequences of non-compliance. Becker's analysis is in a domestic setting where the government has centralized power to enforce. Fines and probabilities of punishment can be directly chosen relatively easily though sometimes with high cost.[11] Also, his analysis considers individual compliance rather than country level compliance so he can ignore collective action problems.

Becker's model is based purely on deterrence where the laws that actors need to comply with and the interests of actors are given. Other approaches are more flexible. Taking a different but complementary approach, the economic literature on contracts starting with Coase (1937) considers how to write contracts and structure institutions when there are information problems and transaction costs.[12] This could be thought of as designing rules that will

---

[9] For a dynamic extension of this model see Harrington (1988).

[10] This is a simplified version. Becker takes account of potential risk aversion or risk loving.

[11] At the international level 'fines' are extremely limited due to the anarchic structure of international relations. Rewards are also limited due to the difficulties with making side-payments between countries. Thus to encourage global cooperation, we need to focus on improving our ability to punish and reward. We can also raise the probability of punishment by having effective compliance systems. Harrington (1988) looks at the case where enforcement instruments are limited.

[12] For an excellent exposition see, Laffont and Tirole (1993). Barrett, Carraro and Siniscalco have written extensively on international cooperation using contract and game theory ideas.

achieve as good an outcome as possible but that are also enforceable.[13] If the agreement is too ambitious it may be impossible to write a contract that will achieve its goals.

2.1.3   Rewards, graduated punishments and voluntary participation

The model of compliance that comes from the contract literature has the following characteristics. By making positive transfers dependent on observable outcomes that are related to compliance effort, the contract encourages compliance effort.[14] In contrast to Becker, the rewards are a continuous function of observed compliance, which allows for the reality of partial compliance. Participation in contracts is voluntary and this constraint is built into the model.[15] This means that each agent must at least in expectation receive a positive benefit from being involved in the contract. These attributes of the contracting model are appropriate to modeling international compliance.[16]

Elinor Ostrom (1990) a political scientist, also supports the idea of gradual punishments that depend on the degree of violation and that take into account the intention to violate the agreement. She bases her arguments on a series of case studies of successful and unsuccessful cooperation. She argues that if some people are forgiven for violations that were clearly beyond their control (e.g. emissions from the fires in Kuwait after the Persian Gulf War) it not only keeps them in the agreement but others will not see it as a weakening of overall compliance.

---

[13]Petrakis and Xepapadeas (1996) consider the problem of compliance as a formal mechanism design problem. They look at a situation where there are transfers to less environmentally conscious countries and individual country emissions are unobservable. However, they assume that total emissions are observable and base their complex mechanism on this. In problems such as climate change or ozone depletion, it is only possible to observe total emissions through the sum of individual emissions. The relationship between emissions and ambient levels is very uncertain and involves lags of emissions and natural sources as well as anthropogenic emissions. Their model would be more appropriate to a problem such as sulfur dioxide in Europe where pollutant movements are better understood and ambient levels are more directly related to local and neighboring emissions.

[14]For example $C = e + \mu$, where C is observed compliance, e is compliance effort and μ is an iid shock with mean zero.

[15]The political science literature also discusses the problem of voluntary participation and its effects on optimal compliance structures (see Downs, 1998).

[16]The law and economics literature also deals extensively with similar problems. Calabresi (1970) develops a theory of accident law and appropriate liability structures. This was further developed by Brown (1973), Diamond (1974a, 1974b), Diamond and Mirrlees (1975) and Green (1976). This literature is dealing with a different and clearer set of institutional constraints to those in an international cooperation problem, but uses a similar microeconomic foundation.

2.1.4   Inability/poor ability to observe actions – poor relationship between effort and consequences

Given that compliance is rewarded based on observable outcomes not effort, agents may put in optimal effort and carry out the best actions possible, but fail to produce the required outcome due to forces beyond their control. In these models the random elements of observed outcomes and hence rewards and punishments are accounted for explicitly. It is optimal to allow for some findings of non-compliance in cases where actions (compliance) are not fully observable, for example, where inventories are incomplete or known to be inaccurate. Unfortunately this means that some actors will be perceived to be out of compliance when they are not really.

Problems also arise when actions are non-verifiable, so that they cannot be used as evidence in a court of law. For example, if rules for inventories are not clear and standardized a country could be formally in compliance by manipulating their data to match the legal requirements even though it is clear to all other states that they were not in compliance with the intention of the agreement. The actual non-compliance is not verifiable. Thus formal law enforcement will be weak.

Our inability to perfectly observe actions, or the appropriateness of actions, and/or the inability to act on the information received (e.g., due to sovereignty concerns) leads to the problem of moral hazard.[17] Although we really want to reward effort to comply we have to reward/punish based on observed compliance, which may not be that closely related. This increases the risk faced by those who really try to comply because their efforts may not be accurately reflected in measured outcomes. This argues for some leeway in compliance; that is punishments may best be applied in a discretionary way to take account of the situation. When punishments are based on poorly observed indicators they are unlikely to be able to be automatic. The disadvantage of non-automatic punishments is that non-compliers may not be punished because it will be impossible to prove lack of effort. Non-compliers will always claim circumstances beyond their control or that the measurements do not accurately reflect their reality. One key way to address all of these problems is to improve the systems for monitoring and reporting.

2.1.5   Repetition and reputation

The non-cooperative game theory literature suggests that cooperation is more likely to be achieved in a repeated game where states can remember and take

---

[17]We are concerned with all forms of opportunism in Williamson's (1985, pp. 47–49) terms, rather than moral hazard in the strict insurance sense. For a recent article, which looks at the general problem of moral hazard in encouraging compliance of non-environmentally conscious countries, see Petrakis and Xepapadeas (1996).

into account the behavior of other states in past periods. This suggests that visibly maintaining data on the compliance records of states and basing compliance rewards and penalties on past behavior is valuable. States need to be able to create a visible reputation for good compliance and cooperation.[18] In a narrow sense this highlights the importance of creating future commitment periods early so that changes in obligations in the second period relative to the initial agreement can be used to reward and punish behavior in the first commitment period. This is only effective to the extent that we can find penalties for non-compliers that do not punish the compliant states. Punishments need to be credible. More broadly it suggests the importance of linking compliance in the climate agreement to other international agreements that are part of the larger international repeated 'game'. States can be broadly rewarded for acting cooperatively.[19]

2.1.6   Equity

A fourth economics literature that is relevant is that of cooperative game theory.[20] This literature focuses on the equity of agreements. In an international agreement, countries may be more likely to comply if they believe that the agreement is equitable. Cooperative game theory takes axioms that are believed to be just and, based on each state's benefits and costs, finds cost sharing rules (and hence commitment targets) that satisfy these axioms. This is clearly important for designing an agreement that countries will sign. For these factors to affect outcomes after states have signed the agreement we have to believe that state's preferences are not fixed. The state will behave differently even when faced with the same incentives depending on the incentives faced by others. The underlying structure of the agreement can have a significant effect on compliance.

Genuine agreement to comply at the time of signing is still not enough to ensure compliance. Cooperative game theory assumes the ability to make binding commitments. Without this ability, the problem becomes non-cooperative once the agreement is signed. Punishments will be part of that cooperative agreement and can be seen as a commitment device agreed to by all parties even though they may in the future apply to themselves. This is a device to build trust. Each state can see that if there are credible, enforceable punishments it is in the interests of each other state to comply. This in turn

---

[18]Kreps and Wilson (1982) and Milgrom and Roberts (1982). Discussed in Fudenberg and Tirole (1993).

[19]In this circumstance we are assuming that the country has agreed to participate in the agreement in the first place; that there are cooperative gains. If not, it is much harder to use other issues to force participation.

[20]See for example, Moulin (1988).

lowers the risks associated with large investments in compliance and creates a virtuous compliance circle.

2.2   Political Science and International Law

There is a long literature in political science and international law on why countries comply with treaties.[21] This literature is also relevant to compliance with an international tradable permit market. Keohane (1984) gives a clear discussion of the problems with enforcing cooperation, using game theory concepts. The cooperation problems arise both because of incentives to not cooperate and because of free riding in enforcement. He discusses changes to the basic structure of the 'game', such as repetition and reputation effects, which reduce these difficulties. The traditional 'common wisdom' approach to compliance in political science comes from a theory of deterrence.[22] The aim of a deterrence-based strategy is to raise the costs of non-compliance by creating a severe, credible threat of punishment (Schelling, 1980). This is equivalent to Becker's approach. These models tend to assume that actors are rational utility maximizers and can effectively control their actions.[23]

Another strand of the political science literature however emphasizes that states have agreed to comply with agreements because they want the outcome. This literature notes that most states comply with most agreements most of the time. The key question is why and whether this will extend to a more challenging agreement on climate change. Do states simply comply because the agreement codifies something they intended to do anyway? Does the agreement have a coordination role where if other states comply it is in the interests of the state to comply? In this situation the agreement would be valuable but the pressure on the agreement once made is slight so compliance is not surprising. States may comply because of the linkage to other issues that are more important to them.[24] States may want the climate agreement to work but there are always incentives for each to non-comply and the agreement needs to build considerable trust. As the aims of the agreement become more ambitious and the costs rise, the interdependence of parties on each other's compliance increases and stronger non-compliance

---

[21]For a concise introduction to the literature see Mitchell (1996). See also Victor, Raustiala and Skolnikoff (1998).

[22]For a recent discussion of this model see Hawkins (1984).

[23]See Braithwaite (1985).

[24]For an excellent discussion of the issues of linkages and 'zones of agreement' see Sebenius (1993).

mechanisms are probably required. For some evidence on this see Downs et al. (1996).

2.2.1   Capacity to comply

Chayes and Chayes (1993) discuss compliance with international law and argue persuasively that compliance is achieved through positive inducements and assistance rather than deterrence and punishment.

The political science literature in general stresses the capacity of agents to comply, and of governments to enforce compliance.[25]   Compliance is by sovereign states but emission reductions are actually done by individuals and firms.   Non-compliance could arise because the country is incapable of implementing and enforcing regulations that limit emissions sufficiently. The private sector could deliberately non-comply with domestic regulation if the government's enforcement powers are not strong enough.   Actual non-compliance is likely to be a combination of lack of effort and lack of capacity to control domestic actors.   If the government does not feel a strong pressure to comply it will be unwilling to impose and enforce costly measures against domestic opposition.

A lack of capacity to comply exacerbates the problems of opportunism and moral hazard, because it is difficult to observe true effort in a case where the ability to control outcomes is limited.   Countries that are found to be out of compliance will tend to claim exceptional circumstances beyond their control even when the reality is a lack of effort.   Compliance policies must either impose risk on innocent states or let some states get away with inadequate effort.   The political science emphasis on capacity leads to similar conclusions to the contracting model where the optimal compliance system not only involves choosing appropriate rewards and punishments but altering the contract to deal with varying capabilities.

2.2.2   Preventing non-compliance

Recent political science literature has begun to explore the effects of institutional design on compliance.   Compliance is modeled as a rational action but one that is constrained by capacity, information and incentives. For example Mitchell (1994a & b) uses the example of intentional oil pollution at sea to argue that in some cases, prevention of non-compliance is more effective than ex-post monitoring and reward or punishment.   He also shows that, sometimes, institutional change can increase the capacity of agents to legally enforce compliance of others as well as their incentives to enforce.

[25]For a good discussion of these issues see Haas, Keohane and Levy (1993).

One major strand of work in political science emphasizes three elements of success in international environmental institutions, 'concern', 'contracting' and 'capacity'.[26] The compliance regime and the agreement as a whole can be constructed to increase and reward concern and commitment to the outcomes. Taking account of incentives and constraints on information, as well as emphasizing improvements in data, creates contracts that leverage the concern states have and the punishments available to maximize compliance. Facilitating compliance by raising the capacity of states to control their sub-state actors in an efficient effective way and to diffuse technology and skills reduces the cost of compliance and the ability of states to claim inability to control compliance.

3   WHAT DID STATES AGREE TO COMPLY WITH UNDER KYOTO?

Under the Kyoto Protocol, industrialized ('Annex 1') countries committed to meet binding emissions limitation and reduction commitments. The specific commitment of each country is expressed as a percentage of base year (usually 1990) emissions and applies for the period 2008 to 2012 (see Appendix 1).[27] These commitments have four functions. First, they will have a direct though small impact on the environment. Second, they have a role in establishing coordination among the efforts of different states. If they are achieved they will begin to establish trust in the cooperative process necessary to achieve long run goals. Third, they begin to establish norms for relative cost bearing both within Annex B and between developing countries and Annex B. Targets are differentiated; they are linked to historical emissions; poorer states take on less stringent targets than richer states.[28] Fourth, by setting clear, relatively immediate targets they have focused policy

---

[26]See Haas, Keohane and Levy (1993) and Keohane and Levy (1996).

[27]Article 3.1 of the Protocol requires Annex B Parties to 'ensure that their aggregate anthropogenic carbon dioxide equivalent emissions of [greenhouse gases] do not exceed their assigned amounts'. Annex I is currently the same group as Annex B. Further, Article 3.3 says that 'net changes in greenhouse gas emissions by sources and removals by sinks shall be used to meet the commitments under [Article 3]'. To be in compliance with these provisions, an Annex B Party must at the end of the commitment period hold assigned amount units (AAUs) equal to or greater than its emissions during the commitment period. Total assigned amount units held will equal the Party's initial assigned amount (including AAUs banked from earlier commitment periods) plus or minus net AAUs acquired/transferred during the commitment period.

[28]People may see the example of 'hot air' as concerning in this context but in fact hot air was not negotiated. It was a mistake resulting from excessive optimism about the future of the Eastern European economies.

attention on the details of designing the domestic and international institutions and regulations necessary to change human behavior. The institutions that are now evolving could have significant effects on the long-term nature of global regulation. At least part of the debate has moved from generalities to specific concrete issues.

Industrialized countries agreed to several other provisions that are designed to ensure that Parties meet their binding emissions commitments, though they do not mandate particular levels of emissions reductions. One such provision requires countries to implement policies and measures (PAMs) to mitigate emissions, though it does not specify what those PAMs should be, while another provision requires industrialized states to have made, by 2005, 'demonstrable progress' toward meeting their Kyoto commitments.[29]

Industrialized countries are also committed under the Protocol to collecting and disseminating information about their greenhouse gas emissions and related policies.[30] Countries will be required to prepare annual greenhouse gas inventories (actually required under the Convention), implement 'national systems' for developing strong inventories and regularly report all information needed to demonstrate compliance with all Protocol commitments.

The development of detailed emissions inventories is key to assessing compliance with short-term emissions limitation commitments. It also has a longer-term role in improving our knowledge of sources of and trends in emissions. It will allow better assessment of future options and the creation of fair agreements. The improved data allow us to identify valuable opportunities for mitigation. Compliance with information provisions is key both for short run compliance and for long run environmental effectiveness.

Finally, the Protocol contains a number of provisions aimed at facilitating cooperation among nations. For example, all countries, both developing and industrialized, are to 'Cooperate in the promotion of effective modalities for the development, application and diffusion of . . . environmentally sound technologies, . . . cooperate in scientific and technical research and the development of systematic observation systems and development of data archives, and cooperate in the development and implementation of educational training programme'.[31]

From here on we will consider directly compliance only with the emission reduction commitments for Annex B and the reporting and monitoring

---

[29]See Articles 2 and 3.2 of the Kyoto Protocol, respectively.
[30]These requirements are in Articles 5 and 7 of the Protocol.
[31]Kyoto Protocol Article 10.

requirements that are essential for assessing compliance with those commitments.

4   HOW CAN WE DETERMINE COMPLIANCE?

4.1   Greenhouse Gas Measurement

The Framework Convention on Climate Change requires countries to file greenhouse gas inventories, and the Kyoto Protocol requires each Annex B Party to develop 'a national system for the estimation of anthropogenic emissions by sources and removals by sinks of all greenhouse gases'.[32] The national system includes institutional and procedural arrangements required to collect, process, communicate and store GHG inventory data. These provisions are perhaps the most fundamental building block for making sure that emissions limitation commitments are met; their purpose is to ensure that GHG accounting is done in a reliable fashion. If GHG emissions inventories are not reliable, we cannot know if Annex B Parties are meeting their emission reduction commitments.

Broadly speaking, emissions for each emissions source category (e.g., carbon dioxide emissions from fuel combustion, methane from landfills) are equal to:

$$emissions = \sum_{activities} activity * emission\ factor$$

Where an activity is anything that generates emissions. For example, burning coal is an activity that would be measured in tons of coal of a certain grade burned over a certain period of time. The emission factor would be the amount of CO_2 expected from the combustion of one ton of that type of coal. Sinks could also be included in the measure where the emission factor would be replaced with a 'sequestration factor'. An accurate measure of total emissions requires good data on activities and emission factors for each activity that reasonably reflect the true emission rate. Each of these will be uncertain for a number of reasons. Activities may be hard to measure accurately. Parties may have to estimate some by sampling. Emission factors may be inaccurate due to lack of scientific knowledge or because the activity categories are broad and in reality emissions vary a great deal within them. This may be particularly true for gases other than CO_2 and for sinks such as land use.

---

[32]Kyoto Protocol Article 5.1

4.1.1   Defining strong national GHG accounting systems

The OECD has described three levels of analysis of domestic monitoring systems, Willems (1999). These are:

- Technical, which refers to measurement/estimation methods and data collection and reporting;
- Managerial, which refers to inventory planning, documentation, quality assurance and quality control, and organization and staffing; and
- Institutional, which refers to coordination among the diverse organizations involved in the GHG accounting process.

National greenhouse gas accounting systems will differ from country to country because they are shaped by historical institutional arrangements and other national circumstances such as the characteristics of energy industries. Regarding emissions from energy use, in general data collection is more complicated in countries with more complex energy sectors (large numbers of energy producers, processors, transports, distributors and users, high volumes of both imports and exports, and other complications such as the use of fuels for non-energy purposes such as chemical production). Energy data collection in the US requires a major surveying effort because of the decentralized nature of energy production and use, whereas in countries with nationalized energy industries (for example, France), energy data collection is naturally centralized.

Despite the fact that high-quality national systems can have different characteristics, it is possible to define a basic set of conditions that characterizes a strong system. Loosely following the OECD's typology, we now describe these characteristics.

4.1.1.1   Technical function. Estimation methodologies: The national system should include procedures to select greenhouse gas estimation methodologies. The methodologies used by a Party should consist of IPCC 'good practices' (see below) or other methodologies that better reflect national conditions, provided that they are compatible with the IPCC guidelines and are well documented.

Collection of activity data: The national system should collect data regularly from all major emissions sources. In addition, countries should employ recognized and appropriate sampling techniques as the basis for collecting information from small sources. With respect to the energy sector, countries should collect data from various points in the fuel cycle production, processing, transport and distribution, as well as from actual emitters. The advantage of such an 'energy balance approach' is that figures for one point in the fuel cycle, for example, production and imports, can be used to check the accuracy of data reported at another point, e.g., energy sales to end users. Performing such reconciliations enables countries to check the accuracy of the energy data used in the national GHG emissions inventory prior to use of these data in the inventory.

Emissions factors: While the IPCC inventory guidelines provide default emissions factors that countries may apply, locally developed emissions factors are likely to provide a more accurate estimate of actual emissions. The good practice guidance states that countries should develop local emissions factors for all 'key' emissions source categories.

4.1.1.2 Managerial functions. Qualified personnel: The personnel who develop, prepare and maintain the national inventory should have appropriate technical capabilities. It is especially important that people with technical knowledge of key emissions source categories are involved in inventory development. For example, people familiar with the energy industry and forest management will be needed. In addition, skilled data managers are needed.

Quality assurance and quality control: The use of quality assurance (QA) and quality control (QC) procedures by the government information collection agency is essential to improving activity data quality.[33] QA/QC procedures can be used to address both technical errors (e.g., mathematical errors, incorrect assumptions and methodologies) as well as procedural errors (due to poor management or inadequate training, for example). We discuss QA further below in the context of the discussion of the international role in ensuring data quality. QC procedures can take many forms, including verification of the mathematical accuracy of reported data, identification of outliers, identification of non-filers, reconciliation to other reports, 'frames maintenance', data sharing with other organizations, and verification of data reported by entities through procedures such as inspection of underlying records and measurement equipment.

4.1.1.3 Institutional coordination. Because greenhouse gas emissions come from all parts of the economy, implementation of the national inventory will require coordination among many organizations. It is important that one organization be designated as having final responsibility for the inventory, that all necessary activities be defined in advance, that the roles of all

---

[33]Chapter 8 of the IPCC draft good practice guidance document defines 'quality control' roughly as the set of internal controls built into the inventory development system to ensure quality, while 'quality assurance' refers to procedures conducted by outside parties to ensure quality.

organizations be clearly defined as well as the role of all staff, and that the lead organization develop timetables for the delivery of information from other organizations.

The role of the international community is to set rules that will reduce overall bias in the estimation of emissions, that create a perception of fair treatment across states, and that avoid the possibility that states can significantly manipulate the way they report emissions to gain advantage. To play this role the international community will need to establish uniform accounting rules and procedures and then audit national greenhouse gas emissions inventories.

4.1.2   International definition of accounting procedures.

The Parties to the Framework Convention have already made great progress in establishing a system of accounting rules and procedures. The first step they took was to officially adopt the Intergovernmental Panel on Climate Change (IPCC) guidelines for developing national inventories (Houghton et al. 1996). These guidelines provide broad guidance on the methodologies to be used in estimating greenhouse gas emissions and removals. They have been in widespread use for a number of years.

Recently, a second step in developing an accounting framework was taken when, in response to a request by one of the official bodies established under the Framework Convention, the IPCC completed a first draft on good practice in inventory preparation and uncertainty management (IPCC, 1999). The purpose of this 'IPCC good practice guidance' document is to provide more detailed guidance on the preparation of national emissions inventories, so that countries 'produce inventories which were accurate in the sense of being neither over nor underestimates so far as could be judged, and in which uncertainties were reduced as far as practicable'. The IPCC good practice guidance provides guidance in a number of areas, including choosing appropriate inventory methodologies, best practices in the development of emissions factors; the collection of activity data, the quantification of uncertainty; techniques for documentation and archiving information, and quality control and quality assurance procedures. It will likely serve as the foundation for the national systems guidelines, though it has not yet been adopted by the Parties to the Kyoto Protocol.

Adoption of the IPCC good practice guidance into the national systems guidelines would help establish a strong greenhouse gas accounting foundation for the Kyoto Protocol. It would help to ensure that countries take a systematic approach to GHG emissions accounting and use appropriate methodologies and reliable information. There are two ways, however, in which the national systems guidelines must go beyond the good practice guidance.[34] First, they must provide a broader framework for inventory development and maintenance than that provided by the IPCC guidance, addressing the managerial and institutional issues discussed above. The good practice guidance focuses on the technical aspects of inventory preparation.

Second, in the area of quality assurance and quality control, the guidance provided in the good practice document is helpful but not particularly prescriptive. Independent review of all technical aspects of inventory development would be useful; auditing of activity data is especially important because it is least likely to be examined by the expert review teams established under the Kyoto Protocol to review the data submitted by countries (expert review teams are discussed further below). The audit of activity data should include examination of the procedures for both collecting and handling data. If the accounting framework is not designed to ensure activity data quality, then a situation could arise where a country was meeting its emissions limitation commitments on paper but not actually making the requisite emissions reductions.

4.1.3 International auditing of national reports

4.1.3.1 Who should do reviews and how? The Kyoto Protocol calls for 'expert review teams' (ERTs) to review the emissions inventories and other information prepared by Annex 1 countries. The review process is to 'provide a thorough and comprehensive technical assessment of all aspects of the implementation [of the] Protocol'.[35] Essentially, the ERTs will be the lead player in assessing whether countries are meeting their commitments under the Protocol, including their commitment to establish strong GHG accounting systems and produce accurate emissions inventories.

The countries that ratified the Framework Convention are now considering a set of draft guidelines for the review of inventories.[36] The guidelines outline three possible approaches to individual reviews; under the most rigorous one, experts nominated by their countries would make a one-week visit to each country being reviewed.

The complexity of the inventory process suggests that the review of inventories and national systems will be time-consuming and resource-intensive. Given this, it is unlikely that teams of nominated experts spending one week in country could conduct the detailed assessment of national systems that is needed to ensure inventory quality. The experience to date in

---

[34]We note that it appears that the parties are working to ensure that the national systems guidelines do improve upon the IPCC good practice guidance in these two ways.
[35]Kyoto Protocol, Article 8.3.
[36]UNFCCC (1999c).

inventory review suggests that the expert review teams probably could conduct a thorough review of methodologies chosen and also take a good look at emissions factors and institutional arrangements, but that they would have little or no time to assess the quality of activity data or of GHG accounting systems in general.[37]   Although the in-depth reviews have identified that key states including the United States, the European Union and Japan would be unlikely to meet the target of 1990 emissions by 2000, they have generally produced descriptive reports that do not identify specific non-compliance. They tend to focus on 'overall' compliance in terms of efforts and actions taken rather than pointing out areas where countries have clearly not met commitments.[38] The expert reviews will need to be more specific to be effective.

We believe that the expert review process will be most efficient and effective if it is designed to allow for participation by independent auditors. Experts nominated by Parties to serve on the ERTs will have special knowledge of emissions estimation and the GHG inventory development process, while public accounting firms and ISO9000 conformity assessment bodies have expertise in data system quality assurance. Therefore it makes sense to consider designing the review process so that the ERTs focus on the subtleties of GHG accounting and institutional arrangements and leave activity-data quality assurance for outside auditors. This division would take advantage of the comparative advantages of the two groups.

The participation of auditors could take many forms. At one extreme, which we refer to as 'pre-certification', countries would be required to employ qualified third party reviewers to assess and certify emissions inventories and national accounting systems – or only key components of such systems, such as the systems generating activity data for major emissions source categories. Nominated experts would still review submitted inventories and bear final responsibility for assessing inventory quality; however, reviews could be less detailed and time-consuming because countries would have already subjected their inventory systems to the scrutiny of independent auditors. At the other extreme, auditors could play a much more limited role, such as performing quality assurance only upon the request of the expert review teams. (We refer to this approach as 'sub-

---

[37]In-depth review teams (IDRs) now review the information (including inventories) submitted by countries under the Framework Convention. These teams typically spend one week in a country. A review of the reports filed by these teams indicates that they have focused on institutional issues and accounting methodologies but have done little examination of the accounting systems generating activity data. For more discussion of the role of In-depth review teams see OECD (1998).

[38]See UNFCCC (1995b) and UNFCCC (1996b) cited in Werksman (1999).

contracting.') By sub-contracting some of their work to outside auditors, the ERTs would have more time to focus on methodological issues, emissions factors and institutional arrangements. The ERTs would directly control the choice of auditors.

One advantage of pre-certification is that it would require less coordination between the auditor and the ERT. The auditor would perform all necessary review and then issue a report; the ERT would then review the auditor's report and determine which areas required further attention. Another important advantage of the pre-certification approach is that it would enable faster identification of non-compliance with national systems, reporting and emissions limitation obligations, because review of activity data quality would by and large be performed prior to the submission of inventories rather than after.

A third possible advantage of the pre-certification approach relates to sovereignty concerns. Some countries might feel more comfortable in opening their books to independent auditors than to UN-led expert teams, suggesting that private auditors might be able more carefully to examine the databases underlying national GHG accounting systems. (It is possible, however, that national attitudes towards the UN and the private sector could be the opposite in other countries.) Of course, Parties would not feel comfortable in using independent auditors in this way unless they first gained confidence in the impartiality and competence of the auditors in reviewing their own and their competitor countries' performance. Such confidence would not exist unless high standards of accountability were set for auditors. We discuss this topic further below.

The principal advantage of the sub-contracting approach is that it would allow for a more careful crafting of the role of auditors since as noted, the auditors would carry out only those tasks assigned to them. As noted, it seems most sensible for the ERTs to delegate activity data quality assurance tasks to auditors. Another advantage of the sub-contracting model is that it would inherently provide an additional layer of review of the work of the auditors, since they would be working for the ERTs. This immediate level of review would not exist if countries hired auditors directly and simply attached a report of findings to the inventory. With pre-certification, if parties choose their own auditors it will be essential that auditors are internationally certified to reduce the risk of parties choosing auditors that will give them a biased, favorable review. The ERTs should also have the ability to challenge the auditor's review if they believed it was inadequate.

One drawback to the sub-contracting approach relates to payment of auditors. Under the sub-contracting approach the auditors would be paid by the UNFCCC Secretariat, which in turn would have to make larger budget requests, while under the pre-certification approach they would be paid directly by Parties. While Parties ultimately would pay under either model, the sub-contracting approach presents the political disadvantage of requiring Parties to ask for larger appropriations for UN activities.

4.1.4   Assuring the quality of work performed by auditors

Regardless of whether the pre-certification approach or the sub-contracting approach is taken, the contribution of private sector auditors to the expert review process would more likely be positive if a system were established to regulate their participation. Characteristics of this system should include the following:[39]

Accreditation: auditors involved in the review process should first have to demonstrate that they are competent to play such a role. Also, they should have no past record of fraud or other malfeasance. Demonstrating competence should involve passing an examination that tests knowledge of any review procedures that they (the auditors) are allowed to implement. One issue that the international community will have to wrestle with is whether accreditation should be controlled by one central body or instead whether Parties should establish their own accreditation authorities. This latter is the approach taken with ISO9000 conformity assessment bodies. While because of sovereignty concerns it might be tempting to leave accreditation to Parties, centralized accreditation would lead to higher-quality reviews. If the process is established to allow Parties to select and accredit their own auditors, then expert reviews must include a review of the credentials of the independent auditors used for quality assurance.

Standardized audit procedures: The expert review process could be strengthened by the development of a set of procedures that auditors are expected to apply in auditing the quality of activity data or other aspects of the national inventory. Indeed, a set of review procedures should be developed to guide all aspects of expert reviews, not just those performed by auditors. While reviewers would of course be expected to exercise their own judgment, they also would be required to document why they did not use standardized procedures in instances when they did not.

Accountability: Several features should be built into the expert review infrastructure to hold auditors accountable for the quality of the services they provide. First, auditors should have to periodically renew their licenses to participate in expert reviews by passing a test. Second, the accreditation

---

[39]In developing these recommendations we reviewed the US public accounting system, the ISO9000 quality management system and the system for assessing the quality of health care delivered by health plans in the US.

body should regularly review on a sample basis the reports issued by auditors, as well as the underlying documents that the auditors have prepared in the course of their review. Third, the accreditation body should have the authority to hear allegations of impropriety against auditors and to impose sanctions if necessary. As already noted, if the auditors were to report to the ERTs rather than working directly for Parties, an additional level of review would already exist.

4.1.5   Summary
Both the pre-certification and sub-contracting approaches appear to provide a workable means to help ensure that the expert review process provides a more thorough examination of the data systems underlying national inventories. The ideal division of duties between expert review teams and independent auditors would be to have the ERTs focus on methodological issues, the calculation of emissions factors, and institutional questions, with outside auditors taking the lead in assuring the quality of activity data. This arrangement would take best advantage of the relative strengths of the two types of reviewers.

The choice between the two methods will hinge on how comfortable Parties are with the use of private sector auditors. The pre-certification model appears to offer a more efficient solution and faster assessment of compliance with Kyoto Protocol accounting and emissions limitation commitments, because it calls for independent review of activity data prior to the filing of inventories. It also creates a more autonomous role for auditors, however. If too many countries are uncomfortable with the idea of opening the workings of their national GHG accounting systems to outside auditors or are concerned that other Parties will not use qualified auditors then the role of auditors in the quality assurance process will be limited. To date, Parties have generally expressed a preference to have independent auditors report to the ERTs.

Standardizing audit procedures, accrediting outside auditors and establishing a system for holding auditors accountable for their work will improve the credibility of the review process and would be necessary regardless of whether auditors evaluated data quality prior to the submission of inventories or after. Accreditation would be especially important if the pre-certification approach were taken, because the expert review teams would have less opportunity to scrutinize the work of the outside auditors.

One issue that we have not yet addressed is the frequency with which detailed reviews of inventories and national systems should be conducted. While inventories and greenhouse-gas estimation methodologies should be reviewed on an annual basis, detailed review of the accounting systems generating activity data could be performed less frequently – perhaps twice per five-year commitment period once a Party has a strong national system in place.[40] This less frequent review is appropriate because serious problems are unlikely to arise once the institutions and procedures needed to produce accurate inventories are in place. However, events such as changes in government and changes in funding levels for inventory development affect the quality of inventories; therefore the expert review teams will have to be alert to such events. Where these events have taken place, the ERTs may want to audit or hire outside auditors to audit national systems more frequently even if the country has had a strong past record.

4.2   Non-compliance with Accounting and Reporting Requirements

A number of options are available for addressing accounting and reporting problems. They include (1) technical assistance; (2) adjustments; and (3) loss of the right to sell permits, which is essentially a deterrent to submitting a low-quality inventory as well as a means of limiting the adverse environmental consequences of poor inventories.

4.2.1   Technical assistance
Every effort should be made to correct inventory problems, both as they arise and after inventories have been submitted. The proper stance of the international community towards inventory problems, at least initially, should be to try to facilitate compliance rather than punish non-compliance. Therefore expert review teams should try to link countries experiencing difficulties to appropriate resources. In addition, the Multilateral Consultative Process (MCP) should also be involved in assisting countries in improving their inventories. The MCP is discussed further below.

4.2.2   Adjustments
The Kyoto Protocol states that in cases where methodologies, accepted by the IPCC and agreed upon by the COP, for estimating greenhouse gas emissions are not used, 'appropriate adjustments shall be applied according to [agreed upon] methodologies'. Parties could fail to use appropriate methodology for small sectors where they have not had the resources or data to make appropriate estimates of emissions because they have been focusing on key sources. They may also be careless and not apply methodology correctly even where they have adequate data. Alternatively they may have large gaps

---

[40]In practice, this will mean that national systems should be reviewed thoroughly prior to the beginning of the first commitment period.

in their inventory because of inability or lack of effort to collect and process adequate data. Adjustments could have two purposes:

- First, the threat of an upward adjustment provides Parties with an incentive for using good inventory practices; and
- Second, adjustments would correct emissions inventories so that a proper basis is established for assessing compliance with emissions limitation commitments.

Assessing compliance requires a comparison of a final, accurate emissions inventory to adjusted assigned amount (initial assigned amount plus/minus net transfer). In essence, adjustments will provide complete inventories wherever possible and will protect the atmosphere from the risk that countries will achieve compliance with emissions limitation commitments by under-counting emissions.

To provide an incentive to produce a high quality inventory, the adjustment process must be very likely to result in an emissions figure that is higher than the figure that would be produced by the Party if it used correct methodology, i.e. very conservative. To produce a figure that is less conservative, for example a best point estimate of actual emissions, would lead to the most accurate current inventories and is consistent with the IPCC good practice guidance for inventories, but would provide too weak an incentive for Parties to use good inventory practices in the first place.[41]

On the other hand, designing the adjustments process to deliver clearly punitive emissions estimates would provide the strongest incentive to produce an accurate inventory and would offer the most protection of the atmosphere. It could backfire, however, if the adjustments were so punitive that they caused Parties that were unable to provide complete inventories to see the compliance system as unjust and to withdraw from the Protocol. The adjustment process should aim to produce emissions estimates that are reasonable estimates of actual emissions yet highly unlikely to understate emissions.

In practice, designing and implementing an adjustments process that consistently delivers conservative estimates of actual emissions will require great care. While ideally, adjustments would be made by applying IPCC good practices, in many cases the necessary data will not exist. Lack of data will probably be the most common cause for the need for an adjustment. If this is the case, then the analysts calculating the adjustments will have to choose other approaches that they think will lead to the best estimate, given

---

[41] *The IPCC good practice guidance* states that the aim of good inventory practices is to 'produce inventories which were accurate in the sense of being neither over nor underestimates so far as could be judged, and in which uncertainties were reduced as far as practicable,' IPCC (1999).

the data at their disposal and resource constraints. Alternatives include predetermined formulae such as inflating base year emissions by some growth factor or estimating emissions based on norms for countries of similar circumstances. To ensure that adjustments are conservative, the analysts will have to use 'inflators' (i.e., they will have to multiply estimates by a number larger than 1), deliberately choose conservative assumptions, and/or choose the high end of the range of emissions estimates they develop for the source category in question. Using inflators is likely to meet political resistance based on the perception that it is intentionally punitive.

Leaving the analysts applying adjustments discretion in choosing methodologies could result in a non-transparent process and therefore to charges that the process is unfair. This could be dealt with by choosing a panel of analysts that all parties agree on, by making adjustments consensual where possible, and by having an appeals process for large adjustments.

In some cases, it may be difficult to calculate an adjustment that can be judged with a high degree of confidence to conservatively reflect true emissions. Further, it is possible that the Parties in question will not agree to the adjustments proposed. This leads us to conclude that adjustments should be viewed not as a solution to all inventory problems or as the sole incentive to produce high quality inventories, but simply as a way of making inventories more complete and accurate, so that compliance with emissions limitation commitments can be better assessed.

4.2.3   Loss of right to sell permits

Since some inventory problems may not be adjustable and Parties might not always agree to the adjustments proposed, other tools will be needed to address inventory problems. Because proper accounting for GHG emissions and removals is fundamental to the success of the Kyoto Protocol and UNFCCC as well as the international emissions trading system, we advocate that Parties failing to meet their accounting and reporting commitments in a significant way lose their right to sell permits in the international trading market. Linking eligibility to participate in emissions trading to compliance with accounting and reporting requirements would give Parties a strong incentive to meet their inventory and reporting requirements, because the right to sell permits is a potentially very valuable one. Parties failing to meet these requirements should be barred from selling permits but not from buying them. Withdrawing the right to buy them would impede rather than facilitate compliance.

The test of whether or not a Party should lose its right to sell permits should be kept simple, and because loss of the right to sell permits is a potentially severe consequence, it should discriminate between material and immaterial non-compliance. We propose that the right to sell permits be suspended if the country in question has failed to use IPCC good practice guidelines for inventory preparation, otherwise failed to implement adequately a national GHG accounting system or failed to meet national inventory reporting requirements for greenhouse gases and source categories that in aggregate account for some threshold level (perhaps ten percent) of its base year emissions.[42]

The application of this rule would mean that Parties that had used inadequate inventory methods for major source categories (e.g., CO_2 from fuel combustion, land use change and forestry) or for a large number of small source categories would be considered out of compliance with their national systems requirements. Parties that had failed to adequately account for one or a few small categories would not. However, it would be useful to establish a mechanism for tracking small inventory problems, so that Parties that persistently make small errors would be subject to consequences such as loss of the right to sell permits if the small errors were significant when taken in aggregate.

The possibility that some inventory problems will not be 'adjustable' or that Parties will not agree to the adjustments proposed means that in some cases questions will remain as to what the country's true emissions are. In these cases it will not be possible to make a determination as to whether a country has met its emissions limitation commitments. This problem suggests that the body imposing penalties for non-compliance will have to have some discretion in imposing penalties, and therefore that all penalties cannot be pre-specified and automatic. Withholding the right to sell ensures that even if the compliance regime fails to adequately respond to non-compliance with emissions limitation commitments, at least the country in question will not be able to 'infect' the compliance positions of other countries by selling them permits.

4.3   Conclusions

Addressing problems with inventories and reporting will require a mix of tools. Technical assistance should be used in all cases, at least as an initial response. Adjustments should be used to correct inventory problems where possible, after facilitative approaches have been exhausted. Larger problems should be addressed through the loss of eligibility to sell permits.

---

[42]National systems guidelines will distinguish mandatory features of national systems from desirable features. Failure to use good practices could be defined as failure to implement mandatory guidelines.

5 HOW CAN NON-COMPLIANCE WITH TARGETS BE AVOIDED?

The combination of a strong inventory, reporting and review regime with a system of serious, credible penalties and rewards would be an effective way of ensuring compliance with emissions limitation commitments. The implementation of such a system may not be possible, however. In particular, the imposition of strong penalties for non-compliance may not be feasible. If this is the case, then it will be important to consider implementing measures that aim to facilitate compliance before non-compliance occurs.[43] The options for avoiding non-compliance include:

- Requiring 'annual surrender' of AAUs to cover reported emissions to date;
- Facilitating compliance through technical assistance, possibly through the Multilateral Compliance Procedure; and
- Emissions trading.

5.1 Annual Surrender

Annual surrender would require each country to submit, at the end of each year, a listing of the AAUs that it had retired to cover its estimate of aggregate CO_2 equivalent emissions in that year or, equivalently, transfer them to a 'compliance account' in the registry system. The official UNFCCC registry as well as individual country registries for tracking AAUs would be altered to reflect the specific AAUs which had been retired and which could no longer be traded or utilized.[44] Parties that had chosen to allow legal-entities to participate in emissions trading probably would likewise require that such entities surrender AAUs equal to their annual emissions.

Annual surrender would be based on interim estimates of emissions within two months of the end of each year of the commitment period, since final estimates of emissions for a given year probably would not be available until the completion of the subsequent year.[45] Hence, each Party would be required, by the end of the subsequent year, to provide a final estimate for each year based on the inventory it produces and to adjust its retirements of

---

[43]For detailed discussion of this issue, and application to the problem of oil pollution at sea, see Mitchell (1994a & b).

[44]For discussion of the mechanism for tracking see Chapter 2.

[45]The data for the inventory of the majority of emissions, for example from energy use, is available very quickly. The long delays in finalising inventories result from small areas of the inventory. Thus interim estimates can be quite accurate. Personal communication with Art Rypinski, US Department of Energy, Energy Information Administration, March 1998.

AAUs accordingly. For example, if the Party estimated emissions as 100 in the first year and retired these but on completing their inventory found that true emissions had been 110, the next year they would retire 10 units more than the interim estimate for the second year.

Annual surrender would promote compliance by forcing the retirement of assigned amount units annually by Parties and by 'legal-entities' (business and other sub-national entities) authorized by countries to trade. Retirement of AAUs annually would provide transparent current information to all Parties and others regarding the pattern of emissions and excess AAU holdings in each country. The annual inventories could provide this information when combined with registry data. To assess a country's likely ability to comply, however, might require looking at global emissions and AAU stocks, which requires extensive analysis. With annual surrender, all countries would be forced to cover cumulative emissions and their access to AAUs to cover future emissions would be more transparent. In any case annual inventories may only be available with a one-year lag and some Parties may be even slower. Annual surrender would force the provision of relatively accurate interim information.

Annual Surrender is also likely to encourage earlier trading and more price discovery. The need to match AAUs to emissions will tend to focus the minds of governments early in the commitment period. They will be more likely to create systems to track their AAU 'cash flow' and 'asset/liability' position. This may lead them to trade to cover emissions as they go and maintain precautionary balances. This will facilitate government learning about trading and also the overall management of compliance. Large-scale global non-compliance resulting from every Party expecting to buy AAUs from the same sources close to the end of the commitment period will be less likely.

Countries close to exhausting their initial assigned amounts prior to the end of the commitment period, or that have allocated a large percentage of AAUs to legal-entities and have insufficient to cover non-trading sectors, would be forced by an annual surrender requirement to purchase AAUs. It will also encourage (though not require) them to make their legal-entities responsible for emissions on an annual basis. The more that trade and assessment of needs occurs, the better will be the information available on the real costs of emissions abatement and the effort necessary to achieve global compliance.

5.2   Facilitation

As noted at the outset of this chapter, the Framework Convention and the Kyoto Protocol both include a variety of provisions designed to promote cooperation among countries. These provisions ultimately should have the effect of reducing emissions, and therefore should help Annex B Parties to comply with their emissions limitation commitments. These provisions cover areas such as technology transfer, coordination and cooperation in R&D, and education and training on the issue of climate change.

A second form of facilitation would be to establish a body or bodies charged with providing technical assistance to countries having trouble complying with their various commitments. This could take many forms, including assistance in preparing emissions inventories (the expert review teams will do this) and expert advice in establishing policies and projects to mitigate greenhouse gases. The Framework Convention established the multilateral consultative process (MCP), and the Kyoto Protocol states that the Parties to the Convention should consider applying the MCP to the Protocol as well, modifying the MCP as appropriate. Although to date the Parties have taken no steps to bring the MCP to life in the context of the Protocol, the MCP could play a role in facilitating compliance with Protocol obligations. The MCP is discussed further below.

5.3   Emissions Trading

Another approach to facilitating compliance is emissions trading, which improves the chances of compliance by reducing the cost of meeting emissions targets. Trading reduces total costs for all Parties, buyers and sellers. Trading reduces the marginal costs of compliance for those who face high costs in the absence of trading and hence are net buyers. Such countries (e.g., Japan, the Netherlands) would have to cut emissions significantly to meet their commitments alone. In the short-term, they may find it difficult to achieve compliance without trading. The achievement of large, cost-effective reductions requires the development of new technologies and changes in capital stock (e.g., in the power sector) and infrastructure (e.g., in public transport). These in turn require large investments with long lead-times. Many reductions involve changes in lifestyles, industrial structures and patterns of growth. They could have significant distributional implications. These investments are likely to have other social and environmental side effects (e.g., concerns about expanding the use of nuclear energy) and also are likely to be politically contentious. Trading can either reduce the need for such changes and/or provide a transitional option to allow changes to occur at a more manageable pace. Because trading enables a Party to improve its compliance position immediately (if the market is liquid), Parties gain more direct control of their compliance and thus enjoy a greater ability to comply. In an efficient market, any buyer can comply by bearing the financial cost of purchasing sufficient AAUs. In contrast, without trading buyers may be politically unable to implement sufficiently stringent regulation, or may not anticipate potential non-compliance early enough to remedy it through additional domestic reductions. Real reductions are more difficult to control than financial transactions. Further, trading makes non-compliance deliberate and hence more credibly punishable. It is easier to enforce compliance in cases where Parties have alternatives to non-compliance.

Trading assists not only buyers; it also provides incentives to selling countries. In the absence of trading, countries with very low costs of compliance (zero costs in the case of countries with 'hot air') will have little incentive to undertake any GHG mitigation activities. With trading, in contrast, these countries can earn a reward for each additional ton of CO_2 equivalent that is mitigated. This reward is the Annex B market price. Because the ability to sell is potentially very valuable, trading has the positive effect of encouraging these countries to undertake low-cost mitigation activities. Modeling indicates that the former Soviet Union could gain more than 1.5 percent of GDP and Eastern Europe could gain nearly one percent.[46] This gain not only induces reductions but also encourages these states to comply and continue to participate.

6   WHO DETERMINES NON-COMPLIANCE?

Determining whether or not a country has complied with a commitment may be ambiguous. Two types of questions about compliance could arise. The first set includes questions of clarification and interpretation as to what compliance actually means in a particular situation. For example, one can easily imagine a country having questions about how to apply the accounting rules relating to land-use change and forestry. Further, some flexibility should be allowed so that countries can be clearly forgiven in extreme circumstances such as the oil field fires after the war in Kuwait. If the exceptions to compliance rules are allowed only in extraordinary circumstances, they will not damage the credibility of the overall system. One way to negotiate exceptions is to have consultative processes to resolve

[46]MacCracken et al., p. 50 (1999).

non-compliance before sanctions are imposed. These processes are a standard part of previous international environmental agreements.

The second set includes situations where countries appear to be out of compliance with their commitments. In these cases the extent of non-compliance and the associated consequences will need to be determined. The penalties that are applied and the process for determining these penalties are intertwined (Werksman 1999, p. 9). If the penalties are more serious, the process becomes more important. Thus it will be critical that this body is seen as fair and representative and that the process leads to just outcomes.

With respect to emissions limitation commitments, serious non-compliance situations include cases where a country clearly does not have enough AAUs to match its net emissions at the end of the commitment period. They also could include cases where inventories are developed using controversial methodologies that have a significant impact on the estimate of total emissions, cases where a state fails to provide an inventory or files one that is grossly incomplete and this cannot be resolved through adjustments, or where a Party fails to meet surrender AAUs annually to match interim emissions estimates. To avoid the concerns of developing countries about coercive penalties these more serious compliance penalties could be defined to apply only to Annex B states. Compliance structures could be differentiated in the same way as obligations.

6.1   Questions of Clarification

Addressing questions of clarification and interpretation has been the role of the Multilateral Consultative Process (MCP) under the Montreal Protocol; the MCP could play a similar role in this context. The stated objective of the MCP under the Framework Convention is to 'resolve questions regarding the implementation of the Convention' by 'providing advice', 'promoting understanding of the Convention', and 'preventing disputes'.[47] It is to be conducted in a facilitative, cooperative, non-confrontational, timely and transparent manner and be non-judicial'. The structure for implementing the MCP is proposed to include a 'Multilateral Consultative Committee' that will 'provide appropriate assistance' by 'clarifying and resolving questions', and providing advice both on the 'procurement of technical and financial resources' and on the 'compilation and communication of information'. This would create a standing committee to hear implementation questions and would effectively create compulsory arbitration. One advantage of the proposed structure for this committee is that it could evolve over time with

[47]UNFCCC/AG13/1998/2, Secretariat, Bonn, Germany.

relative ease. This body could form a preliminary conclusion about compliance and can make specific recommendations to the COP about measures to assist or bring about compliance but the COP is not required to act on these. Publication of these reports could, however, bring about public and diplomatic pressure on non-compliers.

The Multilateral Consultative Process could identify serious cases of non-compliance that they cannot resolve and pass these on to a more formal body that has the power to apply real consequences. For example they could incorporate the body that makes judgments based on expert opinion on necessary adjustments to inventories. Where the inventory problems are considered too great they would pass these on to a body that deals with serious non-compliance. The consequences for non-compliance can probably not be automatic. Before applying serious consequences for non-compliance, some body needs to assess whether the Party should have been able to anticipate the events that caused the non-compliance, whether the Party took adequate precautionary measures, and whether the Party can easily repair the damage they have caused. The MCP could give recommendations on this but may not want to be involved in making binding judgments.

6.2 Determination of Non-compliance and its Consequences

The second set of issues, those where non-compliance appears to have occurred, will require a different approach. If there are going to be substantive penalties associated with non-compliance, then the body that determines and/or enforces those penalties will need to have credibility and power. The Protocol includes provisions to establish both 'appropriate and effective procedures and mechanisms to determine and address cases of non-compliance with the provisions of [the] Protocol' and a dispute settlement mechanism.

We believe that potential non-compliance with emissions limitation and reduction commitments and with inventorying and reporting requirements are of such fundamental importance to meeting the goals of the Convention and Protocol that they should be referred to a permanent 'Compliance Authority' (CA). This body should have the capacity to impose meaningful, binding consequences that have the effect of deterring non-compliance with emissions limitation commitments. Other bodies are inappropriate for a number of reasons: the expert review teams that audit national emissions inventories should play a strictly technical function and should not be empowered to take compliance action in cases where they identify non-compliance problems; although currently the Conference of the Parties/Meeting of the Parties (COP/MOP) has the authorization to legally determine compliance and unleash sanctions, the COP/MOP meets too infrequently and is too unwieldy a body to take action on the various potential compliance situations that could arise; the MCP, because of its facilitative nature, lacks the ability to take strong action.

The Compliance Authority should:

- Be a permanent authority composed of a combination of technical experts and diplomats nominated by countries and selected by the COP/MOP;
- Have authority to consider findings and reports prepared by the expert review teams regarding the compliance of countries with emissions limitation commitments and GHG inventory and review requirements, and to order investigation by the review teams of any allegations regarding compliance that are made by other countries or others with standing;
- Have authority to take specified actions if it finds a Party to be in non-compliance with its accounting, report or emissions limitation commitments, with automatic actions specified where possible; and
- Be structured so that countries may appeal the Authority's decisions to the COP/MOP when compliance actions are stringent. In the case of an appeal, the burden of proof should rest on the appealing country.

The Compliance Authority would respond to potential violations of accounting, reporting and surrender requirements annually, primarily in response to reports filed by the expert review teams or referred from the MCP. Potential cases of non-compliance with emissions limitation commitments would be addressed mainly at the end of the commitment period, because it is only then that compliance with these commitments can be definitively assessed. One can imagine, however, that the Compliance Authority would also respond during the commitment period to behavior that is highly likely to lead to non-compliance with emissions limitation commitments. An extreme example would be where a country sold its entire emissions budget in the first year of the commitment. While the country theoretically could still come back into compliance by buying AAUs, compliance is unlikely.

6.3   Discretion vs. Automatic Penalties

The Compliance Authority could use either discretionary or automatic penalties once it has determined non-compliance. The advantages of automatic punishments are that they provide a certain signal that is an effective deterrent, that they are applied equally across different Parties and that they are applied with no delay. The advantages of discretion are that they can allow for special circumstances that may argue for less stringent punishments; this may be seen as more fair. They may be more likely to acceptable to Parties. If the penalties are automatic and clearly defined the burden of proof, both political and evidentiary will fall on the Compliance Authority.[48] The optimal response may include automatic penalties for unambiguous, clearly defined offences where the compliance consequences are not too serious and discretionary penalties for gross non-compliance that requires serious penalties.

7 WHAT HAPPENS TO NON-COMPLIERS?

7.1 Punishment and Deterrence

Preventive approaches to addressing non-compliance with emissions limitation commitments should be supplemented by deterrents that encourage Parties to comply or punish them for non-compliance (or behavior that will lead to non-compliance). Deterrents could be used during the commitment period or could be sanctions imposed at the end of the commitment period, once the Compliance Authority had concluded that non-compliance indeed had been found to occur. The purpose of sanctions is not to take revenge on countries that have not complied, but rather to deter non-compliance before it occurs. To be effective, sanctions, and the situations in which they will be applied, must be well understood in advance and seen to be credible.

Effective deterrence requires that the punishment times the probability of being punished is greater than the gain from non-compliance, where all are in present values:[49]

Punishment * probability of punishment >(Non-compliance gain) $(1+r)^t$

Where r is the discount rate and t is the number of years between the over-selling (or avoided purchasing) and the punishment. Consider a Party that sells AAUs in 2008 even though it knows that doing so will lead it to non-compliance.[50] Suppose the price of AAUs in 2008 is US$100 per metric ton. If the discount rate is 10 percent and the Party perceives the probability of being caught and punished as 50 percent, the punishment will have to impose

---

[48]Werksman (1999), p. 28.

[49]If states are risk averse the punishment can be a little lower. For the seminal discussion of these issues see Becker (1968).

[50]Of course it is hard to know in 2008 that their behavior will lead to non-compliance. They might know that they will either have to buy back at higher future prices or non-comply. In any case they are taking a risk that they will be unable to comply – the international community ultimately bears this risk.

a cost equivalent to at least $322 if it is not imposed until 2013. The Party may think it can hide the over-selling in its inventory, may believe there is some probability that the Kyoto agreement will collapse, or may believe that even if the agreement holds punishments will not be effectively enforced.

In applying sanctions, it is important to make the level of sanction sensitive to the level of non-compliance: Parties that are barely out of compliance should not face the same non-compliance consequences as those that are egregiously so. A situation should never arise where a Party sees that the punishment it receives will not be reduced even if it marginally improves its compliance.[51] When several different forms of non-compliance are possible, penalties also need to be set appropriately across transgressions. This could create political problems if it were applied to the Protocol and Convention as a whole because the weight of penalties would seem to reflect the importance of different aspects of compliance (Werksman, 1999, p 6). In this narrower context, where the penalties only apply to Annex B Parties, only two major forms of non-compliance, reporting and meeting Annex B emissions targets, are being compared; these are maybe not so sensitive for developing countries.

As a comparison, two broad consequences can be applied under the Montreal Protocol if the MCP process fails to facilitate a solution to a problem. First, a caution would be issued to the non-compliant Party. Second, a meeting of the Parties could agree to suspend the Party's rights and privileges under the Protocol. These rights and privileges particularly include the right to trade obligations through the process of industrial rationalization (see Chapter 1), the right to trade ozone-depleting substances with other Parties, the right of access to the financial mechanism to facilitate compliance, the transfer of technology and involvement in institutional arrangements (e.g. voting rights).

The key case where these procedures were tested under the Montreal Protocol was a case of non-compliance by some economies in transition. The non-compliant Parties were brought into compliance using a combination of the threat of trade sanctions and Global Environmental Facility funding that both facilitated compliance but was also provided in tranches conditional upon monitoring and enforcement of progress.[52] Overall, the effectiveness of these instruments was probably highly dependent on the fact that most countries were in compliance.

A wide variety of possible end-of-period sanctions exist. These include political/diplomatic sanctions, public/moral pressure, economic sanctions

[51]Ostrom (1990), pp. 94–100.
[52]Werksman (1996).

including financial penalties on countries or trade sanctions on GHG-intensive industries, protocol-related sanctions, and trading-related sanctions.

7.1.1   Suspension of treaty voting rights: diplomatic sanctions

Even without non-compliance provisions in the agreement, the Vienna Convention on the Law of Treaties entitles any 'specially affected party' to suspend the operation of the treaty between itself and the defaulting state on the grounds of a material breach of the treaty. The other parties could agree to jointly suspend the defaulting states' treaty privileges. A material breach only occurs where a provision essential to the accomplishment of the object and purpose of the treaty is violated.[53] Suspension could be applied more selectively to imply loss of vote in the Compliance Authority and the COP/MOP. Loss of a vote may seem relatively weak, but it has little cost and so should be employed where appropriate. Suspension of voting rights may be a stronger punishment than it seems. Parties partly sign treaties because they want to be part of the international community and seen to be cooperative independent of their interest in the particular issue.

7.1.2   Publicity for compliers and non-compliers – engage informal compliance pressures

If the compliance authority can unambiguously determine non-compliance a list of compliers and non-compliers (together with the nature and extent of non-compliance) could be made public. This public information can lead to a number of private or bilateral sanctions. Countries will be able to observe each Party's developing reputation for cooperation. They may reward compliers or penalize non-compliers in their other non-climate related relationships. Non-profit groups frequently put pressure on their own governments if they are not complying. In an extreme example, the National Resources Defense Council filed suit against the EPA under the US Clean Air Act for not taking sufficient domestic action to protect the environment during the early stages of the ozone negotiations.[54] Private companies might also reward and punish Parties if they are interested in a corporate image that does not take unfair advantage of the flexibility of the international treaty. They may choose to take account of the likely compliance of Parties they purchase AAUs from even if it is not formally required.

Bilateral and public pressure has advantages and disadvantages. It is rarely applied in an unbiased, fair way. Weaker, smaller countries are more likely to suffer real costs from other Parties as a result of non-compliance.

---

[53]Werksman (1999), p. 14.
[54]Benedick (1991), p. 28.

Countries with strong environmental movements will suffer (or benefit) more from pressure from non-profit groups. The targeting of this pressure would be improved, however, by the transparent provision of relatively unbiased unambiguous indicators of compliance. This may focus informal pressure more effectively.

7.1.3 Economic sanctions

Strict, credible financial penalties that far exceed the cost of compliance would likely be a very effective sanction, though this approach probably is not politically feasible due to sovereignty concerns. Financial sanctions are extremely rare in international treaty law. The success of domestic environmental programs such as the US SO_2 control program has been directly linked to the existence of financial penalties for non-compliance set at a per ton rate that exceeds the marginal cost of achieving emission reductions. Compliance ultimately will depend on the nature and level of domestic incentives for emissions reductions and penalties for domestic non-compliance. The existence, credibility and effectiveness of such domestic regulations, however, will heavily depend on the perceived strength of international pressure for states to comply.

Another economic sanction is trade sanctions. The threat of trade sanctions on GHG-intensive industries is strong but probably not very credible, one reason being that they hurt other countries in addition to those who are sanctioned. Another problem is that trade sanctions are a fairly blunt instrument. They are not responsive to the level of non-compliance; also they are often applied unequally across countries.[55] They have proven valuable in some situations, however; for example, when Russia was out of compliance with the Montreal Protocol, the threat of trade sanctions was one of the levers used to bring it into compliance.[56] Thus trade sanctions should be maintained as a threat for extreme non-compliance but not relied on for addressing more normal infractions.

7.1.4 Protocol-related sanctions

Other sanctions arise directly from the Protocol itself. For instance, the compliance regime implicitly requires purchase of enough AAUs to bring it into compliance at the end of the period if the Party cannot achieve compliance without. This could be made explicit, and if the country does not buy sufficient before the end of the period they could be required to buy more than the amount that offsets its non-compliance. If they were available, and

---

[55]For more discussion of the effectiveness of sanctions see Martin (1993).
[56]Victor et al. (1998).

the threat of requiring more than offsetting purchases was credible, the Parties would not go out of compliance in the first place. The limitation on this approach is the availability of AAUs. If a country were a long way from compliance or several countries were out of compliance, then a global shortage of AAUs could arise.

Another Protocol-related approach would be to reduce future assigned amounts ('allowable emissions') by an amount related to the level of non-compliance (e.g. 130 percent of non-compliance, which implies a penalty interest rate of 30 percent).[57] One advantage of this approach is that it does not depend on the availability of AAUs at the end of the commitment period. To make this approach effective, future assigned amounts would need to be negotiated well in advance of the first commitment period; otherwise, countries that appeared to be on their way toward serious non-compliance would simply try to negotiate more generous future assigned amounts. (One can argue, however, that countries already strive to negotiate the most generous targets possible.) Countries might try to argue that they have very high marginal costs of compliance and, as evidence, present their inability to meet current commitment period targets. This is less credible with an active AAU market. Another, more serious difficulty with this approach is that upon facing very stringent future period commitments, some Parties might choose to withdraw from the Protocol as a whole, making the sanction less credible.

7.1.5   Trading-related sanctions

Finally, emissions trading creates the opportunity to create a number of other sanctions that could be used to spur compliance. These will not improve buyer compliance but could improve seller compliance. They are discussed in detail in Chapter 4. These include first, direct loss or limitation of the right to sell AAUs in future commitment periods.[58] The future privilege to trade is valuable and can thus be used as an incentive for current compliance.

---

[57]This is actually technically equivalent to the unpopular idea of 'borrowing'. Because it would be imposed with a different moral implication and clear penalty, however, it may be more acceptable. No country would actually have the 'right' to borrow; it would have to accept the moral opprobrium and other sanctions that apply in order to take permits from future commitment periods.

[58]One trading-related sanction is already incorporated in the Kyoto Protocol. If an in-depth review team raises a 'question of implementation', the country's right to purchase ERUs from joint implementation is suspended until the question is resolved. This is not a good use of trading sanctions as it further impedes compliance and only harms those who really want to comply. Restricting sales would be more effective. Luckily, because JI is interchangeable with emissions trading for most states (see Chapter 6), and especially for those that are likely to be buyers, this is unlikely to have serious bite.

Second, a compliance reserve would require that every time a trade is made, a percentage of the AAUs sold are put into an account.[59] The compliance reserve would be a percentage of net sales so AAUs could be withdrawn from the reserve when the country purchased AAUs. If the country devolved some trading rights to legal-entities they would have to put AAUs into the compliance reserve, as though these AAUs were sold, until they were surrendered to the government domestically. Once the AAUs are not in the national government's registry account, they do not have a defined national status and the government cannot control their international sale. At the end of the commitment period, if the country were in compliance, then the AAUs would be returned and could be sold. If the country were out of compliance, the reserve would be used to bring them closer to compliance. If some AAUs remained, a share of them would be given back, with the share depending on the degree of initial non-compliance. The compliance reserve offers some prevention of gross over-selling in that in a gross way it limits sales and ensures that some AAUs are available at the end of the period (though these could be sold to other parties in forward contracts). It also is a slight deterrent in that it withholds AAUs from those found to be out of compliance.

An escrow account is similar to a compliance reserve but is denominated in terms of money rather than AAUs. It is akin to a performance bond. Parties would put some portion of the revenue from net sales of AAUs into an account; they could not withdraw it until compliance was proven. This would require that revenue be observable, which would be easy if there were a single market price at any point in time but ;hard if there were heterogeneous AAUs as would be the case under buyer liability (see Chapter 4). If the reserve were a large portion of revenues, clear financial liquidity issues would arise as well as issues of political acceptability. Escrow accounts, like compliance reserves, require significant administrative oversight.

Finally, requiring buyer liability for the validity of AAUs purchased (i.e. for the seller Party's compliance) would increase compliance pressure on the seller but at the cost of high transaction costs. This could be used as a penalty for serious non-compliance. The next chapter discusses buyer liability in depth.

The effectiveness of trading-related sanctions would depend on the relative size of the rewards for non-compliance now and the value of AAU sales in the future. These in turn would be a function of past and future carbon market prices as well as the level of non-compliance in the current

[59]Similar to 'tons in escrow' in Baron (1999a).

commitment period and the level of expected sales in future periods. One problem with trade-related sanctions is that, like economic sanctions, limiting trade hurts buyers as well as the non-compliant sellers because the price of AAUs will rise. This may limit the credibility of threats of severe AAU trading limitations.

One strength of trading-related sanctions is that they strike a middle ground in toughness between financial penalties on countries and more diplomatic approaches to non-compliance. Penalties such as suspension of selling rights might be effective because they dispense tangible, calculable punishments; however, they are not so severe as to be politically untenable. They also help prevent future non-compliance by sellers. These mechanisms would be easier to apply and thus more credible because they represent a withholding of rewards rather than a punishment.

7.1.5.1 Bilateral trading-related sanctions: Even without buyer liability, AAU buyers could voluntarily include private sanctions against non-compliance by the seller in contracts to trade AAUs. If they were voluntary, the sanctions could be purpose-designed to apply to a narrow definition of compliance within the control of the selling party if they were a sub-state actor or legal-entity. These contracts could be enforced under international commercial law applicable to private transactions. They would significantly strengthen overall compliance. Experience with the WTO suggests that bilateral disputes at the state level that are addressed using carefully tailored forms of compulsory and binding arbitration could also support the multilateral framework.[60]

8 CONCLUSIONS

A strong compliance system is essential for ensuring that the emissions limits agreed to at Kyoto are met and also for the effective functioning of the international emissions trading system. The compliance regime gives value to the AAUs that are traded.

We believe that an effective compliance regime will include a variety of components, including strong accounting and reporting infrastructure, measures to prevent non-compliance, efforts to facilitate compliance, incentives and deterrents, and moral pressure. Responses to non-compliance should be graduated, serious cases of non-compliance should be met with tougher consequences than modest cases of non-compliance. Sanctions

[60]Werksman (1999), p.17.

should be strong enough to deter non-compliance – in other words; they must impose a burden that is substantially greater than the benefits of not complying. Sanctions will have greater deterrent force when they are automatic and known in advance.

Our specific recommendations for the structure of the compliance regime are as follows:

8.1 The GHG Accounting Infrastructure Must Include

Accounting guidelines that ensure that: estimation methodologies, emissions factors and activity data used are reliable; personnel involved in national emissions accounting have proper training; and necessary institutional relationships are in place.

A system for auditing national emissions inventories that enables reviewers to take a close look at all aspects of countries' national GHG accounting systems, including the systems generating activity data. Reviewers should include both experts nominated by countries and independent auditors. The latter could pre-certify inventories before they are submitted for review by nominated experts or instead, they could work for the nominated experts. The ideal approach would have expert review teams focusing their attention on areas such as estimation methodologies and emissions factors, which require expertise related to greenhouse gas emissions, and outside auditors focusing on the quality of activity data, where they have expertise.

A process for making adjustments to inventories where the estimates made by countries are incomplete or do not use IPCC or better methodologies. Ideally, adjustments would be conservative, i.e. high, estimates of true emissions; in practice, ensuring that this is the case could be very difficult.

A provision for loss of eligibility to sell AAUs during the commitment period for material failure to meet accounting and reporting commitments. This consequence should be imposed only where countries have failed to meet basic accounting and reporting requirements for material emissions source categories.

8.2 Preventive Measures Should Include

Annual surrender of AAUs to cover emissions for the year based on interim estimates. This would improve information flows, encourage early development of markets, provide governments with experience in managing compliance and help prevent over-selling by taking out of circulation AAUs that had already been 'spent'.

Facilitative measures such as technology transfer programs, coordination and cooperation in R&D, and education and training on the issue of climate change.   These measures are already required under the Protocol.   In addition, mechanisms such as the Multilateral Consultative Process and the Expert Review Teams should provide technical assistance to countries having trouble complying with their commitments.

8.3   The Infrastructure for Deterrence Should Include

- A permanent 'Compliance Authority' which has the capacity to legally determine non-compliance and impose meaningful, binding consequences should be established.   The decisions of this authority should be transparent to facilitate and target informal responses to compliance and non-compliance.
- Suspension of voting rights in the COP/MOP and compliance authority.
- Mandatory purchase of more than offsetting AAUs to come into compliance during a six-month true up period after the commitment period.
- The reduction of assigned amount in the subsequent commitment period, 'with interest' in response to non-compliance with emissions limitation commitments.   Serious non-compliance would best be met through strong financial penalties on countries, but this may not be politically feasible.
- A graduated set of sanctions that includes (in addition to reduction of future assigned amount): first, a compliance reserve on future sales; second, buyer liability on future sales; and, finally, loss of the ability to sell AAUs for more serious cases of non-compliance.

We believe this approach combines a strong accounting foundation with an appropriate mix of prevention, facilitation, and deterrence.

4 Additional Compliance Issues Arising from Trading

Suzi Kerr[1]

1 INTRODUCTION

A strong credible compliance regime is the cornerstone of any effective environmental regulation be it domestic or international. Unfortunately strong compliance is also the Achilles' heel of all international agreements. International law is heavily dependent on the goodwill of states that voluntarily comply and on the will of powerful states to enforce it on the recalcitrant. Treaty compliance cannot be determined by strong financial penalties but, as discussed in the previous chapter, must be sought through a range of instruments that prevent extreme non-compliance, facilitate compliance and provide incentives through both carrots and sticks. No compliance regime can, however, generate compliance if the signatories do not strongly support the treaty. Ultimately, the cost of achieving the goals sought and the perceived equity of the relative contributions of different states will limit the level of cooperation that we can support. International emissions trading (IET) creates opportunities to strengthen compliance with the Kyoto Protocol and raise the level of potential cooperation but also poses new risks.

We expect that most countries will intend to comply if they choose to ratify. Experience suggests that most countries do comply with international agreements; however, past agreements have not involved such high costs of compliance so past experience may not apply to the case of climate change.[2] Experience also suggests that international law works best through rewards and facilitation of compliance rather than strong sanctions.[3] Compliance regimes are set up to address problems with marginal Parties. In this Chapter we often stress ways to control self-interested actors. This does not imply

---

[1] This Chapter incorporates many ideas developed in an earlier paper (Kerr et al. 1998).
[2] Victor et al. (1998).
[3] Chayes and Chayes (1993).

that we regard all countries as 'guilty until proven innocent' but simply that the reliable countries are not the focus of compliance attention. This does not mean, however, that if we have inadequate compliance rules, only the marginal players will be affected. If some Parties begin to cheat, other countries will suffer competitive disadvantage and will feel like 'suckers' for complying. The treaty as a whole will be undermined. Parties may only ratify if they feel confident that others will comply. Effective agreements require trust, but trust is easier to generate and sustain when Parties have strong, credible incentives to behave cooperatively. How will trading affect these incentives?

Trading's greatest positive effect on compliance is that it lowers compliance costs. Estimates of the carbon prices needed to achieve compliance in Annex 1 vary dramatically. As an indication, however, with no trading the likely taxes range from $10 to $1,075 per metric ton (1990 US$; low EU estimate to high Japan estimate).[4] With Annex 1 trading, the tax required will be same in all countries and will probably be between $20 and $225. This carbon price is the cost of additional emission reductions or marginal compliance. In Japan and the EU, trading could lower the marginal cost of compliance by 75–80 percent. The estimates of total GDP loss in 2010 in the US, Japan, the EU, Canada, Australia and New Zealand combined from meeting Kyoto range from US$83bn to $486bn (1990 US$).[5] With trading they fall to $38–$219bn or less than half. With the costs of compliance falling by 50 percent overall and up to 80 percent on the margin in some countries, trading dramatically reduces the pressures for these countries to not comply.

Trading lowers the marginal and total costs of compliance for those who faced high costs in the absence of trading and hence are buyers. Trading unambiguously increases their willingness and encourages them to comply. In addition, without trade, improving compliance in a given country requires real reductions in that country. These cannot be achieved quickly because they require policies to be created and investments to be made. In contrast, with trading and a liquid market, a state's compliance can be improved immediately by purchasing additional assigned amount units (AAUs) from another state. Compliance becomes more directly controllable by states, which gives them greater ability to comply. It also makes non-compliance deliberate and hence more credibly punishable.

In contrast, without trading, countries with very low costs of compliance (zero costs in the case of countries with 'hot air') have little incentive to not

---

[4] Calculated from Stanford Energy Modeling Forum results, Weyant and Hill (1999).
[5] Calculated from Weyant and Hill (1999).

comply. With trading, the reward for each AAU sold is the Annex I market price. This has the positive effect of encouraging these countries to undertake low cost mitigation actions. If the international compliance framework is not strong, however, they may also gain the same reward at no cost by over selling AAUs, i.e. selling AAUs that they need for their own compliance. Overselling and hence non-compliance by low emission reduction cost states is made possible through trading.

Under an effective compliance regime a party has no incentive to over-sell AAUs, i.e. sell AAUs that are required to cover its own emissions. Sellers that do not comply are subject to the same punishments as any other non-complying party. The initial seller of an AAU, or the 'issuer' is automatically liable for the sale if it needed that AAU for its own compliance. However, because participation in the Protocol is voluntary and international enforcement instruments normally are weak, compliance with the commitments is uncertain for all parties and may be especially weak for some sellers. The benefits to parties of AAU sales may be greater than the penalties for non-compliance. Because of the possibility of a weak international compliance regime, it has been suggested that something additional to, or different from, the basic issuer-liability model might be required.[6]

One key IET design issue that must be decided is the issue of liability, or whether portions of assigned amount (AAUs) that have been traded are valid if the issuer of the AAUs is found to be out of compliance with its emissions limitation commitments at the end of the commitment period. The country that initially sells one of its AAUs is always liable for its own compliance. In addition, the buyer could be made liable for the compliance of the seller from which the AAU they are purchasing originates. The country of origin of every AAU would need to be identified.

Table 4.1 shows a possible pattern of trading among countries. State A is a net seller. It is able to emit 100 under its Kyoto commitments but only emits 80. This allows it to sell 20 and still be in compliance. State B is a net buyer that is in compliance. State C, a net seller, and State D, a net buyer, are both out of compliance. Each of C and D is subject to compliance procedures. Under buyer liability, any AAU that originates from either C or D could also be invalid.

---

[6] Article 17 of the Kyoto Protocol states that the Parties must define the 'principles, modalities, rules and guidelines' for international emissions trading (IET.) At the Fourth Conference of the Parties the Parties agreed that this rulemaking process should be completed by the Sixth Conference of the Parties.

Table 4.1   Impact of trading on compliance

State	Business-as-usual emissions	Kyoto commitment	Post trading target	Actual emissions
A	90	100	80 (seller)	80 (in compliance)
B	70	50	60 (buyer)	60 (in compliance)
C	70	70	60 (seller)	65 (out of compliance)
D	60	20	40 (buyer)	45 (out of compliance)

Suppose State C sells two of its AAUs to country B and then State B sells one of these to State A. When State C is out of compliance in 2012, both State A and State B hold invalid AAUs. With issuer-only liability, only State C would be punished. With buyer-liability, all three states would face some punishment. It is also possible that the invalidation of AAUs could put either State A or State B out of compliance. Alternatively AAU issuers could be required to purchase insurance from accredited agencies before they sell them. In this case, once an AAU was insured it would be the same as any other insured AAU. If State C was out of compliance, it would be punished and its insurer would have to pay compensation to the international community or provide AAUs from another source. Will either of these options raise overall compliance? If so, at what cost?

Finally, trading offers significant benefits to sellers and may even make participation in the Protocol profitable for some.[7] It certainly lowers the cost of participation. Offering the opportunity to trade may enhance participation in the Protocol. Threatening to withdraw this opportunity may provide a valuable, relatively credible punishment for non-compliers. It is particularly powerful for sellers for whom the costs of participation are low or even negative. For buyers it is less powerful; a buyer that has been unable to comply even with the ability to trade may decide to withdraw from the Protocol altogether if it is not allowed to trade and the costs of participation become even higher. Thus rewards and punishments relating to the right to trade could be powerful for sellers but probably not for buyers.

1.1   State and Legal-entity Trading

Above we have talked about the compliance of states, which are Parties to the Protocol. Actual emission reductions are carried out by legal-entities or 'legal-entities'. The states will create domestic policies and enforcement

---

[7] A country does not need to have 'hot air' to profit from the Protocol. They simply have to have profit from sales greater than the cost of emission reductions to achieve their own compliance.

mechanisms to induce and enforce reductions by legal-entities. These policies and measures could include anything from energy efficiency standards, labeling requirements, or subsidies to public transport through to carbon taxes and tradable allowance systems. Legal-entities may also participate in international trading if their state devolves the power to trade to them. This would probably be done by creating a domestic tradable allowance system that puts a cap on the emissions of the entities, gives them AAUs equal to the cap and allows them to trade domestically and internationally as long as they surrender AAUs equal to their emissions each year.[8] The international compliance pressures imposed on the state will be passed on to legal-entities through the state's attempts to ensure domestic compliance.

Trading shifts emission rights from the selling country's target to the buying country's target. The shift could be implemented through state level trading or legal-entity trading. Responsibility for achieving the new, post-trading, emission targets depends partly on the allocation of liability when a selling country does not meet its post-trading target. This responsibility will be passed down to legal-entities. If a state is out of compliance, all AAUs sold by its legal-entities are subject to invalidation under buyer liability. This clearly affects legal-entities in State C, the seller that is out of compliance, but it also affects those in D. Although D is a net buyer it probably contains some legal-entities that sold AAUs. Those legal-entities that bought from C or D will lose unless their government takes on the risk.

Non-compliance where the country is a net seller does not imply that entities, entitled to trade through an allowance system, over-sold relative to their emissions and domestic targets. Maybe the other sectors of the economy did not meet their domestic targets and the state did not buy enough AAUs to compensate. Any discussion of the compliance effect of trading, and particularly of buyer liability, needs to take account of the relationship between states and legal-entities. A state's mitigation strategy is only as effective as its ability to control its legal-entities, whether they are trading or simply carrying out domestic reductions. Conversely, under buyer liability, the validity of the AAUs a legal-entity sells depends on the compliance of the state.

---

[8] The right to sell could also be devolved through a number of other mechanisms in combination with a tax or other policies and measures. See Chapter 6 on potential links between domestic and international regulatory systems.

1.2   Criteria for Assessing Compliance Options

The goal of the Kyoto Protocol is to make progress in reaching an environmental objective. Therefore the primary concern should be how the compliance system contributes to environmental effectiveness. Environmental effectiveness requires that countries are accountable for their compliance with the targets they accepted.

A second goal is to achieve environmental goals at the lowest economic and social cost possible. This requires that the private sector be actively engaged in seeking and implementing emission reduction activities. To do this effectively they must face a reasonably stable investment environment with relatively simple and predictable regulatory requirements. This allows them to make long-term investment plans. Effective international trading can lower costs dramatically. For trading to work well, transaction costs must be low, and all actors must have competitive access to the market. A flexible Annex I emissions market could potentially involve an enormous volume of trade as states and legal-entities continuously respond to new information and opportunities. An active competitive market will provide useful price signals, will allow the development of derivatives such as futures and options and will allow buyers at the state and sub-state level to comply in a flexible way.

A direct cost of the Protocol is the cost of administration. Some proposed options for the compliance regimes would require complex monitoring and tracking. This imposes costs on the international community and the monitored states. It also tends to raise complexity, which increases uncertainty and raises trading costs and tends to reduce trading efficiency. Because the Protocol is negotiated and voluntary, the costs of compliance may not affect only current welfare but also the stringency of future environmental targets chosen. Thus the impact of the compliance regime on costs is important for economic welfare and environmental effectiveness.

Finally, in the early years of the program, building confidence that others will participate fairly and that the environmental goals will be reached is critical. The Kyoto Protocol is the most ambitious international environmental treaty ever created. The international emissions trading system is the first on this scale. This means that there is a lot of uncertainty about how countries will comply and how trading will operate. What effects will different compliance options have on countries' confidence in each other's behavior?

How can we design trading to take maximum advantage of the opportunities to enhance compliance and avoid the problems that exacerbate non-compliance? This chapter first looks at how to design trading to maximize the potential for facilitating buyer compliance and at using the ability to trade as an incentive for compliance. To control the risk of overselling we look at two basic approaches: directly preventing or limiting overselling, and deterring overselling through monitoring combined with punishments and rewards based on the level of compliance observed. In discussing deterrence we particularly focus on the issue of who to punish if non-compliance is detected. This issue is widely referred to as 'buyer liability'. The chapter focuses primarily on economic considerations related to the use of these mechanisms and does not look closely at legal and institutional issues.

2   FACILITATING BUYER COMPLIANCE

In Table 4.1 country B is a country (e.g. Japan, the United States, or the Netherlands) that will have to cut emissions significantly to meet its commitment alone. State B may find it difficult to achieve compliance without trading. Large efficient reductions require the development of new technology, changes in capital (such as electric utilities) and infrastructure (such as public transport). All of these require large investments with a long lead-time. Many reductions involve changes in lifestyles, industrial structures and patterns of growth. They will probably have significant distributional implications. The investments are likely to have other social and environmental side effects (e.g. concerns about expanding the use of nuclear energy). They are likely to be politically contentious. Either they will fail to achieve the goals or they will need a long lead-time to consult, plan and implement changes. Trading can either replace these changes or provide a transitional option to allow changes to occur at a realistic pace.

For trading to provide a reasonably priced, secure alternative to domestic compliance, the market needs to be liquid. Countries need to be able to buy large numbers of AAUs easily at any time. No country knows exactly how many they will need so they also need to believe they can sell any excess with little cost. A stable price, good quality early price signals and issuer-only liability reduce the risk associated with trading and lower buyer compliance costs still further.

Controlling market power and putting the minimum necessary controls on derivatives markets (futures, options etc.), i.e. those that apply to other similar markets, will increase the volume of trade, provide price signals, provide options for controlling risk, and increase price stability. All these things will make buyer compliance easier and more controllable.

When a state more easily controls compliance, enforcement of compliance is facilitated. Any seller can comply by controlling their sales. In an efficient market, any buyer can comply by bearing the financial cost of purchasing sufficient AAUs. In contrast, without trading buyers may be politically unable to implement sufficiently stringent regulation, or may not anticipate potential non-compliance early enough to remedy it through additional domestic reductions. Real reductions are more difficult to control than financial transactions. It is easier to control non-compliance by 'commission', that is, non-compliance where parties have alternatives to non-compliance. They can control compliance, and hence when they don't comply they do it deliberately. 'We have recognized that the efficacy of a threat may depend on what alternatives are available.'[9]

Buyer countries are, by definition, those who have taken on more stringent targets. They accepted these because they are more committed to addressing climate change. This could be because they believe they would be severely hurt by climate change, because they are highly concerned with their international reputation or because their population is strongly environmentally conscious. In any case, they can be assumed to want to comply. How important is facilitating their compliance relative to enforcing the compliance of other less committed actors?

The Parties to the treaty enforce an international treaty. It primarily relies on moral suasion and international pressure. If powerful countries are clearly in compliance, they are in a strong moral position to put pressure on others. Therefore it is key to ensure that a core group of countries that are highly committed to the treaty achieve compliance themselves. Then they will have the incentive and the international standing to pressure others. With the best will in the world, however, some key countries will not be able to achieve compliance without effective trading.

3 AVOIDING OVERSELLING THROUGH PREVENTION AND FACILITATION

Trading facilitates buyer compliance and can provide an extra incentive for sellers to comply but it also creates an additional incentive for sellers to non-comply by offering a reward for over-selling. In Table 4.1, State C is out of compliance at the end of the commitment period and has oversold. How could this have been avoided or reduced? Four approaches are possible: prevention, facilitation, feedback and deterrence.

Deterrence is an excellent compliance tool if it is effective because it allows the maximum possible flexibility in compliance strategies. States can

[9] Schelling (1980), p. 6.

choose unconventional approaches and take risks that yield benefits even if these would appear to outsiders likely to lead to non-compliance. Sometimes, however, compliance cannot be perfectly observed, or is observed at great expense or with a long lag, parties cannot be held fully liable for non-compliance ex-post, parties may non-comply by mistake, or sanctions are limited. In these cases, preventing non-compliance and limiting its extent have a real role.[10]

3.1   Prevention

If State C had been prevented from selling it would never have been found out of compliance. Less dramatically, its selling could have been limited and compliance may have been achieved. In the extreme, preventing trading will prevent overselling. However nearly all prevention measures come at significant cost. To maximize their effectiveness we should apply them only where they have the most impact. One possibility is to apply them at the beginning of the market and then relax them as confidence grows and patterns of compliance are established.

Two risks are competing here. The first is the risk that over-selling will be so severe that the market and Protocol will collapse or be rendered ineffective. The second is that if trading is too limited, a liquid market will never develop, the gains from trade will be largely forgone and high compliance costs will cripple the Protocol. A middle ground may prevent extreme non-compliance but take the risks necessary to allow an active liquid market to develop quickly.

One possibility is to impose preventative measures only on those that have shown by their previous behavior that they are likely to be gross non-compliers. For example, gross non-compliers in the first commitment period could be banned from selling, or their sales could be subject to buyer liability or an insurance requirement, in the second period.

The approach we choose, the balance between prevention and trust, may itself influence a state's intentions. States are voluntarily participating in the Protocol and may be more committed to it if they see themselves as an active equal member of the international team. Feeling trusted by others may be a key element of this.

Some basic safeguards may be appropriate before allowing sales. First, the country must clearly have a functioning registry that meets international

---

[10]For detailed discussion of this issue, and application to the problem of oil pollution at sea, see Mitchell (1994a & b).

standards.[11] Second, they must have greenhouse gas inventories of sufficient quality to assess compliance.[12]   These might be seen as minimum preconditions for selling. Without them, sellers could oversell and we would never know and never be able to punish.

Some would argue for more stringent preconditions. These could include having a timely system for monitoring emissions during the commitment period so the seller can accurately assess the number of excess AAUs they hold. They could also include having an adequate domestic monitoring and enforcement system, particularly if the right to sell is devolved to sub-state entities. While there are arguments in favor of such preconditions, they are difficult to define. The problem of assessing the adequacy of these systems could create extreme uncertainty in the market, particularly if it cannot be swiftly resolved. Preconditions that require judgment and interpretation are also open to political manipulation if some Parties wish to block others from trading or paralyze trading completely.

One simple option to limit overselling is to simply not allow countries or legal-entities to go into overdraft in their AAU registries. This does not prevent 'short' sales in the derivatives market but means that the international community will not accept such sales as binding until the transfer actually occurs through a registry. This tool would be simple to implement and would have no economic cost. However, it will only avoid extreme risk taking and non-compliance.

Two other options that have been proposed to prevent overselling are the 'permanent reserve' and 'annual surplus' trading.[13]   A permanent reserve requires that we estimate likely emissions over the five years in advance and then require that the Party hold enough AAUs to cover these emissions until the end of the commitment period, at which time any excess could be sold; this is equivalent to the assigned amount not changing more than a fixed amount from that in Annex B. The required reserve could be updated each year based on actual inventory data. 'Annual surplus' trading is similar in that it requires that we define annual assigned amounts that sum to the five year assigned amount (a simple, but not necessarily good, rule would be to set the annual assigned amount at 1/5 of the total). Each year each state would be allowed to sell only after it had filed an inventory. It could only sell the difference between the annual assigned amount and the inventory. Both of these options would directly stop large amounts of overselling though some may still occur if emissions are higher than anticipated.

[11]For a discussion of the functioning of these registries see Chapter 2.
[12]Monitoring and reporting requirements are discussed in detail in Chapter 3.
[13]Baron (1999a).

A fourth option would be to ban selling from countries that are talking egregious risks during a compliance period.[14]   The feasibility and effectiveness of this option depends on how feedback is provided during the commitment period and how we can assess egregious risk taking.   We discuss some problems with this approach below.

3.1.1   Effects of prevention options on market function, legal-entity trading and economic cost

The limit on overdrafts in registries would have no effect on legitimate trade. It affects states and legal-entities equally so would not affect the level of trading chosen.   In contrast, the permanent reserve and annual surplus trading could affect trading significantly.   These two options both set limits on total national sales.   For example, if only AAUs in the national government's own registry could form part of the permanent reserve, this would place strict limitations on the government's ability to allow legal-entities to trade. Devolved AAUs that were included in the permanent reserve would have to be limited to being traded within the country; then the state would maintain control of them and could prove that it held the permanent reserve.   Similar issues would arise with annual surplus trading.   Either the state must be the sole seller or the ability to sell internationally would have to be allocated either on a first-come-first-served basis or through another rationing system. This would affect not only net sellers but also those in the country that are thinking of buying.   An actor that buys may not have the option to sell internationally again before the end of the commitment period if it finds it has excess AAUs.   They could still sell domestically but may receive a much lower price.   This would discourage precautionary buying and would lead to a bias toward state trading and hence a thinner less liquid market.

Fixed selling limits, such as through a permanent reserve or annual surplus selling or through 'supplementarity' limits would make prices and AAU availability unstable as large countries pass their selling thresholds each year. AAU demand and supply would be impossible to predict.   It would raise the complexity of trading for all actors and would require additional administrative restrictions on registries both at the international and domestic levels.   It would separate the domestic and international AAU markets making AAUs heterogeneous depending on where they are held, thus reducing overall liquidity.   The effects on economic efficiency would not be nearly as great as banning trade altogether but could be severe.

---

[14]This is often referred to as the 'red light' component of the 'traffic light option'.

3.2   Facilitation and Feedback

In Table 4.1 State D's compliance was improved by its ability to buy AAUs. Advice and technical assistance may have helped State D reduce its own emissions further, also improving compliance.

Feedback on progress during the commitment period could play a facilitative function by identifying in advance countries with problems so that they can increase their own efforts and seek help from others. It could also play a punitive role. Countries that are deemed to be on a highly risky path could be prevented from selling more, or if a buyer, subjected to international pressure to reduce emissions further and buy more AAUs.

A simple feasible form of feedback is annual surrender of AAUs. This mechanism would require each state to surrender, within three or four months after the end of each year, AAUs equal to their interim estimated annual emissions. These estimates would not be as precise as final national inventories but they would be fairly accurate since their energy-related CO_2 component probably could be based on final annual energy statistics. The number of AAUs surrendered annually could be 'trued up' when full inventories were complete. Annual surrender (similar to the 'annual retirement' mechanism described in Baron (1999a)) would identify gross non-compliers early and also provide information on the global demand and supply of AAUs for future years.[15]

Another potential form of feedback would be to monitor holdings of AAUs relative to expected future emissions. For example, at the end of year two, state A will have surrendered two years' worth of emissions (say 36). If it continued to emit at the same rate it would require 18 per year or 54 for the next three years. If it had only sold ten it would still be in good shape to cover its future emissions,

$$Holdings = 100 - 36 - 10 = 54$$

If, however, it had sold 40 it would be taking a serious risk and probably would have to buy back many AAUs. The international community may wish to put a limit to risk taking and suspend the right of Parties like A to sell, because high levels of risk-taking behavior will tend to lower confidence in the Protocol as a whole. It is very difficult to define unacceptable risk taking, however.

One difficulty with this form of feedback arises with countries that devolve control over some AAUs to legal-entities. These actors may hold their AAUs out of their national registries even though they fully intend to

---

[15]This is discussed in more detail in Chapter 3.

bring them back when they need them for domestic compliance. Are these movements of devolved AAUs counted as sales when assessing a state's level of risk or are they counted in the state's holdings of AAUs? Neither option is likely to be an accurate reflection of the true situation.[16] This problem, combined with our inability to determine the true risk probably makes any formal action based on this feedback inadvisable.

4   DETERRING OVERSELLING

Deterrence is designed to encourage effort to comply and discourage deliberate non-compliance. If compliance is clearly observable in a timely way, parties can perfectly control their compliance, and strong credible punishments can be imposed on non-complying parties, deterrence is sufficient to ensure a high level of compliance. As discussed in Chapter 3, effective deterrence requires that the punishment times the probability of being punished is greater than the gain from non-compliance where all are in current values.[17]

*Punishment * probability of punishment >(non-compliance gain) $(1+r)^t$*

where r is the discount rate and t is the number of years between the overselling and the punishment. For example suppose the AAU price in 2008 is US$100 per metric ton. If the discount rate is 10 percent and the state perceives the probability of being caught and punished as 50 percent the punishment will have to be at least equivalent to $322 if it is received in 2013. The state may think it can hide the overselling in its inventory error, may believe there is some probability that Kyoto will collapse and may believe that even if Kyoto holds punishments will not be effectively enforced.

All sanctions that apply to non-compliers with the Protocol as a whole will apply to over-sellers. These are summarized in Table 4.3. In the next section we discuss how these punishments could be leveraged further to apply to the buyers of invalid AAUs to increase the severity of punishment.

---

[16]Similarly a holding of AAUs by an entity within a country may not necessarily mean it is available for compliance purposes. An entity holding excess permits cannot be expected to be more likely to sell domestically than internationally. If permits are globally in short supply at the end of the commitment period a party's compliance may be at risk even if entities within the party own sufficient permits to cover total national emissions.

[17]If states are risk averse the punishment can be a little lower. For the seminal discussion of these issues see Becker (1968).

**4.1   Selling as a Reward for Compliance – Suspension of Selling as a
          Punishment**

The ability to sell is potentially very valuable to sellers. For example, the
former Soviet Union could gain more than 1.5 percent of GDP and Eastern
Europe could gain nearly 1 percent.[18] The risk of jeopardizing future selling,
either having it banned or curtailed, could offset potential current gains from
overselling. The more efficient and liquid the trading market is, the greater
are the legitimate gains available to Annex I sellers.[19] Consequently the
potential punishment is also stronger. Restricting the ability to sell cannot
only be a severe punishment but it is also probably feasible. Removing a
privilege or reward is generally an internationally acceptable form of
punishment where imposing a fine is not (Chayes and Chayes, 1993). The
punishment is also controllable by the international community.

Withdrawing or curtailing selling rights could be a severe and feasible
punishment but is it credible? If a seller is forced to withdraw from the
market because of previous non-compliance, many legitimate sales will be
prevented as well as the invalid sales. If the seller is 'large' (e.g. Russia),
they affect the market price and the market price will rise when they exit.[20]
This hurts buyers. States may have ratified the agreement on the assumption
that the large country will be selling AAUs. They may no longer be happy to
comply. Buyer countries may put pressure on the international community to
not enforce the punishment when non-compliance arises.[21] The punishment
is more likely to be credible if it is graduated so that not all sales are limited
unless the non-compliance is flagrant and on a huge scale. This reduces the
cost of punishment to buyer states, makes it more likely they will agree to
enforce the punishment, and hence makes the threat of punishment a more
effective deterrent. Threats to limit selling could be effective but are limited
by buyers' willingness to enforce them. Using limits on the ability to buy is,
in contrast, unlikely to be effective. It is only punishing if they want to
comply very strongly and in this case there must be a compelling reason for
their non-compliance. If they are out of compliance even with the ability to
buy, it is only likely to make things worse.

---

[18]MacCracken et al. (1999), p.50.

[19]With an effective seller cartel, or even a single country acting to influence the market price,
    sellers may do even better than in an efficient market (Chapter 8 on Market Power). They will
    not benefit from other market imperfections, however.

[20]The price will also rise because of the removal of invalid AAUs but we assume that Parties
    support this rise in the interests of the agreement.

[21]For extensive discussion of this problem see Martin (1993).

4.2 Compliance Reserve or Escrow Account

Two other punishments could be created through the trading rules themselves, a compliance reserve (similar to 'tons in escrow' Baron, 1999) or an escrow account (similar to a performance bond). A compliance reserve requires that every time a trade is a made a percentage of the AAUs sold be put into an account.[22] These could be withdrawn if the country buys again. The compliance reserve would be a percentage of net sales. At the end of the commitment period, if the state is in compliance the AAUs are returned and they can sell them during the 'true up' period. If they are out of compliance, the reserve is used to bring them closer to compliance. If some AAUs remain, a share of them is given back, with the share depending on the degree of initial non-compliance. The compliance reserve offers some prevention of gross overselling and offers an incentive to moderate non-compliers to improve compliance; this increases the number of AAUs the reserve returns to them. For moderate non-compliers, increases in compliance lead to more than one for one increases in the number of AAUs returned.

For example, suppose the compliance reserve is 10 percent and the penalty rate is 50 percent. Then country A from Table 4.1 who on net sells 10 would deposit 1 in the compliance reserve (see Table 4.2). A is in compliance at the end of the period so would receive its unit back and would be able to sell it to non-compliers or bank it for the second commitment period. Country A faces no direct disadvantage from the reserve. In contrast suppose there is a country E that sells 20 units and deposits 2. At the end of the period E is one unit out of compliance (Case (i)), a moderate non-complier. It would forgo one unit of its reserve and would receive 0.5 units back. It has an incentive to improve its compliance. If it had not been out of compliance it would not only have received the one unit it lost but would have received the other entire unit. By improving initial compliance by 1 it would have gained 1.5 at the end of the period for a net gain of 0.5. Country C from Table 4.1 on the other hand is a more serious non-complier. If it improves its compliance (moves from case (i) to (ii)) it is worse off when only the compliance reserve is taken into account. Of course it is also subject to other penalties, which reduce as C's compliance improves.

The compliance reserve withdraws tons from the overall pool until compliance is initially assessed. This makes it harder for countries to achieve compliance in the first place. Thus while we could raise the percentage

---

[22]AAUs that are devolved to legal-entities authorized to sell could be counted as 'sales' until they are surrendered to the government to match emissions. Then legal-entities would not have to have compliance reserves – they would be automatically covered.

required for the compliance reserve this would have serious efficiency consequences. A compliance reserve also has a crude effect on limiting sales. For example a 10 percent reserve limits total sales (and devolution to legal-entities at any point in time) to 90 percent of AAUs. This is unlikely to be binding. The compliance reserve requires international oversight of government accounts in registries to ensure that reserves always match net 'sales'. This adds a layer of administrative complexity. A compliance reserve can be effective for discouraging low-level non-compliance but not large-scale non-compliance. If many instances of minor non-compliance have similar effect on confidence in the agreement as a few cases of larger scale non-compliance this could still be valuable.

Table 4.2 Deterrence effects of a compliance reserve

	Sales	Compliance reserve	Extent of non-compliance (1)	Units not returned (2)	Net gain = (1)-(2)
Country A	20	2	0	0	0
Country E (i)	20	2	1	1.5	-0.5
Country E (ii)	20	2	0	0	0
Country C (i)	20	2	5	2	3
Country C (ii)	20	2	4	2	2

An escrow account is similar but is denominated in terms of money rather than AAUs. Some portion of the revenue from sales of AAUs would be put into an account and could not be used until compliance was proven. This requires that revenue is observable (easy with a common market price but not easy with heterogeneous AAUs). If the reserve is a large portion of revenues, it raises clear financial liquidity issues and also issues of political acceptability. Both compliance reserves and escrow accounts require significant administrative oversight.

Table 4.3 Compliance options for reducing overselling with seller-only liability

Prevention of overselling	Preconditions: good quality inventories and registries.
	Ban overdrafts in registries. Require permanent reserve. 'Annual surplus' trading. Ban trade after egregious risk taking 'red light' option.
Facilitation	Make AAU market as liquid as possible to assist buyers to come into compliance and sellers to return to compliance. Advice and technical assistance.
Feedback	Annual surrender of AAUs based on preliminary emission inventory data. Track state and global expected emissions against total AAU holdings (including or excluding devolved AAUs).
Deterrence	Political/diplomatic sanctions take away votes in the governing body of the COP; publicly identify compliers and non-compliers. Economic sanctions impose trade sanctions on GHG intensive industries; impose financial penalties. Treaty related sanctions require purchase of offsetting, or more than offsetting, AAUs if they are available at the end of the period; reduce future assigned amounts. Trading related sanctions return only a fraction of the compliance reserve or escrow account; deny or limit ability to trade in subsequent periods.

Table 4.3 draws on Chapter 3 and the earlier discussion to summarize the options available to enhance both buyer and seller compliance without utilizing additional liability options. The effectiveness of these options affects both the value and the cost of making additional actors liable for overselling.

5   OPTIONS FOR ALLOCATING LIABILITY

The issue of liability for invalid trades must be viewed within the larger context of the overall compliance regime for the treaty and for trading. If the compliance regime is strong, countries are less likely to be out of compliance so trades will not be invalid and liability will be moot. If compliance instruments are considered too weak to control overselling by some states, however, it may be desirable to broaden liability in some situations so that penalties can be applied to more actors when a state oversells. These other actors will put pressure on the seller to not oversell. Where we refer to sellers here we mean the initial seller of the AAU or the 'issuer'. Even if a particular AAU is sold several times, its validity depends on the compliance of the first seller.

The selling Party should always be held liable, even if another actor is as well.[23] Punishing for acts that are fully controllable is the most effective form of punishment so sellers should always be held liable to the greatest extent possible. No extreme punishments are likely to be available under the Protocol, so the chance of over-punishing a seller is slight.

Making other groups liable in addition to the seller may improve compliance. These groups include buyers and insurance companies. If the buyer is liable it means that, if a selling state is out of compliance at the end of the commitment period, the AAUs it sold are no longer valid and cannot be fully used by buyers for their own compliance. Each sold AAU may be devalued in proportion to the level of non-compliance. In addition the buyer could face penalties. Variations of buyer liability make only a subset invalid (e.g. the most recently sold AAUs are invalid).[24] The buyer is now partly responsible for the seller's compliance. Liability is passed on with the AAU if the AAU is sold on the secondary market.

Insurance companies could be made liable if insurance from an accredited insurance agency were compulsory for sales.[25] The insurance company would accept some liability in return for a premium. If the seller goes out of compliance, the insurance company undertakes to provide the AAUs in their place. Voluntary insurance, such as buyers may seek to protect themselves

---

[23]It would be technically possible to not hold the seller liable for the permits sold by allowing them to claim them back without penalty if they are out of compliance (this is proposed as an option in the OECD/IEA paper). However, this would create perverse incentives to sell because there would be no risk to the seller. It would magnify uncertainty in the market and forgo the most important avenue of compliance pressure.

[24]This is generally called last-in-first-out or LIFO. Haites (1998) discusses various options.

[25]It would be essential to require international accreditation of insurance companies because otherwise companies could be created to offer insurance that would be unable to pay up in the event of default. The sellers who purchase insurance would not be concerned about this as the insurance company is liable to the international community not the seller. Insurers would need to hold certain capital ratios relative to their exposure and possibly portfolios of AAUs.

under buyer liability, makes insurance companies responsible to buyers but not to the international community. The buyers are still ultimately liable.

It is important to examine the role of legal-entities in the assignment of liability. Because states are the signatories of the Kyoto Protocol, they are ultimately responsible to the international community for compliance. It is companies, individuals and households, however, who actually emit. International emissions trades can be carried out by the state and/or by legal-entities that have been given authority to trade by the state. If states devolve authority to trade (together with responsibility to meet domestic caps) they are still responsible for outcomes, so they have a strong incentive to monitor and enforce the compliance of legal-entities. Thus while international rules will apply to states only, states may hold legal-entities responsible.

Thus the three key liability options are:

1   Only the seller is liable;
2   The seller and buyer are both liable; and
3   The seller is liable and is required to hold insurance.

Option 2 could incorporate any degree of liability on each, including 'double' and 'shared' liability (Baron 1999a). Option 3 is equivalent to making the buyer hold insurance because in that instance the seller would have an incentive to procure the insurance for them. The seller can provide more information to the insurer about their likelihood of compliance so will get a lower premium. It would probably be unwise to require both buyer liability and insurance together. Under buyer liability the buyer may demand that the seller finds insurance but this would be voluntary not compulsory.

These options could be applied to all sellers or only to a subset where there are strong reasons for concern. For example additional liability could be imposed on a seller where serious questions about the state's ability to meet its target have been raised, or in the second commitment period, if the seller was out of compliance in the first period. In choosing liability options we must tradeoff increased seller compliance against higher costs and reduced buyer compliance.

5.1   Analysis of Liability Options

5.1.1   Effects of buyer liability and insurance on seller compliance

If buyers or insurance companies are liable for sellers' compliance, they will put pressure on sellers to minimize their own risk. We must be careful, however, not to draw too close a parallel to private markets such as financial markets where buyers have a direct interest in the validity or quality of the good they purchase. In emissions trading markets buyers are only concerned about the compliance of sellers to the extent that they think the international community will catch sellers that are out of compliance and that they will face punishment for it. The effectiveness of buyer liability depends partly on the effectiveness of international monitoring of seller compliance but also on the marginal compliance pressure buyers face. If buyers are unlikely to comply the additional punishments they face if AAUs they have bought are made invalid because of seller non-compliance may be slight. If punishments for non-compliant buyers are expected to be weak, buyers will put little pressure on sellers because the consequences of buying invalid AAUs are not severe. Similarly insurers only care about seller compliance if they believe they will actually be forced to pay up for non-compliance. Buyer liability and insurance do not replace stringent international monitoring and severe, timely punishments for non-compliance.

Buyers and insurance companies can affect seller compliance in two ways. First, and most directly, they can write contracts with sellers that are enforceable under domestic law. These contracts would provide compensation and/or punish the seller if the seller goes out of compliance. Buyers could choose the domestic law that is strongest. The effectiveness of this strategy depends on the strength of international contract law. Second, by choosing the amount to buy and from whom (who to provide insurance to and what premium to charge them), they provide incentives to sellers both to improve the likelihood of future compliance and to provide information to convince others of their intended compliance. Sellers perceived to be reliable will be able to sell AAUs for a high price or will face low premia. Sellers perceived as unreliable may be unable to sell AAUs or obtain insurance. They will be precluded from trading. Buyers and insurance companies will use all the information they have about sellers' likely compliance and will actively seek more.

Buyer liability or insurance will, if effective, give rise to the growth of new private services to monitor seller compliance, enforce contracts and share risk. For example rating agencies may rate AAUs from different countries. Insurance companies may offer private insurance for buyers against the risk of seller default. These institutions will raise the quantity and quality of information flows about compliance and increase transparency.

5.1.2   How effective will this pressure be?
This pressure will raise compliance on trades that do occur by excluding highly risky sales and encouraging other sellers to improve their compliance probability. How much will it raise compliance? How accurately will these pressures reward sellers' efforts to comply and exclude highly risky sales? How many of the trades excluded would have been good trades?   This

depends on how much information buyers have about countries' future compliance and how much direct enforcement pressure they can impose.

Here it is worth diverting a moment to consider who is actually doing the buying and selling. Trading can be carried out either by states or by legal-entities under authority and with responsibility devolved to them through domestic regulation. Ideally the typical trader will be a legal-entity. The presence of legal-entities in the market increases market liquidity, reduces market power and ensures that trades are not based on political considerations.

A legal-entity has the ability to use domestic law so the effect of direct contracting depends on the strength of both countries' legal systems. If the deal involves a company in the selling country, however, that company will probably be unwilling to sign a contract where they get punished if their country is out of compliance in five years time. The sub-state seller has little control over his or her own compliance with the contract.

From the buyer's side, how much will a company know about a country's compliance, especially when non-compliance could happen suddenly in the last year of the commitment period? The type of information that would be valuable is emissions inventory data (made available in a timely way through annual surrender), government holding of AAUs (observable through the system of tracking registries), policies planned or actually implemented and their level of enforcement and efficacy, current levels of investment and planned investment, and new technologies coming on line. Finally, and most critically, they need information on the state's planned future sales or purchases. Regardless of emissions and current holdings, these are what will ultimately determine compliance. How committed is the seller country to compliance? This will be most clearly expressed through the domestic compliance penalties and the historical record on enforcement of other environmental regulations and achievement of past targets.

A problem unique to buyer liability is the possibility of cascading default or the 'domino' problem. Suppose buyer A sells to B who sells its own AAUs to C. If A goes out of compliance, some of B's AAUs will be invalid and this may put B out of compliance. But then some of C's AAUs are also invalid and they may in turn go out of compliance. An actor considering purchasing C's AAUs must not only assess C's intention to comply but the quality of the entire chain of sales that can affect C's compliance.

Buyers may employ brokers and rating agencies to collect information for them, significant uncertainty will remain. Insurance agencies will face the same information problems. Proof of a selling entity's intention to comply, or even that an entire sector will be in domestic compliance, does not provide any assurance that the party will comply.

One problem that may arise is that collecting and analyzing information about a country is an expensive up-front cost so buyers and brokers may focus their efforts on large sellers. Small states may be perceived to be risky simply because information on them is less available and understood.[26]

In summary, either buyer liability or a requirement to hold insurance will lead to higher seller compliance. We can always reduce risks of seller non-compliance by banning trade though. There are no sellers if there is no trade. With no trade, overselling does not exist. This leads to much higher compliance costs overall. Buyer liability or compulsory insurance will exclude some trades that would have been desirable. How much would trading be affected by buyer liability or compulsory insurance and what would the impact be on the costs of mitigation?

5.2   Effects of Buyer Liability or Compulsory Insurance on Market Function and Operational Simplicity

Buyer liability and compulsory insurance can raise costs both directly and, more importantly, indirectly. Costs rise directly through information collection and contracting costs. To the extent that these directly lead to greater compliance they may be justified. However, if buyers (or insurance companies or brokers and rating agencies working for buyers) are not the most efficient information collectors or information is duplicated, these costs may be higher than necessary.

More importantly, even after all the information has been collected and analyzed and contracts are written, buyers and insurance companies will still face high risks. Buyers etc will not be able to accurately predict compliance. This means that buying AAUs will be riskier so they will bias toward countries undertaking more secure mitigation options. This is not a problem if the trades really are risky, as society wants to minimize risk. However, many trades will seem risky when in fact they are not but the seller cannot prove that. These trades may be excluded when they should have gone ahead. The exclusion of these sales means that valuable mitigation opportunities in seller countries will not be exploited and buyers will have to implement more expensive domestic options.

These risks will apply to every trade, even on the secondary market, under buyer liability because the liability is passed on with the trade. In contrast, with compulsory insurance, it only applies to the first trade when the initial seller must find an insurance agency. After that future sellers face no

---

[26]To a certain extent this occurs in currency and capital markets where thin (small) markets are unstable and tend to pay a risk premium.

obligation and buyers face no risk. The insurance is carried with the AAU after the first sale. This seems to be an advantage of compulsory insurance. With insurance, however, only a limited number of accredited agencies will exist and they will be reasonably homogeneous actors with similar information and abilities. Buyers, in contrast, could be any actor on whom a state can enforce a regulation. They could be companies, states or brokers and other intermediaries. Although liability is passed on with AAUs as they are on-sold under buyer liability any buyer in the chain could offer a guarantee of their validity to future owners. They could voluntarily purchase insurance. Insurance agencies have not so far expressed interest in being involved in insuring AAUs on a large scale. The potential level of moral hazard and hence non-diversifiable risk involved is much higher than with most activities that are insured. Buyer liability almost certainly dominates compulsory insurance. Compulsory insurance may completely paralyze the market.

Because states ultimately bear liability for non-compliance, under buyer liability they may choose to control the purchases of their legal-entities. This would allow them to manage the risk but would seriously constrain the market and may introduce an undesirable political element into trading.[27]

Another indirect cost of buyer liability arises through the AAU market. If buyers are liable, every AAU will have to identify the original seller and the date of first sale (for a liability system that invalidates AAUs based on the order of sale). This means that each AAU will be unique when traded. There will be no single 'market price' of AAUs and every contract will need to specify country of origin and date. This will limit the liquidity of the market and slow the rate of information transmission about the global cost of mitigation. AAUs will not be able to be traded on commodity exchanges. It will make the market more vulnerable to market power and manipulation and will disadvantage less sophisticated traders because they won't know the appropriate price to ask or offer. Assessing the value of investments in emission reductions will be less certain.

Overall the costs of compliance will rise. How much they rise will depend on the strength of the overall treaty compliance provisions that independently encourage seller compliance. If compliance is generally good, buyer liability will involve less risk and so will have a smaller effect on costs; however, if compliance is already high it is also less valuable. The rise in costs will also depend on the sophistication of information collection and dissemination and of market processes. A more sophisticated market will assess risk more

---

[27]For more discussion of this, see Chapter 8 on Market Power.

accurately and will resolve some of the problems arising from heterogeneous AAUs. Even a sophisticated market, however, cannot predict sellers' or buyers' future intentions perfectly.

5.3   Effect of Higher Costs on Environmental Effectiveness

Higher compliance costs are damaging in themselves; they may also negatively affect the environment. Faced with an illiquid AAU market, with high AAU prices or even lack of availability, buyer countries will be forced to do more compliance at home. This domestic mitigation may have uncertain results (e.g. from policies and measures such as efficiency standards or taxes) and may be politically unacceptable. Buyer liability could reduce buyer compliance, which has the same environmental effect as seller non-compliance. If AAUs are not available, it is more credible for a country to say that it was 'unable' to achieve compliance. Non-compliance would be a non-deliberate act of omission, which is harder for the international community to influence than a deliberate act of commission (not buying AAUs that were available at a given price).

Another effect of higher costs on the environment is that, if they anticipate high costs of compliance, countries may choose not to ratify the Protocol in the first place. In the longer term, countries will be less willing to take on stringent targets if AAU prices are high, AAU supply is uncertain and costs of compliance are high.

If buyers are not effective enforcers of seller compliance, increased seller compliance with the Protocol may come at the cost of current buyer compliance and future environmental achievements.

5.4   Effects of Buyer Liability on Competitive Access to the AAU
         Market Efficiency

Under seller liability only, AAUs will be homogeneous and with a large number of actors (many states and involvement of legal-entities), and standard free trade protections, any actor will be able to sell or buy AAUs at the common international AAU price.

Introducing buyer liability or insurance requirements makes AAUs heterogeneous. This has four key effects on the AAU market. Each of these effects may lead to differences in access to the AAU market.

First, heterogeneous AAUs imply heterogeneous prices. The value of AAUs will be non-transparent. This could create direct opportunities for one buyer to contract with a seller to exclude other buyers and gain competitive advantage. The seller would simply agree to charge other buyers a very high price in return for a large purchase contract. Because there would be no 'market price' it would be difficult for the other buyers to prove that they are being excluded. If the market is illiquid, these types of exclusions may have real effects on the excluded countries' compliance costs.

Second, when AAUs are heterogeneous and risky, buyers will need to exert a significant effort to assess and monitor each seller country's compliance; for each trade they will need to write and enforce an extensive contract. A buyer country may choose to incur this fixed cost only in a limited number of countries. They may try to be the predominant or even sole buyer from that country. This would allow them to control the country's total level of selling. They could get the seller to contractually agree not to sell more than a fixed amount to others (or none at all). Then they could assess and control the seller's likely compliance more easily.[28]

Having a sole purchaser contract with a country would also allow the buyer to capture the benefits of efforts they put into improving the country's compliance. For example, a buyer may assist the seller to set up a good registry and timely inventory system and to design and implement effective abatement policies. These measures may be taken purely to minimize risk and lower transaction costs but they would dramatically lower market liquidity and could lead to non-transparent non-competitive behavior.

A third effect of heterogeneity that partly offsets the previous tendency towards heavy reliance on a few sellers is that when AAUs are risky, buyers (state or sub-state) may want to diversify by buying from several different states. Non-transparent prices, fixed costs of trading and the need to diversify to control risk may be particularly harmful for smaller buyers and sellers. Small buyers and sellers won't know what price to offer or accept; they will face higher risk because they won't be able to make such in-depth assessments of risk and will be less able to diversify. Small buyers are unlikely to be in a position to dominate buying from one country and hence lose the potential advantage of direct control of compliance. Small sellers may be faced with few potential buyers and hence receive a poor price for their AAUs. Small buyers and sellers will face higher marginal costs of compliance (buyers) or gain less profit from emission reductions (sellers). The bias against small buyers and sellers may lead more states to choose to trade as states rather than through a multitude of legal-entities. Buyer countries may also choose to control their legal-entities' purchases to manage the state's liability risk. This would reduce the liquidity of the market and politicize trading.

---

[28]Of course the seller country may not agree to this type of contract for sovereignty reasons.

Finally, one option to guarantee competitive access would be to force all traders to go through open exchanges. This option would be precluded with heterogeneous AAUs because each trade must involve a bilateral contract.

The effects of compulsory insurance would be much less severe for the liquidity of markets and competitive access. Once a seller had procured insurance, the AAUs would be homogeneous. Of course insurance would still have dramatic effects on the volume and efficiency of trade. Fair access issues would arise with respect to insurers. If some sellers were unable to obtain insurance at a reasonable price, they would be completely excluded from the market. Buyers would simply be competing for a much smaller volume of AAUs.

5.5   Effects on Confidence in the AAU Market and the Protocol as a Whole

The effectiveness of any international agreement ultimately depends on the trust states have in each other's compliance. States that have voluntarily ratified an agreement tend to comply if they believe that the agreement is equitable and that all other states will comply. If, however, they believe that other states are cheating, or likely to cheat, by overselling, by deliberately buying AAUs from unreliable states, or by taking insufficient domestic measures and making insufficient purchases, their own commitment to compliance will be weakened. In the early years of the Protocol when commitments are untested, building and maintaining trust is critical.[29] This argues for strong compliance measures. What does it imply for liability? If, because of inexperience with trading or because some large sellers are perceived as unreliable, states are particularly concerned about non-compliance arising through trading, adding buyer liability or compulsory insurance may raise confidence in the early years. However, if the fear is that countries with more stringent targets, buyers, will not achieve compliance, facilitating their compliance through a liquid AAU market may raise confidence.

The issue of liability for over-selling is intimately associated with the compliance regime under the Protocol. If there is an effective compliance regime in which all market participants believe that parties will be held accountable for non-compliance, then market players can be expected to comply and emissions trading can be expected to ease compliance through reducing costs and maximizing opportunities. However, a number of

---

[29]Problems of this nature are often modeled as 'coordination games' where everyone wants to cooperate if others will but do not want to comply if others do not.

arrangements additional to the basic seller-liability regime may be necessary if an effective compliance regime is unlikely to be implemented.

6   CONCLUSION

Trading can cut compliance costs in half and reduce marginal costs of compliance by up to 80 percent in some key countries.   This directly facilitates compliance and will make it more likely that a core group of key powerful countries will clearly be in compliance.   Clear compliance gives these countries the standing to effectively pressure other countries to come into compliance.

For the countries that are less committed to the treaty trading lowers the net cost of participation and may even make it profitable for some countries. This encourages participation and encourages compliance in the first period in order to be able to continue to benefit from trade in the second and future commitment periods.

On the other hand trading creates an additional possibility for non-compliance.   Sellers cannot comply by selling more AAUs than they have excess.   This selling is theoretically unlimited in contrast to non-compliance by buyers where the highest their emissions will rise is to the business-as-usual level.   Overselling by even one country will potentially affect emissions control efforts in all countries as it will lower the AAU price and hence the marginal reward to emissions control.

Only a few countries are likely to exploit this opportunity to profit from overselling.   Most countries have joined the agreement in good faith and are able to control their own behavior and are likely to try to honor agreements even under different governments.   Although some countries may oversell a little by mistake (possibly by underestimating their domestic emissions in a non-trading sector) instruments to control overselling are primarily aimed at few risky states.

A range of instruments could be used to reduce the risk of overselling. The number used will depend on the level of risk assessed in the context of the overall treaty compliance framework and the types of states that declare an intention to trade.   Some states that do not believe they can control their trading may choose not to fully engage in trading.   In particular, some may choose not to empower legal-entities.

The instruments can probably be ordered as follows in terms of their environmental benefits net of cost.

1   Strongest possible overall treaty compliance regime.
2   Strong inventories and credible registry as preconditions for trading.

3   Loss or limitation of trading rights in second period as punishment for over-selling in first commitment period.
4   Ban overdrafts in any account, state or legal-entity, in official registries.
5   Low level compliance reserve or escrow account.
6   Permanent reserve set at low end of likely emissions.
7   Buyer liability.
8   Compulsory seller insurance.
9   Annual surplus trading.

Options 1–4 have no real economic cost and therefore should certainly be included in any system. How far further down the list the trading compliance regime should move is a matter of judgment of the value of rapid market development vs. early confidence in trading compliance, the risk and importance of buyer non-compliance vs. the risk and importance of seller non-compliance, and the value of low costs that could lead to greater participation and future environmental stringency vs. the risk of a breakdown in confidence if too many actors are perceived to be cheating. Different participants have different assessment of these tradeoffs. These assessments will change with time as the institutions to support the Protocol develop, countries' compliance strategies take shape and the costs of compliance and commitment to compliance become more apparent.

5 Inclusion of all Source and Sink Categories in International Emissions Trading

Tim Denne[1]

1   INTRODUCTION

This chapter addresses the extent to which all gases, source and sink categories, as included in the Kyoto Protocol, can and should be included in international emissions trading.

The Protocol has established targets for Parties on the basis of an aggregate of emissions of six gases specified in terms of CO_2-equivalents. Global Warming Potentials (GWPs) have been developed to measure the relative contribution of each gas to atmospheric heating (radiactive forcing) over a specified time period, this enables emissions of different gases to be added together, e.g. under the approach chosen, 310 tonnes of N_2O is equivalent to one tonne of CO_2.[2] In addition, the Protocol states that net absorption by certain categories of sinks shall be used to meet these numerical targets.[3] Table 5.1 lists the six gases included in the Protocol, their relative contributions to total emissions and their main sources.

The development of commitments for six greenhouse gases from a wide range of source categories rather than simply CO_2 both increases the total emission reduction requirement, thus benefiting the atmosphere, and reduces

[1] I am grateful to Suzi Kerr, Ned Helme, Catherine Leining and Tim Hargrave for comments and to all members of the CCAP's International Emissions Trading Dialogue for comments on an earlier manuscript.
[2] For discussion of the concept of Global Warming Potentials see Houghton et al. (1996).
[3] The Protocol requires Parties to use the net changes in greenhouse gas emissions by sources and removals by sinks resulting from human-induced land-use change and forestry activities, limited to afforestation, reforestation and deforestation since 1990, measured as verifiable changes in carbon stocks, to meet the commitments (Article 3.3). If land use and forestry constituted a net source of emissions in 1990 these are included in the Party's assigned amount (Article 3.7). It also introduces the potential for other categories of sinks to be included from agricultural soils and land-use change and forestry categories (Article 3.4).

the unit costs for a given level of reductions.[4] Figure 5.1 illustrates this with two cost curves. The first is for measures that tackle CO_2 emissions only; a given percentage reduction target would achieve emission reductions equal to Q1 at a unit cost equal to P1. If the commitments are extended to all gases, the cost curve is lower but the reduction requirement increases from Q1 to Q2. The average cost of achieving emission reductions equal to Q2 reduces to P3 if measures across all sources and gases are used but, if measures are targeted at CO_2 only in order to achieve Q2, unit costs increase to P2.

Table 5.1 Main sources of greenhouse gases included in the Kyoto Protocol

Gas	% of Annex I	Main Sources
Carbon Dioxide (CO_2)	80.4	Fossil fuel combustion
		Industrial processes (e.g. cement manufacture, lime manufacture, steel production)
Methane (CH_4)	12.6	Coal mining
		Natural gas systems
		Agriculture (ruminant animals, manure management, rice cultivation)
		Landfills and wastewater treatment
Nitrous Oxide (N_2O)	5.7	Fossil fuel combustion
		Industrial processes (adipic and nitric acid manufacture)
		Agriculture (agricultural soils and manure management)
		Waste combustion
Hydrofluoro-carbons (HFCs)	0.4	Substitution of Ozone Depleting Substances (ODS)
		HCFC-22 production
		Semiconductor manufacture
Perfluoro-carbons (PFCs)	0.3	Substitution of ODS
		Aluminum production
		Semiconductor manufacture
Sulphur Hexafluoride (SF_6)	0.6	Semiconductor manufacture
		Electrical transmission & distribution
		Magnesium production

Source: http://www.unfccc.de. Data are percentages of 1995 totals; where data are unavailable, 1990 data are used.

---

[4] This assumes that targets are set in order to reduce emissions of the aggregate of all gases included to 5 percent below 1990 levels whether it is CO_2 only or six gases.

Figure 5.1 Hypothetical average cost curves for greenhouse gas emissions reduction

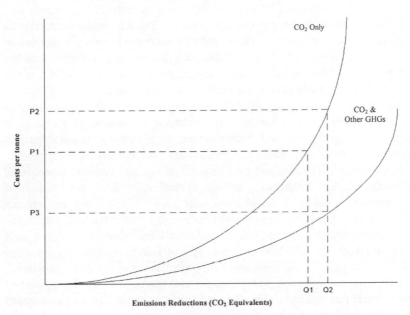

Reilly et al. (1999) modeled these cost impacts for different world regions. They found that, in addition to reductions in unit costs, for Annex B countries as a whole, total costs were $27 billion less for tackling all greenhouse gases than for tackling CO_2 only, despite the need to reduce emissions further. This result applied across all regional groups (US, EU, Japan, other OECD) with the exception of Central and Eastern Europe where costs rose slightly. Other analysts have similarly shown cost reductions from inclusion of non-CO_2 emission reductions in the overall program.[5] Tol (1999) suggests that the cost reductions associated with including methane emission reductions alone are about the same magnitude as the cost reductions associated with international trading of CO_2.

Despite the advantages in terms of cost-effectiveness, there are a number of monitoring and measurement difficulties that the multi-gas approach introduces, which might mean some of these benefits are lost. In comparison with the main source of anthropogenic greenhouse gas emissions, CO_2 from fuel combustion, many other greenhouse gas and source category combinations have much greater levels of uncertainty in measurement. Because of this uncertainty, emission inventories or national systems may not

---

[5] See Hayhoe et al. (1999) and Harvey et al. (1999).

record the real level of emissions and international inventories may not record the real extent or even direction of change in emission rates. Of particular concern is that Parties could bias their inventories deliberately in a way that favors their compliance assessment. Further, under international emissions trading, deliberate biases might be used to increase the number of assigned amount units (AAUs) available for sale. In these circumstances, the cost reductions from including the widest range of source categories are not from the low cost abatement opportunities but from cheating.

Arguably, levels of uncertainty surrounding measurement of some sources may be sufficient to stop Parties from including all sources or all gases in domestic trading systems and from allowing certain entities to participate in international emissions trading. Particularly where there is a difference between entity-level emissions monitoring systems and national inventories, including entities within the trading system may limit the ability of governments to control risks of non-compliance. Compliance assessments are based on national inventories and it is possible that there would be legal-entity compliance but not national compliance where different data are used at the different levels. However, this type of risk is no different from the risks of other policies and measures being insufficient to achieve compliance. It is an issue for domestic policy makers and not necessarily the subject of international rule-making. This chapter focuses on those issues of concern to the international community.

2   UNCERTAINTY

2.1   Sources of Uncertainty

Emissions of greenhouse gases are measured either directly, e.g. using emissions monitors, or, more typically, are estimated on the basis of emission factors. Using emission factors involves two types of data:

- Activity data, e.g. the quantity of fossil fuel burnt, cement produced or fertilizer applied;
- Emission factors, i.e. the emissions associated with a unit of activity.

The estimate of emissions is a product of these two factors. Across the full set of source categories included in the Kyoto Protocol, there are very different levels of uncertainty associated with the different data sets used to make these calculations reflecting random or systematic ('bias') errors. Bias errors tend to dominate.[6] Random errors result from imperfections in the data

---

[6] United States Department of Energy (1998).

collection process and computational errors; they make trends difficult to distinguish from 'noise'. Bias errors will be approximately the same size each year and are caused by excluded sources, which will bias downwards, changes in definition, and double counting which will bias upwards. Bias errors are hard to detect without applying multiple estimation techniques. A fuller description of some of these error sources is given below.

- Evolving Definitions. For example, emission inventories are meant to measure 'anthropogenic' (human-caused) emissions. Although in most cases it is obvious whether emissions from a particular source fall within this definition, there are a number of ambiguous cases, and the range of accepted definitions has shifted over time.
- Emissions Sources Excluded. An estimate that excludes some sources will be biased downward by the amount of the excluded source. It is probable that there are still sources in many or all countries that have not yet been identified and escape inclusion in both the estimates and the list of sources excluded.
- Incorrect Models of Emissions Processes. An estimate based on a belief that emissions are caused by (or can be estimated from) a particular activity or process can produce large, systematically biased errors if the emissions are actually caused by some other process. The incorrect method can produce estimates that are considerably higher or lower than actual emissions and have different time-series properties.
- Errors in Emissions Factors. Errors in emissions factors can have diverse causes, the most common of which are definitional errors, sampling errors, and measurement errors. These errors can be either random or systematic.
- Errors in Activity Data. Activity data are also subject to definitional errors, frame errors, sampling errors, and measurement errors, which can be either random or systematic.
- Computational Errors. Computational errors can exist in the estimation of emissions factors, in the calculation of emissions, or in the computation of the underlying activity data by the source organization. Although any single computational error will usually produce a systematic error, computational errors as a group tend to produce small random errors in the estimate.

Biases influence estimates from the different source categories in very different ways. Emissions of CO_2 from fuel combustion, for example, are estimated on the basis of fuel use data, fuel carbon coefficients and assumptions regarding the proportion that is fully oxidized. Data on quantities of fuel combusted are collected for a number of different reasons, including international reporting requirements and as the basis for energy taxation in many countries. Energy is a very significant component of economic activity and effective data systems have been developed over many years. Energy consumption data are typically very accurate.

In contrast, fugitive fuel emissions, such as leaks from natural gas pipes are measured on the basis of samples, e.g. in the US, statistical sampling techniques are applied to 'model' facilities to derive emissions factors for all the major components in the natural gas system.[7] This introduces scope for both random and bias errors. For example, the choice of model facility might not reflect a true average.

For ruminant methane emissions (enteric fermentation), typically animal numbers are estimated from population surveys which may involve self-reporting or infrequent results. Very few experiments have been undertaken to estimate emissions per animal so emission factors may be biased in either direction.

Data systems are likely to improve as the Kyoto Protocol is implemented and the requirements for measuring compliance are clarified. However, some source categories are inherently more difficult to measure with accuracy and there will always be significant differences in levels of uncertainty.

2.2   Levels of Uncertainty

The IPCC inventory guidelines provide an illustrative assessment of the relative levels of uncertainty between emission sources (see Table 5.2).

The least uncertain emission sources are for CO_2 from fuel combustion (energy) and industrial processes. Absorption of CO_2 by sinks has high levels of uncertainty. Agricultural emissions have high levels of uncertainty, particularly N_2O emissions from soils. Levels of emission measurement uncertainty differ among countries also, reflecting different methodologies for inventory compilation and, in aggregate, the relative contributions of different source and sink categories. For example, compared with the Annex I average of 80 percent (Table 5.1), CO_2 is 95 percent of the total inventory in Luxembourg but only 35 percent in New Zealand. IPCC approaches to inventory compilation are required for national inventory reporting under the Convention. Steps are being taken to improve the quality of emission estimates including the IPCC/OECD/IEA program on good practise in inventory preparation, the encouragement of bottom-up inventory approaches and of country-specific emission factors. However, estimates will still have significant uncertainties even after these improvements.

---

[7] US Environmental Protection Agency (1999).

Table 5.2 Uncertainties due to emission factors and activity data

Gas	Source Category	Emission Factor	Activity Data	Overall Uncertainty	% of Annex I Emissions
CO_2	Energy	7%	7%	10%	79%
	Industrial Processes	7%	7%	10%	2.5%
	Land Use Change & Forestry	33%	50%	60%	-11%
CH_4	Biomass Burning	50%	50%	100%	0.03%
	Oil & Nat Gas Activities	55%	20%	60%	3.2%
	Coal Mining & Handling	55%	20%	60%	1.5%
	Rice Cultivation	¾	¼	1	0.1%
	Waste	$^2/_3$	$^1/_3$	1	3.0%
	Animals	25%	10%	25%	2.9%
	Animal Waste	20%	10%	20%	0.7%
N_2O	Industrial Processes	35%	35%	50%	1.0%
	Agricultural Soils			2 orders of magnitude	2.9%
	Biomass Burning			100%	0.01%

Note: Individual uncertainties that appear to be greater than ±60% are not shown. Instead judgment as to the relative importance of emission factor and activity data uncertainties are shown as fractions which sum to one.
Source: Greenhouse Gas Inventory Database;
http://www.unfccc.de/resource/index.html

2.3 Impacts on the Atmosphere, Costs and Compliance

Uncertainties mask the differences between measured and 'actual' emission rates. They can mean that:

- Where emission rates are under-estimated, countries will do less than would be needed to meet the targets if emissions were measured accurately, and the climate suffers;
- Where emission rates are over-estimated, firms and/or national economies face higher costs than they would if actual emission rates had been measured.

Because Kyoto emissions commitments are specified for an aggregate of six gases, uncertainties in measurement of emissions from one source category affect what can be emitted from all other source categories. For example, if landfill methane emissions are under-estimated, energy CO_2 emissions can be increased while maintaining measured aggregate emissions to below the assigned amount. As emissions from all source categories are included both in the base year (1990) and the commitment period, the bias problem is limited to the extent that there is consistency in measurement approach and no significant change in emissions. Systematic biases in emission estimates are probably of similar magnitude and the same direction in both periods. The obvious exception is absorption by sinks which is excluded from the base year for commitments under the Kyoto Protocol.[8] For sinks and for source categories for which there is a significant change in emissions, there can be a more marked difference between measured and actual emission rate changes with implications for compliance assessments.

Table 5.3 illustrates the issues for a country for which the 1990 inventory has emissions totaling 100 Mt, made up of 80 Mt from low uncertainty and 20 Mt from high uncertainty source categories. The country has net sequestration of 10 Mt from sinks each year during the commitment period. The country's target is 8 percent less than this, i.e. 92 Mt but this is increased to 102 Mt because of the contribution of sinks.[9] The country can increase its emissions from low uncertainty sources by 2 units to 82 and still be in compliance.

Where high uncertainty emission sources are biased upwards non–deliberately (by 60 percent which is the IPCC estimate for pipeline methane), i.e. at the top end of the uncertainty range, 1990 emissions are estimated at 112 Mt and the new commitment period target is biased upward to 113 Mt (i.e. 112 less 8 percent = 103 and plus 10 from absorption by sinks). The high estimate of emissions from high uncertainty sources requires that emissions from low uncertainty sources only increase to 81. The net environmental effect of this bias with no change in the level of activity in uncertain activities is a small positive gain. Where emissions from high uncertainty sources are biased downwards, the total allowed emissions are reduced to 91 Mt but emissions from low uncertainty sources can rise to 83 Mt causing a net environmental loss of 1 Mt. These losses are small because they affect both 1990 and commitment period emissions in similar ways.

---

[8] Except for countries in which land use change and forestry was a net source of emissions in 1990.

[9] The Conference of the Parties has decided (Decision 9/CP.4) that net absorption by sinks will increase the assigned amount rather than reduce the inventory total.

Table 5.3 Impacts of biases on compliance assessments

Bias	Emissions Source	1990 million tonnes	2008–2012 average million tonnes	
No bias	Total emissions	100	92	
	Sinks		10	
	Total allowed emissions		102	
	Low uncertainty (e.g. energy CO_2)	80	**82**	
	High uncertainty (e.g. Methane from pipelines)	20	20	
	Total actual emissions	100	102	
			Reported	Actual
Upward bias in methane	Sinks		10	10
	Total allowed emissions		113	102
Net damage = 1	Low uncertainty	80	**81**	81
	High uncertainty	32	32	20
	Total emissions	112	113	101
Downward bias in methane	Sinks		10	10
	Total allowed emissions		91	102
	Low uncertainty	80	**83**	83
Net damage = 1	High uncertainty	8	8	20
	Total actual emissions	88	91	103
Reduction in methane with upward bias	Sinks		10	10
	Total allowed emissions		113	102
	Low uncertainty	80	97	97
	High uncertainty	32	16	10
	Total reported emissions	112	113	107
Net damage = 5				
Upward bias in sinks	Sinks		16	10
	Total allowed emissions		108	102
Net damage = 6	Low uncertainty	80	88	88
	High uncertainty	20	20	20
	Total reported emissions	100	108	108

In contrast, if emissions are biased upward and the country decides to reduce emissions from high uncertainty sources the net environmental damage is increased. Allowable emissions are 113 but reducing reported uncertain emissions by 16 (10 in reality) allows an increase in certain emissions by the same amount. The net environmental damage from the combination of a change in the 1990 emissions baseline and the change in reported inventory is 5.

Although sinks are a small component of total emissions, because of their exclusion from the base case, the full level of uncertainty is reflected in allowed emissions in the commitment period, whether it is from random or systematic errors. Upward bias in sinks (by 60 percent as estimated by IPCC) increases allowed emissions by 6 and hence leads to net environmental damage of 6.

There are a number of implications for compliance. If there is no systematic or deliberate bias, the effects of uncertainty can be in either direction and result in under or over-estimation of residual emissions. However, parties might deliberately manipulate emissions data in order to ease compliance. Under a compliance regime with penalties, there is an incentive to bias emission estimates to avoid these penalties. Where a Party expects to reduce emissions in a certain category, the Party would benefit from upward bias of those emission estimates. It would benefit even more through upward bias in the base year and downward bias in the commitment period. Such bias would ease compliance and reduce the need for domestic measures or allowance purchases.

Because of the potential for strategic bias, errors will not even out over Parties. Rather, they will lead to systematic environmental losses. They will also lower efficiency by putting excessive emphasis on uncertain sources if reductions in them are systematically over-rewarded. The potential for bias also has equity implications because some may cheat while others do not.

Truly random errors will tend to even out over time, sources and Parties so there will be no aggregate environmental damage. There will still be an efficiency cost because reductions from some sources are likely to be over - or under-rewarded. There may also be equity and competitiveness impacts if different countries provide different rewards for the same real reductions.[10]

Ensuring good data systems will be a vital component of the compliance regime.[11] It requires both good reporting formats and methodologies plus stringent reviews of data. If significant changes in emissions from uncertain sources were identified in emission inventories, this would suggest the need for especially detailed assessment and review of national methodologies and data sources.

---

[10]These implications are discussed in detail in Kerr and Pfaff (2000).
[11]See Chapter 3.

2.4 How Does Uncertainty Create Problems under Trading?

Trading can increase problems associated with uncertainty in two ways.

- the opportunity to sell AAUs increases the incentives for net sellers to bias;
- the opportunity to sell AAUs may lead to increased emission reduction activity in uncertain source categories.

2.4.1 Increased incentives for bias

The incentive for deliberate bias may be greater where Parties or entities can sell AAUs: they might make use of uncertainty to cover some portion of the AAUs that had been transferred to other Parties. Where there is no opportunity for international sales of AAUs, the incentive to bias is limited by the level of emission reductions required to meet the domestic target. Where there is the opportunity to sell AAUs there is no limit to this incentive as all AAUs made available can be sold.

In contrast, for Parties or entities that are buyers in aggregate, there is still an incentive to bias emission inventories deliberately under international emissions trading, but it is reduced relative to the situation without trading, because the costs of compliance, and the benefits of biasing, are reduced through access to AAUs at the international market price.

The extent to which these factors balance each other out depends on whether net buyer or net seller countries are more likely to bias inventories.

2.4.2 Increased emission reduction activity among uncertain sources

Trading allows sellers to release AAUs through additional emission reductions from uncertain source categories. For individual countries and in aggregate, the existence of trading is likely to change the balance of emission reductions among source categories in addition to between countries. For example, country A may have more low cost opportunities than country B but the least cost opportunities in country A might be in limiting N_2O from agricultural soils rather than switching fuels for electricity generation from coal to gas, the next least cost opportunity in country B. Under trading with this example, more emission reductions are undertaken from agricultural N_2O opportunities and fewer from energy CO_2.

These effects can be in both directions leading to under or over-estimates of emissions and more or less emission reduction activity, depending on the relative costs of control.

2.5   Trading and its Effects on Improving Certainty

Rather than exacerbating uncertainty problems, emissions trading may reduce them. This is for two reasons. First, legal-entity trading is likely to lead towards a more detailed approach to emissions inventory compilation. The data required to check AAU requirements at the entity-level are likely to enhance the data systems established for the national inventory and to become an important component of the inventory system itself. This may improve the inventory and ensure a better match between the national inventory and measurements made at the entity-level.

Second, in aggregate it will reduce the costs of compliance and thus the incentives for biasing emission estimates downwards. Because entities, and ultimately Parties, can purchase AAUs at a price less than or equal to costs of the marginal domestic emission reduction, there is a lower benefit to deliberate bias. However, trading will change which Parties or entities have the incentives to bias, concentrating incentives on those that are net sellers of AAUs. If these are countries that have worse inventories and are inherently more likely to bias their emissions estimates, then the problem is worsened.

2.6   How can the Problems Relating to Uncertainty be Addressed?

Uncertainty problems can be tackled directly, through addressing the causes via improvements to inventories. They can also be tackled indirectly through measures that seek to prevent the wider implications and effects of uncertainty, for example by introducing restrictions on AAU sales from uncertain source categories or through liability rules.

2.6.1   Improving inventories
Improving inventory methodologies will have benefits for the compliance regime under the Kyoto Protocol with and without trading.[12] It might include:

* Standardizing the emission factors used. Maintaining emission factors from 1990 until the end of the first commitment period should, in theory, remove a means for strategic bias. However, there are situations where emission factors should change over time but are maintained. For example, if a landfill's emissions were based on an average waste content but an individual landfill had a changing waste mix, actual emissions might rise but would not be measured as such if the single emission factor was maintained. Justification needs to be provided in

[12]See Chapter 3.

inventories for emission factors, whether they have been retained from the base year or not. However, in periodic reviews of national inventories, particular attention needs to be given where emission factors have changed.

- Improved measurement and monitoring, including moves towards direct measurement of emissions rather than calculation. In addition, there would be greater confidence in the inventory if it were subject to independent audit.[13]

- Expert reviews could particularly examine how reductions in emissions from uncertain sources have been achieved to see if there are reasonable causes, deliberate or not, that explain the reductions.

As noted above, the introduction of emissions trading may provide positive incentives for the improvement of inventory methodologies.

2.6.2 Restricting trading

A number of options to restrict a source category from selling AAUs are discussed below.

2.6.2.1 International rules on what sources can sell AAUs International rules on which emission source categories can be the source of AAUs for sale, do not eliminate the potential for governments to bias inventories in order to increase sales of AAUs.

For international emissions trading, the unit of trade is an assigned amount unit (AAU). Because assigned amounts are specified for an aggregate of six gases it is not possible to differentiate to which gas or source category AAUs 'belong'. If a Party sells AAUs while its agricultural soil emissions reduce, it is not possible to link these events. The reduction in emissions from agricultural soils may reflect business as usual, whereas the ability to sell may be more linked to reduced growth in energy-related CO_2 emissions.

Where governments trade, there is a clear potential for under-estimates of emission rates, because of uncertainty, to be used to release AAUs for sale. The amount made available for sale is the net difference between the national assigned amount and the national inventory total. But, even if a Party allowed legal-entity trading for a limited number of source categories, the problem remains because the units of transfer are domestically fungible. For example, the volume of sales of AAUs from the electricity generation sector will be a function of the initial level of allocation (assuming grandfathering), the international price of AAUs and the cost of emission reductions. Where an electricity company is selling AAUs this may reflect a generous

---

[13]Chapter 3 and Hargrave et al. (1999b).

allocation. The generous allocation may have been made possible through deliberate biasing of emission estimates for other sources. Under these circumstances, any restrictions on sales from entities for which emission estimates are highly uncertain, will not limit the effects of deliberate bias.

Similarly, where a Party introduces non-trading policies and measures to tackle an uncertain source and emissions fall, the resulting freed-up AAUs can still be sold, either through initial over-allocation of AAUs to more certain sources that are involved in trading or through government trading.

Restrictions might be put in place through international rules limiting sales to some proportion of assigned amount. For example, if uncertain sources[14] made up 10 percent of a national inventory then sales might be restricted to 90 percent of total emissions or some proportion thereof. However, given the proportion of the aggregate of six gases that energy-related CO_2 (which has low uncertainty in measurement) makes in most Parties, this would not be an effective strategy; no country will legitimately be able to sell this many AAUs in any case.

Alternatively, Parties might need to demonstrate that they had placed fewer AAUs on the market, i.e. had allocated fewer AAUs to entities, than a proportion of their total assigned amount equal to the proportion of source categories with low levels of uncertainty in their base year inventory. For example, the Party in Table 5.2 would only be able to place 80 million AAUs on the market. This would be equivalent to not allowing entities in uncertain source categories to sell. However, this does not isolate the AAU market from the uncertainty nor the ability of the government to bias emissions data in the same way as it could if the emission source was included in the permit system. Because ultimately a Party is judged by a comparison of emissions and assigned amount, uncertainties are reflected in the total national demand for AAUs. Trading sectors can over-sell AAUs and the Party still be in compliance when total emissions from all source categories are measured; this means that measurements of changes in emissions in uncertain sources still count in assessing the quantity of AAUs that can be sold.

Uncertain source categories might be restricted to project-based trades. Project-based trading would ensure there was a well-measured subset of emission reductions within an uncertain source category, probably using a different methodology from that used for the inventory. For example, measurements of emission reductions for landfill methane capture might be made from direct monitoring of quantities of emission captured. However, this will not change the overall level of uncertainty in the aggregate measure

---

[14]An uncertain source would need to be defined on the basis of some expert estimate of measurement uncertainty; it is likely to differ by country.

of landfill methane emissions and will not limit the influence of biases on compliance assessments.

2.6.2.2 Source-specific targets The only way to prevent 'leakage' between traded and untraded source categories would be by requiring Parties that wish to sell AAUs internationally to introduce legally-binding targets for those sectors or source categories that are allowed to trade (sell) internationally. Two targets or caps might be used, one for high uncertainty source categories, the other for low uncertainty source categories. This would require Parties to estimate, before the beginning of the commitment period, where they were going to achieve their emission reductions across the different gases or source categories in order for them to set appropriate sectoral targets. These definitions might be based on an assessment of the quality of the Party's inventory and ability to measure activity data pursuant to the requirements for data quality included in the Kyoto Protocol (Articles 5, 7 and 8, or some set of best practise guidelines).

Source categories that could sell would have legally binding caps or assigned amounts which could be increased or decreased following sales or acquisitions of AAUs. The non-trading source categories would not be able to sell (although they might be able to buy). This does not completely eliminate the Party's ability to deliberately bias the emissions data to improve compliance but requires that they know how they will do so from the beginning of the first commitment period, e.g. by setting targets that can be met through data manipulation.

In order to eliminate this possibility, target setting would need to be subject to international scrutiny. This might open up the possibility of very protracted negotiations of similar complexity to the Protocol itself. In addition to the practical constraints, this type of restriction introduces a number of inefficiencies to the trading market. In particular, it requires a Party to choose between two types of potential for efficiency gain, that associated with inter-gas 'trade' via aggregation using global warming potentials (GWPs) and that associated with inter-Party trading.[15] Introducing source-specific targets limits a Party's ability to increase emissions from one source at the expense of another. Both aggregation and international trading offer significant opportunities for Parties to reduce the overall costs of achieving commitments.

---

[15]As noted above, Richard Tol (1999) suggests that the cost savings from allowing reductions amongst other gases are as great as those from inter-country trading of CO_2. This suggests that efficiency is maximized through allowing greatest flexibility with respect to how marginal increases in emissions are offset.

In comparison with improvements to inventories, requiring separate targets on the basis of source emission measurement uncertainty is an unnecessary complexity.

2.6.2.3 Buyer liability   Buyer liability is a system whereby sales of AAUs can later be invalidated if the selling Party is found not to be in compliance with its emission limitation and reduction commitments, i.e. if its emissions are higher than its assigned amount. A number of proposals have been made for how buyer liability might be introduced in order to prevent over-selling of AAUs either as a compliance penalty or a permanent feature of the compliance regime.[16]   Under buyer liability, inventory biasing entails considerable risks for buyers who may have to return AAUs purchased from countries that had biased their inventories if these biases are later identified. Whereas this provides some disincentive for deliberate bias, there are a wide range of disadvantages to buyer liability – particularly its effects on market function through creating differentiated AAU markets. Buyer liability and its implications are discussed in greater detail in Chapter 4.

3   CONCLUSIONS

The aggregate or basket approach adopted for targets under the Kyoto Protocol, enables emission reductions across all gases, source categories and sinks to contribute towards meeting commitments.   This will maximize economic efficiency through providing the greatest number of opportunities for emission reduction.   This approach provides an incentive to reduce the emission intensity of current activities and to reduce activity levels of emission-intensive sectors.   It means that the least cost pathway to meeting emission limitation commitments can potentially be discovered for all Parties and entities.

However, the basket approach introduces a number of uncertainties to the measurement of compliance under the Protocol because of the level of uncertainty associated with emission measurement from a number of source categories.   Thus uncertainty is inherent in the Protocol, and it is the aggregate approach, not trading, which introduces the potential for the bias of inventories to ease compliance.

Trading can exacerbate the bias problem where it results in greater emission reduction activity (or greater measured reductions) from sources with high measurement uncertainty, or provides a greater incentive for Parties to manipulate their inventories.   Where measured emissions from uncertain

[16]See Baron (1999b) and Haites (1998).

sources are less than actual emissions, the requirement for AAUs is reduced and more AAUs can be sold. The possibility of selling AAUs clearly introduces some additional incentives to bias emission estimates.

Under current rules it is not feasible to limit or prevent trading of AAUs from uncertain sources because AAUs are domestically fungible. Biasing emission estimates from an uncertain source can be used to enable greater allocation of AAUs to more certain source categories.

The only way to stop Parties from using the high level of uncertainty of some source categories to bias the comparison of inventory and AAU holdings, would be to set separate emissions caps for those sources that are allowed to trade internationally. This is effectively breaking up the basket that has been approved for commitments under the Kyoto Protocol to a gas-specific, source category-specific set of targets, or two targets, one for relatively certain source categories allowed to trade and one for uncertain sources that cannot. There is a clear efficiency loss from this restriction as it reduces some of the potential options for identifying least cost emission reduction opportunities.

Fully preventing strategic bias would require international agreement on the specific targets for individual sources within Parties as it is possible for a government to anticipate or plan how it will bias inventory data in the future and use this information in setting targets. The development of these source targets would be a complex analytical and negotiating task.

Introducing separate targets is an unnecessary and inefficient approach to dealing with uncertainty issues. It removes from parties the flexibility to seek least cost emission reduction opportunities wherever they exist. In contrast, a more appropriate and proportionate response is through improving data systems and their quality control. This might be achieved through:

- Ensuring consistency of emission factors, and activity data sources across base year and commitment period;
- Thorough expert review of the causes of reductions in emissions from uncertain sources;
- Better matching of inventory approach and the approach to measuring emissions at the entity-level.

Trading itself may ease the uncertainty problem as it is likely to lead towards development of a more detailed and more accurate emission estimation approaches which will improve the overall level of accuracy of national inventories and national systems. Also, under international emissions trading, because buying AAUs may be a lower cost option than emission reductions, the incentive to bias emission estimates downwards may be reduced.

3.1 Implications for the Rules for International Emissions Trading

The rules should not introduce any language that restricts any emission source or sink category from contributing emission reductions in a way that enables AAUs to be sold.

Good inventory data and national systems are key to confidence in the trading system and to ensuring against selling through inventory biases.

Measures which encourage independent review of national inventories, e.g. via auditing prior to presentation or ex-post justification will give further confidence in emissions data and compliance assessments.

6 Domestic Greenhouse Regulation and International Emissions Trading

Suzi Kerr[1]

1 INTRODUCTION

The efficiency and effectiveness of Kyoto ultimately depends on the implementation of effective domestic policies. To gain the full benefit from international trading, those domestic policies need to be responsive to the opportunities in the international market and facilitate low transaction cost international trading.

Current empirical modeling assumes that emissions are reduced at least cost at the national level. Estimates of marginal costs with no trading range from $100 to $1,100 (1990 US $ per metric ton), in Japan and the EU and $75 and $400 in the US.[2] With Annex B trading, marginal costs are expected to be between $10 and $220. All these estimates are lower bounds if countries do not use efficient policies. Modeling also assumes that when international trading occurs it is competitive and frictionless (with the exception of specific modeling of market power and restrictions on trade such as supplementarity). None of these assumptions are likely to hold in reality. Incorporating frictions in the international market would raise the estimates of marginal cost of emission reductions under trading considerably.

Kyoto, as any other international agreement, is an agreement among sovereign nations. This means that the agreement is as non-prescriptive as possible. In particular each nation retains domestic sovereignty over instrument choice. This is an unavoidable feature of international agreements. States would not, in an environmental treaty, sign away their control over domestic regulation that affects all sectors of their economy. Domestic sovereignty means that we will see a wide range of domestic responses to the need to meet international targets. As long as reporting and monitoring of outcomes is standardized this does not matter from a short-run

---

[1] Some of the ideas in this chapter developed from discussions with and earlier work on the integration of domestic trading and non-trading instruments by Tim Denne.
[2] Weyant and Hill (1999), pp. xxxi–xxxii.

environmental point of view. It may, however, reduce efficiency and create competitiveness issues (see Chapter 7). These could reduce the stringency of future targets. On the other hand, domestic sovereignty could have some benefits. Different policies will be most efficient and feasible for different countries especially in the short run. This will depend on their existing policies, the sources of their greenhouse gases and their political and regulatory culture. Also, given that much uncertainty remains about effective domestic greenhouse policy, having different states implement different approaches could be valuable as experimentation. This Chapter focuses on the impact of varying policies on states' abilities to trade efficiently.

Efficient trade has advantages for both the state making the trade and for all other countries involved in the agreement. As with any form of trade, increasing trade benefits both buyers and sellers. Buyers can reduce their domestic costs of compliance while sellers profit from selling Assigned Amount Units (AAUs) for more than the cost of reducing emissions. Trading between the more developed states in Annex B and the countries in transition, such as Russia, will improve the dynamic efficiency of the agreement by providing an effective mechanism to transfer skills and technology.

Efficient trade also has the advantage that it reduces any impacts of the agreement on fair competition in goods. If all sectors in all countries trade competitively (i.e. do not have limits on trade or exploit market power) marginal costs of emission reduction are equalized and the increased marginal costs of production of goods truly reflect the cost of greenhouse emissions involved in production. No sector in any Annex B country gains an artificial cost advantage.

Improving each country's efforts to improve its link with the international market will have impacts on the general efficiency of the market and ultimately the mitigation effort. Increased volumes of trade by more atomistic actors (i.e. actors that cannot affect the price) will reduce price volatility, increase liquidity and reduce the risk of involvement in the market. They will reduce the ability of large players to exert market power.

Improved access to AAUs in the open market will reduce the cost and risks involved in compliance. If countries and entities have the option to buy AAUs, the risk of accidental non-compliance is dramatically reduced. Having an additional compliance option with highly transparent prices and quick response also reduces financial risk. This would ultimately increase compliance and may encourage future participation by states outside of Annex B. An efficient international market does not require that all countries have identical domestic regulation. It requires that domestic regulation be sufficiently integrated with the international market to ensure enough international trade to equalize marginal costs among countries; it requires also that domestic instruments lead to equalization of marginal costs within countries.

Hahn and Stavins (1999) discuss the theoretical implications of trade among countries with different domestic systems. Many papers look at the design of domestic climate policy (see for example Stavins, 1997a). This Chapter looks more deeply at the reasons why domestic systems will and should differ and the different ways domestic policy design can facilitate international trade and lessen the impacts of these differences on the international market. This Chapter starts by describing three ways that trading might occur within Annex B. The Chapter outlines the potential objectives of national governments in designing domestic regulation. It then outlines the basic regulatory options and why and how they may be used in combination. The main section of the Chapter discusses options for integrating domestic systems with Annex B trading. We start with the simple case of a domestic tradable allowance system and then consider other regulations that are, or could easily be, based on clearly defined quantities of emissions, then clearly defined prices for emissions, and then other regulations. We conclude by considering strategies for domestic regulation that will meet varying domestic objectives in the short and long run but also facilitate a transition toward more efficient integration with international trading.

2   HOW CAN TRADE WITHIN ANNEX B OCCUR?

Formally two forms of trade exist within Annex B, International Emissions Trading (IET) and Joint Implementation (JI).[3] International Emissions Trading is essentially trade in AAUs where each country faces a binding target so the AAUs traded are not specific to a project or sector. Joint Implementation is project-based trading where units traded are associated with specific emission reduction projects. It is not clear if the rules on trade will be different between these forms (see discussion in Chapter 9). In Chapter 3, Hargrave, Kerr, Helme and Denne suggest that states should be able to sell through IET only if they can meet monitoring and reporting requirements.

---

[3] International Emissions Trading occurs through Article 17 of the Protocol. Joint Implementation among Annex B states occurs under Article 6. This must be distinguished from the pilot program Activities Implemented Jointly created under the Framework Convention that involved developing countries also and was often referred to as Joint Implementation. Annex B parties will engage in trading with developing countries through the Clean Development Mechanism.

It also is useful to distinguish trading by governments, sometimes known as international transferable quota trading, and trading by legal-entities or sub-state actors.[4] Trading by a government, whether buying or selling, simply requires that a government agency is made responsible for this function. Governments would probably trade through IET directly by simply buying and selling AAUs. While governments could, in theory, trade efficiently on behalf of their country they would be extremely unlikely to. Efficient trading would require that they know the expected marginal costs of abatement in their country over the commitment period. They would use this, combined with the international prices, to determine how many AAUs to buy. Efficiency would also require that they could optimally handle the risk and uncertainty associated with trading when their assessment of marginal cost, and hence their AAU demand, would be continuously reassessed and where prices in the market are fluctuating. Even if governments knew how to trade efficiently, government trading could be influenced by political considerations and could lead to market power (see Chapter 8). They may also be influenced by a desire to maximize revenues from carbon taxes.

Even if a government traded efficiently given expected national marginal costs, unless governments passed on these price signals to all domestic actors through domestic regulation it would not lead to cost minimization within the country; marginal costs would vary throughout the economy. If a government allows its legal-entities to trade internationally on their own behalf, the government does not need to know very much about marginal costs of abatement and abatement opportunities. They can focus on institutional issues and on monitoring.

Legal-entities could trade through IET or through JI projects.[5] Trading through IET requires that governments devolve AAUs to legal-entities through domestic regulation such as a tradable allowance program or project-based trading or that legal-entities have directly bought AAUs from the government (or contracted to buy them for the government) and sell them on their behalf. We will look at the latter simpler case first. If a government knows that it has excess AAUs and wants to sell them efficiently it could tender them to its own private sector and let them sell them on the market in the best way they can. This may be more efficient than the government directly engaging in AAU trade. If the government knows it will have a shortfall and needs to cover that for some sectors, it could contract with private entities to purchase some AAUs on behalf of government. In both these cases brokers, expert at dealing with price risks and liquidity issues,

---

[4] See Hahn and Stavins (1999), Tietenberg et al. (1998) and Joshua (1998).
[5] In the global market they could also buy certified emission reductions through the Clean Development Mechanism. This is not part of Annex B trading so is not discussed here.

could simply handle transactions more efficiently. This would not solve the problems of how the government decides how many to buy or sell or how to equalize domestic marginal costs.

With a domestic allowance system, or a tax or other system with a allowance option (see later), legal-entities are being given responsibilities for limiting emissions as well being devolved the right to buy and sell allowances. If they are allowed to directly trade on the international market (the domestic allowances are the same 'currency' as AAUs) they will make their own judgments about future marginal costs and demands. They will sell through IET but could buy from other Annex B states either through IET or JI. For IET, the government would simply need to make the legal-entity the legal owner of the AAUs they hold. For buying through JI the government may set conditions on buying if ERUs (emission reduction units created through JI projects) are not directly equivalent to AAUs (e.g. if they have some buyer liability). Governments may not let them be used as direct replacements for AAUs in domestic compliance because the government ultimately bears the risk that the JI projects are not valid. Invalid ERUs could push the state out of compliance. The state might require that the legal-entity purchase insurance or provide security. Legal-entities will abate and trade until their marginal cost equals the international AAU price.

If the government does not devolve AAUs to some sectors they may still allow them to sell through individual projects (JI or IET) and possibly buy through JI or IET. Selling through individual projects essentially requires the government to devolve AAUs to legal-entities on a project-by-project basis.[6] The government must have an apparatus for approving project-based sales because they directly affect national compliance through the national AAU budget. For legal-entities to buy AAUs or ERUs they need an incentive.[7] In a tradable allowance program they can use the AAUs to meet their regulatory obligations. With other forms of regulation they will buy only if they can exchange AAUs for a reduction in their regulatory obligations.

IET with legal-entity trading would be sufficient for efficiency if all countries engaged in IET and all sectors were involved. Some sectors will not be involved, however, because the regulatory form will preclude their direct participation in trading even through projects that receive JI-type credit or use allowances to replace stringent non-economic regulations (see later section). Some countries will not use IET, even in project-based form, because they may not have strong enough monitoring regimes to meet

[6] In a tradable allowance market this apparatus is not necessary because checks on the relationship between additional abatement and permits sold are built into the allocation, monitoring and surrendering of allowances.

[7] Private entities may also buy for speculative purposes but these AAUs will never be surrendered to their government. They will be resold.

international standards or because they may not feel that they can trust their domestic regulatory systems to control sales. [8] They may still use JI because it is controlled by international rules. This would mean that the state faces less risk of non-compliance if it has difficulty controlling legal-entities. Therefore, for efficiency, all countries will need to have some ability for legal-entities to buy JI credits even if they sell through IET always. How well these flexible mechanisms link domestic abatement opportunities to equalize costs internationally depends critically on domestic regulation.

3   DOMESTIC OBJECTIVES

Governments combine a number of different objectives in designing regulation. These are summarized in Box 6.1. Economic analysis emphasizes the efficiency of regulation.[9] Will the regulation achieve governments' objectives at least cost to the economy? This includes static efficiency - providing incentives for different actors to reveal and act upon their private information about static costs of abatement. It also includes dynamic efficiency – providing efficient incentives for research and development and adoption of new technologies.[10] A regulation that is flexible in response to changes in technology, tastes and resource use reduces the need for government to change the policy as conditions change. Flexibility improves efficiency over time and also minimizes disruption to regulated entities. Issues other than economic efficiency also influence governments.

To enact regulations, governments need to have sufficient support. Thus the interests of particular powerful lobbies may influence the form of regulation. These groups could be generally powerful or could be critical to forming a coalition on a particular issue.[11] Related but not identical, governments are generally concerned about the distributional effects of policies and particularly about 'winners and losers'. This concern could be for political feasibility reasons or for deeper equity reasons. This concern also could lead governments to subsidize particular sectors to increase their international 'competitiveness'.[12]

---

[8] In Chapter 9 Kelly and Leining argue that these countries should use JI with the same emissions additionality requirements as CDM. During the Pilot Phase of Joint Implementation the US has had an office specifically to facilitate the purchase of JI credits by private actors.

[9] Here we are really considering cost-effectiveness because the actual environmental goals are given by the international agreement and may or may not be efficiently set.

[10] For a discussion of the dynamic efficiency of different instruments see Fischer et al. (1998b).

[11] For discussion of the political economy of the US Acid Rain program see Joskow and Schmalensee (1998).

[12] These issues are discussed in depth in Chapter 7.

Box 6.1 Domestic objectives

Efficiency
- Static efficiency
- Dynamic efficiency

Flexibility

Distributional effects
- Political feasibility
- Winners and losers relative to status quo
- Vertical and horizontal equity

Limitations on government capability and resources

Existing regulatory structure
- Fixed costs of creating new monitoring regimes or legal frameworks,
- new regulations will interact with existing ones,
- existing regulations may be substitutes,
- or complements – e.g. address non-price barriers

Ancillary benefits

Cultural approaches to regulation

Opportunity to raise more revenue

Attitudes toward certainty of compliance
- Different perceptions of their certainty

Governments need to implement regulations and frequently face limitations on capability and resources. Regulations that are less administratively demanding are often preferred.[13] For example, some regulations require monitoring that may not be feasible. Currently it is not feasible to measure methane emissions from livestock accurately. Even though the most efficient regulation would provide incentives for farmers to alter their herds to reduce emissions, regulation will have to be based on average emissions levels and thus will not provide these incentives.

Another major element that affects government's choice of regulation is its existing regulatory structure. Some of this effect is related to the fixed costs of creating new monitoring regimes or legal frameworks. Existing ones can be adapted to new tasks. It may be efficient to build on existing structures that have been tested and accepted and that are well understood. They may be felt to be certain. For example the US is likely to use the Environmental Protection Agency (EPA) and/or the Department of Energy (DOE) to implement climate regulation rather than creating a new body even

---

[13]In some situations the opposite is true. If the bureaucracy is a powerful interest in itself it may seek forms of regulation that increase their discretionary power and require that government builds and sustains large bureaucracies. Bureaucrats often oppose market-based instruments because they become limited to a monitoring role.

though these are not tailor-made for the job. European monitoring may be based on the CORINAIR monitoring system created to deal with other pollutants such as SO_2. They may choose to use the Large Combustion Plant Directive to identify plants to be regulated in an initial round of regulation (see Box 6.2).

Box 6.2 European large combustion plant directive

The Large Combustion Plant Directive (LCPD) provides one means for defining which plants could be included in a European trading system and possibly for the initial allocation of allowances (using the emission limit values). The LCPD introduces bubble limits and emission limit values for SO_2, NO_x and particulates for combustion plants greater than 50 MW.[14]

In 1990 in the 29 European countries that reported, large point sources accounted for 1,728 million tonnes of carbon dioxide, or 36 percent of total carbon dioxide emissions (Radunsky and Ritter, 1996). Included in these, there were 582 power plants with capacity of greater than 50 MW thermal, 611 industrial combustion plants greater than 50 MW thermal, 219 refineries and 184 chemical plants.

Another aspect is that new regulations will interact with existing ones in other areas, either as complements or substitutes. Most countries already regulate energy extensively. Non-GHG energy-related policies are aimed at issues such as local pollution issues and energy security. Some existing policies, such as information programs, address non-price barriers to energy efficiency and will be directly complementary to market-based GHG regulation. Other policies will still be relevant and will be substitutes to greenhouse policy. For example, countries that are strongly concerned about energy security might implement a strong program to produce hydro or other renewable power energy prices. Countries where local pollution is an issue may have very stringent energy efficiency regulations in some locations. These policies may lead to effective marginal costs of GHG abatement that exceed the optimal level under GHG policy. These programs may be substitutes for GHG regulation and make GHG goals easier to meet.

Governments need to take care to avoid inequitable inefficient double regulation. This could arise where fuel taxes are used to encourage energy efficiency and reduce urban smog and a carbon tax equal to the international AAU price (or a domestic allowance system) is added on top. The marginal cost of abatement would be equal to the sum of the taxes, which is much too high. In contrast, if firms were required to meet minimum energy efficiency

[14]Council Directive 88/609/EEC of 24 November 1988. The European Commission (2000) Green Paper discusses the way existing EU policies could be used as the basis for an EU GHG trading system.

standards and then were required to pay a carbon tax on every unit of fuel, the marginal cost would be determined by whichever of these was binding.

Box 6.3 Illustration of potential use of existing policy

European Integrated Pollution Prevention and Control Directive (IPPC)

Under the IPPC Directive, particular industrial activities must obtain a permit that includes emission limit values based on best available technique. The IPPC Directive does not explicitly cover any of the six GHGs included in the Kyoto Protocol. The list of substances covered is, however, only 'indicative', requiring the permit to include emission limit values for pollutants 'likely to be emitted from the installation concerned in significant quantities'. Member States may thus include GHG emissions in their implementation of the IPPC Directive, and are even forced to do so if these emissions are 'significant'.

The IPPC Directive requires energy efficiency to be taken into account. This introduces some limited controls on greenhouse gas emissions, viz. those associated with the efficiency of energy conversion. There is some degree of conflict between energy efficiency goals and the reduction of other pollutants that needs to be weighed up in the current assessment of best available technique. Introduction of specific GHG regulations might take away the need to consider energy efficiency explicitly.

Administratively and procedurally speaking, there is wide scope for relating the operations of the IPPC and emission trading systems. Although not explicitly required to do so, Member States may cover the emission of GHGs in the IPPC permits. These could be used as performance standards. Alternatively, emission limit values might be considered analogous to an allocation (grandfathering) of greenhouse gas emission allowances, which would then be tradable. National authorities with the resources and skills to administer IPPC permits would be well placed to manage the issuing, monitoring, verification and compliance within a tradable allowance market.

All the arguments above are related to efficiency implications of existing policies and structures and complementary goals and policies. Countries also have different cultural approaches to regulation. While these can and do change over time and with circumstances they can have significant implications for the development of regulation. The US has seen an evolution from a very hands-on command-and-control approach to regulation in the 1970s to the development of market-based instruments such as the Lead Phasedown and the Acid Rain program from the mid 1980s.[15] While the tension between direct and market controls still plays out in the US GHG debate, market-based approaches are seriously considered. In contrast, Europe still primarily uses command and control methods to limit pollution (e.g. the IPPC directive discussed in Box 6.3) so its recent discussion of the

[15]Stavins (1997b) discusses the Acid Rain Program. Kerr and Newell (2000) outline the history of the lead phasedown.

use of tradable allowance markets is a major innovation and is likely to face considerable cultural opposition from bureaucrats, environmentalists and business.   Europe on the other hand has been a major proponent of carbon taxes (with existing taxes in Scandinavia and Austria and a proposed carbon levy in the United Kingdom) so it may be more likely to use a tax or to auction at least a proportion of allowances if it creates an allowance system. The US has a history of grandfathering.

Japan has a history of close relations between government and industry and their GHG plan will probably reflect this by mostly relying on voluntary agreements and industry goals.   Japan also has a history of self-sufficiency and might be unwilling to depend heavily on international trade to achieve compliance for cultural and historical reasons.[16]

Australia and New Zealand are frequently more innovative in policy and may be most likely to implement an upstream tradable allowance system as part of their GHG policy. New Zealand has been seriously considering this approach since before 1996.[17]

An issue that is of concern to business is that governments may see GHG policy as an opportunity to raise more revenue.   Europeans certainly have seen carbon taxes as a possibility for 'eco-tax' reform.   While this is presented as replacing existing taxes with environmentally motivated taxes, business is concerned that the new taxes will simply raise the tax burden. New taxes could certainly raise compliance costs. One of the key arguments in favor of raising revenue from regulation is that this revenue can replace that from highly distorting taxes such as taxes on labor and savings without creating any additional distortions.   For a given level of regulatory stringency, the argument for using regulatory instruments that raise revenue is strong.[18]

Some people believe that the 'revenue recycling' benefits would make it worth raising eco-taxes even beyond the level required for domestic compliance. If labor taxes are highly distorting relative to carbon taxes, carbon taxes are not simply good GHG policy, they are good revenue policy. Countries may choose to 'over-comply' with Kyoto in order to raise more government revenue. For this to be efficient, a substantial 'double dividend' must exist. The existence of a double dividend is empirically very uncertain. US evidence suggests there is not one in the US but European evidence is more varied.[19]   If some countries decide to raise carbon taxes above the

[16]Email conversation with Naoki Matsuo.
[17]Young et al. (1998) discusses Australian policy.   The New Zealand Ministry for the Environment (1997) outlines early New Zealand thinking on permit markets.
[18]For a summary of the evidence on this sec Cramton and Kerr (1999).
[19]For the US see Parry et al. (1998). For general discussions see Bovenberg (1997) and de Mooij (1999).

levels of international AAU prices, this will have implications for trading. They will not allow firms to opt out of the tax by buying permits even though the firms would like to. Perhaps they would allow a tradeoff between paying the tax and buying AAUs with a premium, for example 1.1 AAUs for every unit of emissions exempted from tax.

Finally different countries have different attitudes toward certainty of compliance in the short and long run. Different policies offer different levels of certainty. In the short run, a properly monitored and enforced tradable allowance market offers complete certainty on emissions levels in contrast to a tax or to policies that control technology or product standards which have highly uncertain effects. In the long run, the effect of a tradable allowance system or tax on R&D and adoption of new technology depends on firms' expectations about the continuity and future stringency of the system. If future regulation is highly uncertain, firms may choose short-run approaches to compliance. This may not lead to long-term non-compliance but, by making future costs higher, could make governments unwilling to accept stringent targets. A government may believe or want to ensure that the regulation is more certain than the private sector believes; it may want to have policies that will reinforce that. The government can try to commit their state to supporting stringent future targets by choosing abatement options that have high fixed costs up front but then lead to low future costs. A policy that directly subsidizes R&D or requires adoption of a new technology guarantees a certain level of investment that will lower future costs. More investment and R&D is not necessarily efficient, however, and the type of investment and R&D induced may not be efficient so this could raise costs significantly.

Not only may policies differ in terms of their actual level of certainty, people also have different perceptions of their certainty. Many people who are unaccustomed to economic approaches are deeply skeptical of the idea that simple price changes with no coercion will lead to significant long-term changes in behavior. Empirical evidence suggests that responses to price signals are significant but cannot say if they are efficient.[20]

These objectives and concerns will play out in different ways for different countries, sectors and gases. Even a country like the US that may use a domestic tradable allowance market for most of its carbon-dioxide emissions is likely to treat methane emissions and land use differently. Countries may choose different sets of instruments and may also choose different levels of integration with the international market. Although complete integration is efficient it may endanger revenue goals, decrease competitiveness of some industries and reduce government control over the way that sources abate (e.g. short term vs. long term options).

---

[20]See Newell et al. (1999) and Kerr and Newell (2000).

4   KEY DOMESTIC REGULATION OPTIONS

In this section we briefly describe the menu of instruments available and the domestic objectives they may help to achieve. This section does not aim to be an introduction to greenhouse regulation or environmental regulation. Readers seeking more detail on these instruments should see Stavins (1997a) or, for a textbook discussion, Tietenberg (1995), Pearce and Turner (1990) or Hanley et al. (1997). The next section will discuss how these can be integrated with international trading.

4.1   Economic Instruments

Economic instruments function by increasing the price of emissions, or close proxies to emissions directly. They create the 'missing market' that leads to inefficient levels of emissions in an unregulated market. The key forms are tradable allowances, taxes and subsidies.

To create an economic instrument the government needs to define how emissions will be measured. If emissions can be directly monitored (the US Acid Rain program does this for SO_2) or a perfect proxy exists (fossil fuel combusted is a near perfect proxy for CO_2 in the absence of feasible sequestration options) allowances should be defined as quantities of emissions or the proxy. This is best. If emissions cannot be monitored directly and no perfect proxy exists the regulator may be forced to use an imperfect proxy.[21] This means that the private entity will not have perfect incentives to reduce emissions because some actions will not affect their measured emissions. For example a loose proxy for agricultural methane would be the number of sheep, cows, pigs etc. A better proxy would also take into account the breed and the feed used (free range, corn fed...). If the proxies available are too poor, a non-economic instrument may be preferred.

Second, the government needs to define the point of regulation, that is, which legal-entities will be required to hold allowances or pay a tax to match measured emissions. Ideally this will be chosen to cover as wide a range of measured emissions as possible while minimizing the number of entities regulated. For CO_2 this is generally quite a long way upstream (closer to the point of production than consumption).[22]

A domestic tradable allowance market operates in much the same way as an international market.[23] Creating a tradable allowance market requires that

---

[21]For discussion of the use of imperfect proxies see Fullerton and Metcalfe (2000).
[22]For analysis of this in the US context see Hargrave (1997) and Smith et al. (1992).
[23]For a concise discussion of design issues relating to domestic markets see Fischer et al. (1998 a and c).

government creates property rights to emit and enforces these. The allowances can be grandfathered or sold into the private sector; the regulator requires regulated entities to surrender allowances equal to their emissions at regular intervals. These allowances must be tradable among entities and preferably through time (banking). A tradable allowance market can equalize the marginal costs of abatement across all regulated entities. It also leads price signals to be passed forward and backward through the·economy to all entities that affect the creation of emissions through their consumption or production behavior.

A slightly different form of tradable allowance market is an offset or credit market where allowances are not defined in advance but are created through sequestration or abatement activities. This is a· project-based instrument where government will need to have rules and bureaucrats to approve each offset or credit created. This can be a useful instrument where emissions or sequestration are not easily measurable over the whole economy but the gains from providing incentives for some abatement projects are high.

Sometimes governments choose to regulate activities that are very loose proxies for emissions. For example governments may require a certain percentage of electric power to be generated from renewable sources. They may allow this requirement to be traded among electric utilities so that utilities with the best renewable opportunities produce all the renewable electricity for the industry. This will not lead to efficient abatement even though trading occurs; trading is in a loose proxy not in emissions.

A tax is economically very similar to a tradable allowance market but the price passed on to regulated entities and hence through the economy is directly set by government rather than determined by the market. The same entities can be taxed rather than requiring them to surrender allowances. To address climate change, a tax would ideally be on emissions or the carbon content of fossil fuel as a proxy. Many countries however have pre-existing taxes on energy measured on a thermal basis (e.g. BTU) or consumption of specific fuels. Changing these may be politically and possibly administratively difficult.

Some countries including Denmark, Finland and Sweden, already have carbon taxes. In addition, most governments tax or subsidize energy. Carbon taxes have been established in a similar way to an upstream allowance system, i.e. taxes are levied largely on fossil fuel use. In all countries there are significant exemptions to the tax system for energy intensive industries that are competing internationally. To date most of the debate in Europe has been related to introducing EU-wide carbon taxes although they are now seriously considering a tradable allowance system.[24]

[24]See European Commission 2000.

A subsidy is effectively a reverse tax. The efficiency implications are identical but the distributional and revenue implications are very different. Subsidies are most commonly achieved by providing tax breaks. These are attractive politically because they are a non-transparent way to spend money. Usually the tax breaks are not related directly to emissions but to R&D relating to pollution abatement or to forestry development. These do not have the direct efficiency advantages that emissions-related instruments have but may address sources of emissions/sequestration that are not easily measured. They may potentially address non-price problems of research such as need for coordination, high risks and poorly protected intellectual property rights.

At their best, economic instruments provide strong incentives for static and dynamic efficiency throughout the economy. They are an extremely flexible instrument that responds easily to changes in economic and technological conditions. Tradable allowances offer political flexibility through the ability to give away valuable allowances. Taxes and allowances can often use existing monitoring systems and taxes can use the existing tax administration. Both require little knowledge of abatement by government.

4.2   Non-economic Instruments

Non-economic instruments have five potential roles. First, they can address efficiency where there are non-price barriers to abatement such as information problems or public goods. Second, they can fill regulatory gaps where monitoring needs do not allow the use of economic instruments. Alternatively, for some gases (e.g. SF_6 in some countries) there may be so few sources that it is not worth designing general regulation that covers them. Third, they can fill a political need by creating a perception of dynamic efficiency; they can force investment and adoption of pollution reducing technology although this may in reality not be efficient or effective. Fourth, they can deal with distributional issues in a flexible, non-transparent way; they allow deals with politically powerful groups that might otherwise not be acceptable. Finally, existing instruments tend to be non-economic; these may be adapted to climate purposes in the short run at least because of their low political and administrative fixed costs. This section discusses four common types of non-economic instruments and their roles.

4.2.1 Standards
One superficially simple way to regulate is to require production processes to use prescribed technologies and products to meet certain standards. Governments may require the closure of inefficient coal-burning electric utilities or their conversion to gas. If the government knows the most

efficient abatement technologies this is an efficient policy. This is unlikely even in the short term; in the long term it is impossible for government to know all potential technologies and processes that could be developed to abate efficiently. If government cannot use economic instruments, or does not believe that firms and consumers will respond efficiently to those signals because they are short-sighted, lacking in information or simply irrational, this may be a second-best instrument. Electrical appliances, motor vehicles, electric utilities and house construction are often regulated in this way.

One justification for minimum efficiency standards for appliances and building codes is that consumers and firms do not have good information on the return to purchasing more efficient products or making new energy efficient investments. Even if they had the information, the cost of processing it and making good decisions would be too high. Standards avoid the need for consumers and firms to do this calculation and hence may be efficient.

Another classic problem is the distinction between landlords who make energy investment decisions and tenants who face the price of energy and hence the effects of market-based instruments. Building codes are aimed at alleviating this problem. Many people also believe that consumers do not pay adequate attention to fuel efficiency of vehicles because it is a small part of the total bundle.[25] Fuel efficiency standards aim to address this. Market-based instruments can reinforce the effects of non-market instruments. High energy prices make efficient buildings and cars more attractive to tenants and consumers. Builders and appliance manufacturers do not have the incentive to increase efficiency themselves unless consumers and firms are willing to pay more for energy efficiency.

Standards are simple to understand and familiar; the costs are hidden and the successes are visible. Monitoring is often relatively simple though defining the standards efficiently is not.

4.2.2 Information policies
Another way to address this issue is to require that the information be provided in an easy to understand way. Thus car manufacturers are required to provide information on fuel efficiency and, in the US, appliances are marked with their efficiency relative to other similar appliances or given a star if they are high efficiency. Low efficiency manufacturers need to be forced to provide this information and the government, or another credible body, needs to check that the information provided is accurate. Information programs clearly can be complementary to trading; they assist in the

[25]For a summary of the evidence on this see the Kyoto Special Issue of the Energy Journal, (1994).

functioning of markets through making a wide range of market actors aware of opportunities for emission reduction options.

A second role is putting indirect pressure on firms through the disclosure of information about their activities.[26] Another role for information is an education role. By letting people know about the causes and implications of climate change they may change their attitudes. They may change their behavior directly or they may be more supportive and accepting of climate regulation.

Information and education policies would be complementary to other forms of regulation, especially economic instruments. Informed consumers will respond more to higher energy prices and higher energy prices will increase the value of the information in consumer's decisions.

4.2.3   Public goods, coordination and high risks
Some of the efficient forms of abatement require direct government involvement. The first is where an 'abatement public good' is involved. A classic example of this is the knowledge that flows from research and development. If this knowledge is publicly available it can be diffused quickly and developed efficiently. Making knowledge available requires government funding of R&D or purchase of relevant patents. Another public good role that government usually plays is in the development of roads and other transport infrastructure. Key investments in these areas can have large impacts on emissions. Increased efficiency of roads will tend to increase driving and GHG emissions (though it may lower local pollution by reducing congestion). Investments in rail, public transport and pedestrian amenities may lower emissions. Redesigning cities to reduce travel needs may require government coordination.

General government regulation policies can have significant though indirect effects on emissions. Liberalization of energy markets may lower energy prices and hence increase emissions but it may also allow more flexible movement toward alternative fuels. Structural reform in the economy, such as the removal of subsidies, can have significant effects. Removal of energy subsidies of various sorts, including protection of heavy industry, will tend to reduce emissions. Other structural reforms may enhance economic growth and increase emissions. These policies could complement economic instruments or could make compliance harder to achieve.

Coordination may also play an important role in the diffusion of major new technologies. Many people argue that renewables and alternatives to

---

[26]For a clear discussion of the different roles of information and evidence on their effectiveness see Tietenberg (1999).

fossil fuel require a minimum scale before they will be efficient. Government can help create infrastructure for electric vehicles or hydrogen. By subsidizing wind power, they could help develop the industry to a self-sustaining point.

Finally, some major new technologies are highly uncertain and require large investments to set up. Even if they are a good idea, the private sector may not be able to absorb such a large risk. Some government involvement in risk sharing may be appropriate. This is less of an issue if large multinationals are able to be involved.

4.3   Voluntary Agreements and Imposed Regulation

To date, many of the climate policies implemented or agreed involve 'voluntary' agreements. For an example see Box 6.4. These are not a different form of regulation in themselves but involve a different type of incentive. In a voluntary agreement firms or industries agree to take certain abatement actions, or to reach a certain level of abatement or efficiency. Their motivation to do so is threefold. First, they want to avoid government regulation. Speaking positively, they believe that they can achieve the goals more efficiently without regulation; cynically, a voluntary agreement puts off regulation for a few years. Second, they want to influence the form of regulation. By creating their own regulation within the industry they may affect the design of the binding regulation they finally face. Firms would generally like to have flexible regulation and would like to avoid high compliance costs. This is a major driving force behind companies' involvements in Joint Implementation and the development of self regulation such as British Petroleum/Amoco's global emissions trading program.[27] Third, some companies are genuinely public spirited and recognize their responsibilities in protecting the environment. They are also concerned about their corporate reputation.

For those not motivated by higher concerns, the incentives offered by voluntary agreements are weak and uncertain. The outcomes if companies do not meet their goals are not clearly specified or even credible. They are unlikely to lead most companies to bear very high costs or make very large investment. Even if some companies would be willing to make real changes, they find it difficult to do so if they do not believe their competitors will be similarly motivated. Investments in Joint Implementation are very small; domestic actions under the Climate Change Action Plan in the US have had little impact on the trend in emissions.

[27]For details see http://www.bpamoco.com/climatechange.

Box 6.4 Voluntary agreements

The Netherlands Covenant for Benchmarking Energy Efficiency requires large Dutch firms to achieve levels of energy efficiency equal to the best of international firms. In return, the government will exempt these firms from national energy taxes, and other energy efficiency or CO_2 limitation requirements. This agreement allows these firms to increase their production so long as their energy intensity is kept low. These firms might be willing to convert this agreement into a responsibility to hold allowances coupled with an allocation of allowances based on some level of agreed future activity rates. However, this is a complicated negotiation and, given the current rights of the entities involved, is likely to require the government to grandfather more than a proportionate share of AAUs to this sector. This will need to be compensated by tighter regulations elsewhere in the economy or through government purchase of AAUs, ERUs or CERs from other countries.

5 INTERACTION OF DOMESTIC REGULATIONS WITH ANNEX B TRADING

How can different domestic instruments integrate with international trading? In this section we discuss what is necessary to allow legal-entity buying and selling under different regimes. We start with the simplest systems where allowable quantities of emissions are defined at the source level, then look at cases where the price of emissions is clearly defined for each source. Finally we consider the plethora of instruments with poorly defined quantity and price at source level.

5.1 Regulations that Define Clear Quantities of Allowable Emissions

5.1.1 Domestic tradable allowances

If a domestic allowance market is created, all that is required for international trading is to make the allowances that are traded domestically identical to AAUs and allow legal-entities to both buy and sell. To allow entities to buy from countries selling through JI, the government will have to define the terms under which ERUs can be used for domestic compliance. If ERUs are subject to buyer liability until they are confirmed internationally, the government will probably want to mimic this domestically by not allowing legal-entities to use them for compliance until they are equivalent to AAUs. The legal-entities are choosing to take on the risk by buying the ERUs when they could buy AAUs. They also can have knowledge about and possibly control over the project that generated the ERUs. This makes it efficient for the legal-entities to assume that risk rather than their government.

Will the government want to integrate perfectly with the international market? The government will probably not want to restrict sales of AAUs unless they do not believe their domestic compliance system is strong enough. If they restrict sales they would be subsidizing marginal production costs by lowering domestic allowance prices. If they restricted buying, they would raise domestic allowance prices, which would give their companies a competitive disadvantage but might also lead to more domestic R&D and technology adoption. The government may also be concerned about undermining the agreement by purchasing AAUs from dubious sources even if they are not legally liable. If the government is auctioning allowances domestically and strongly believes in a double dividend from revenue recycling, it might want to limit international purchases to keep auction prices high.

5.1.2 Emission performance standards

Many countries have regulations that aim to encourage energy efficiency (rate of energy use per unit of production) and reduce rates of emissions. For example, in the Netherlands, industry has agreed to be as efficient in terms of emissions as the highest world standards (see Box 6.4). If these standards are quantified they imply a certain level of emissions for each level of output. These types of standards can be translated into allowance quantities that could be tradable. The simplest approach (though not the best) would be to allocate allowances regularly based on an emissions factor times output in say a quarter. Firms would be required to surrender allowances to match their emissions but could sell excess allowances or buy additional allowances either domestically or internationally.[28] Firms would have a direct incentive to agree to a program of this type and it would improve efficiency relative to performance standards. The problem with this program is that it uses an output-based form of allocation, which is inefficient because it operates as an output subsidy. The more output the firm produces the more allowances they receive.[29]

More generally regulations that involve emissions rates could be translated into programs with fixed quantities of emissions that can be traded. This could be done on a project-by-project basis or industry-wide and could be done year-by-year or in perpetuity. Project-by-project determination of baselines involves high transaction costs and is likely to lead to strategic behaviour and rent seeking which is costly. Year-by-year determination of baselines is also costly because of the need for annual negotiations and because firms will behave strategically to try to affect their baseline.

[28]This is the form of the US lead phasedown tradable allowance market.
[29]For a discussion of the efficiency problems with output-based allocation see Fischer (1997).

Creating general rules across industries and time that allow international trading would be most efficient. If these rules are created, however, why not simply create a domestic tradable allowance market?

If governments have other motivations for regulating the rate of energy use, such as local air pollution concerns, they may limit buying of allowances beyond a certain level by making rates tradable only to a limited extent. Essentially each source would face a minimum efficiency level and also a tradable allowance system. This would encourage abatement beyond the minimum efficiency level, which is favorable, and avoid very high costs but also ensure that local air quality goals are met.

Governments do not gain revenue through rate-based regulation so would definitely gain from international trading. International trading would ease national compliance costs with no impact on the net national AAU budget. Additional emissions would be matched by purchases while additional abatement would be matched by sales. If trading led to lower overall efficiency rates, domestic R&D and adoption may be lower but of course this may be optimal.

5.2   Regulations that Define a Clear Cost of Emitting

5.2.1   Taxes

The infrastructure for the existing tax systems might be used as the basis for an international or domestic trading system, e.g. monitoring and reporting systems might be transferable. Typically taxes have operated upstream, e.g. at the point of import of the fuel or of extraction. Thus these would most easily integrate with upstream trading. Downstream actors could still purchase or be grandfathered AAUs and trade them to upstream energy suppliers as part of negotiated energy contracts.[30] The policies required to allow legal-entities facing a tax system to trade are different depending on whether the tax is above or below the international AAU price.

It is relatively easy to allow taxed sources to purchase AAUs internationally. They will only want to do so when the tax is relatively high. The government simply needs to allow them to purchase AAUs to match their emissions and surrender the AAUs instead of paying tax. This is valuable for the government if they do not want to adjust their tax regularly to match international AAUs' prices. It creates an automatic safeguard against high domestic compliance costs, which protects the competitiveness of firms. This type of system is quite closely related to a 'hybrid' system

---

[30]Suppliers of high sulfur coal to electric utilities were active in the US Acid Rain market, buying allowances to bundle with the coal and allow the utilities to immediately offset the sulfur in the coal.

where firms face an allowance system but can pay a tax instead of purchasing allowances where the price is too high.[31] Neither provides emissions certainty but both protect against high compliance costs.

Taxes with an AAU opt-out will provide at least as much compliance certainty for government as taxes because any increase in emissions due to the opt-out will be matched by AAUs. Even if all sources opted out of the tax, the government would have enough AAUs to cover the emissions in the sector. In contrast, when legal-entities are paying the tax, the government will have to purchase AAUs with the tax revenue if the country is not reaching compliance with domestic measures alone. If governments want to keep taxes high for revenue-raising reasons, however, an opt-out will undermine their objective. They will receive AAUs instead of higher valued tax revenue.

Allowing taxed sources to sell AAUs internationally is more complex. This becomes an issue when domestic regulation is less stringent than international targets; i.e. the tax is below the international AAU price. If legal-entities are allowed to sell AAUs they must have a cap or baseline that they can sell relative to. They cannot be allowed simply to pay extra tax for the emissions that are implied by their sales; this would lead to uncontrolled sales when the tax was below the AAU price and the government would not be receiving enough tax revenue to buy back AAUs for compliance. The desire to buy AAUs is limited by emissions; selling is potentially unlimited.

Low taxes, or even tax exemptions, may be set to give concessions to some industries. However, sources in these industries will be willing to abate more, until their marginal cost is equal to the international AAU price, if they are able to sell the corresponding AAUs. The government would need to set source-level caps where if the source emits less than the cap they can sell the difference. When they emit more than the cap they pay the tax on all units of emissions. If they emit less than the cap and sell the excess, they should not also pay less tax (i.e. they should pay tax on the cap level not their actual emissions) or they would be receiving a double reward. They are essentially buying the extra AAUs from the government by paying the tax for them even though they sell them rather than use them. If the government does this it almost may as well introduce a domestic tradable allowance system.

5.2.2 Subsidies
Some countries may choose to subsidize low emissions energy sources or provide positive incentives for improved energy efficiency rather than taxing emissions. In particular, countries may subsidize renewable energy. These

---

[31]These systems are discussed by NZ Ministry for the Environment (1997), Denne (1999), Kopp et al. (1999) and Pizer (1999).

policies may with some work provide a clear price for abatement. The difficulty is that subsidies are not directly related to emissions abatement but rather to production of emission-free energy that may replace fossil fuel based energy, or to adoption of new technology that improves energy efficiency. The new energy may not replace energy from old sources one-for-one but may reduce energy prices leading to greater total energy use. Energy efficient technology does not affect energy prices directly (though by decreasing demand it may lower prices) but it does reduce the costs of energy intensive production so may lead to increased output. These effects would need to be estimated to allow legal-entities to claim AAUs that they can sell in lieu of receiving subsidies. This could be done using general rules or on a project-by-project basis.

5.3   Other Regulations

Many forms of regulation are not easily amenable to integration with trading. Some of these are complementary to trading and thus can run alongside trading with no efficiency loss. For example, information programs and product standards may address non-price barriers to energy efficiency. Higher energy prices, induced by an allowance system, will reinforce these programs; they will amplify the effect of higher prices.

Other forms of regulation are similar in effect to market based instruments and could be replaced by them to improve efficiency. However governments may choose to stay with them for a variety of reasons as discussed above. Does this mean that these sectors cannot benefit at all from international trading? No, not necessarily. First, the government can try to set the stringency of these regulations to roughly approximate international stringency. If the government got this right, the sources would not want to trade even if they could. This requires that the government allocate part of its national AAU budget to these non-trading sources and may require that they buy additional AAUs to cover high emissions if abatement costs are high. Alternatively, if abatement costs are lower than anticipated, these sectors may need less than their initially allocated share of national AAUs and the government may be able to sell some AAUs or allocate them to other sectors. The government would be trading on the sector's behalf.

5.4   Project-based Trading

The government could allow a very limited sort of legal-entity trading through project-based trading. In the past this would have been JI trading but under current rules it could involve domestic projects that free up AAUs at the national level; these can be sold under IET.[32] If the sources want to buy AAUs and relax their regulation the government could agree to exchange AAUs for more lenient regulation. The rate of exchange could be source and project specific. A baseline of expected emissions under the regulation would need to be defined for each source. Actual emissions could be monitored or estimates could be used. This is clearly a costly way to trade but would be more efficient than no trading and may provide the experience than facilitates a later introduction of more flexible instruments.

For example, energy efficiency standards such as building codes are used in most countries to limit energy demand. An opt-in to trading might be applied through allowing firms that do not meet the standard to purchase allowances to make-up the difference. Builders might purchase allowances to cover the expected additional emissions associated with the additional energy use. This would require quantifying the expected emissions if they meet the standards. Any project that might have been considered under the Activities Implemented Jointly pilot program could be considered here.

5.5   Voluntary and Negotiated Agreements

Voluntary and Negotiated Agreements typically are developed on the understanding that, if industries meet the targets agreed, governments will not regulate firms that have signed the agreement. This applies, for example, to the transport agreement with European Automobile Manufacturers Association (ACEA) and the energy efficiency agreements with industry in the Netherlands.[33]

The voluntary target might be turned into a binding target; the target would be used to set the number of additional allowances that the government would distribute in the domestic trading system, probably through grandfathering to the firms currently in the negotiated agreement. Alternatively, if there were no domestic trading system or if the agreement was not easily translated into an AAU equivalent, an industry or firm level 'project' could create a binding baseline and reductions beyond or short of that could be traded through JI. The firms might wish to accept a binding target in exchange for the right to trade if they believed that the target that

---

[32]For more discussion of project-based trading see Chapter 9.
[33]As defined in Directive 70/156/EEC.

they had agreed to in the voluntary agreement was relatively low cost to achieve (i.e. less than the allowance price at the margin). This would enable firms to make additional reductions below targeted levels and to sell the allowances that were surplus to requirements. A government might wish to do so because it would provide incentives for additional emission reductions beyond that included in the voluntary agreement; it also provides much greater certainty of achievement.

5.6   Opting-in to Trading

Even if the existing form of regulation does not define clear quantities, some sources could be integrated in international trading through individual sources opting to take on caps that allow them to trade either through IET or Annex B JI.

The US SO_2 trading system was established for the largest coal-fired power plants throughout the US. It allows combustion sources, not required to participate in the Acid Rain Program, the opportunity to enter on a voluntary basis and receive their own acid rain allowances.[34] Sources are allocated allowances to cover their emissions on the basis of historical energy use and allowed emission rates. By reducing emissions below its allowance allocation, an opt-in source will create unused allowances, which it can sell. In addition, and more importantly empirically 'Phase II' utilities that were not required to participate in the early years of the program were allowed to opt in and sell if they made reductions.

This opt-in approach might provide a model for a similar approach to integrate sources into international trading. Individual firms might choose to opt out of other regulations and into trading. For governments this might be desirable because, for sources that are in the trading system, there is greater certainty of emissions being limited to the capped level of emissions. For entities, sources opting in to trading may be doing so because, if they do, they are exempt from the requirements of the other regulations and the allowance price is less costly than the policies and measures that they would otherwise face. Alternatively these sources may do so because they can profit from additional emission reductions by selling the excess allowances they can generate.

The downside of a voluntary opt-in program is that firms self-select. The firms that choose to accept caps are those for whom the caps are generous relative to their actual emissions. The cap may not exceed their uncontrolled emissions but it is high enough that they can make a profit by abating and

---

[34]Combustion sources are defined as fossil fuel-fired boilers, turbines or internal combustion engines.

selling the excess. This program could lead to much higher emissions than anticipated.[35]

6   CONCLUSION

Domestic flexibility in instrument choice is important because countries have different existing regulations, political priorities and constraints, culture, and economic structure and hence structure of emissions sources. In the short run it will be practical and efficient for countries to use a variety of domestic instruments even though Kyoto will not achieve its theoretical minimum cost. Some of these instruments will integrate easily with international trading while others will not.

In the long run, it will be efficient for most countries to use market-based instruments and ideally domestic allowance trading for most sources. This will make domestic regulation efficient and will ensure a liquid, efficient international market. Even in the long run, however, not all sources will be covered only by market instruments. Some sources are too small or difficult to be worth monitoring directly. In other cases, non-market instruments will be complementary to trading.

In the long run, government activity will ideally focus on monitoring and enforcing a domestic allowance market. Discretionary regulatory attention could focus on emissions from sources that are not directly monitored, or public goods associated with efficient abatement, and on large scale, high-risk activities or activities that require economy-wide coordination that is beyond the scope of private actors. Government will continue to have a legitimate role in these areas.

In the short run, the challenge is to create feasible domestic policies that achieve compliance and facilitate a transition toward efficient trading. Governments need to avoid creating vested interests opposed to domestic trading, either in the bureaucracy or the private sector. Although many policies may be used in the short term, these should not be entrenched making long term achievement of the goals of the Framework Convention on Climate Change prohibitively expensive.

Trading can be combined with any domestic instrument but may depend on government trading on behalf of the sector. Taxes can fairly easily be combined with the ability to buy AAUs but not with the ability to sell. For large projects the government may decide to allow project-based trading even if the underlying regulation is non-economic. With any instruments other than trading, trading will be highly imperfect and marginal costs in these

---

[35]These issues are discussed in detail in Montero (1997).

sectors will not be set equal to the international price. This can raise serious competitiveness concerns particularly where the government is creating a significant subsidy through lenient regulation. The more firms are able to trade internationally on their own behalf, the less the form and stringency of domestic regulation will be an issue of international concern.

If few firms are able to trade internationally, the implications for international liquidity and AAU market function could be serious. Markets function best when many small price-takers operate with low transaction costs. If a significant amount of trading is done through governments, market power may arise as an issue and trading may become a political rather than an economic activity. Domestic sovereignty in instrument choice may have political and efficiency advantages and may be unavoidable in the short run; encouraging legal-entity linkages with the international market, through domestic trading or opt-ins to trading from other instruments, will help reduce costs, will reduce competitiveness concerns and will reduce the potential for market power.

7 Fair Competition and Annex B Trading

Suzi Kerr

---

1 INTRODUCTION

This chapter addresses the effect of the Kyoto Protocol on fair competition and the possible ways that Annex B trading may affect this.[1] By fair competition we mean that competition among firms is based on the true economic costs of production and is not distorted by subsidies. Fair competition also requires that firms have free access to markets, and that governments avoid creating non-tariff barriers. An unfair competition problem arises when regulation raises the costs of production of one firm more than that of another firm in the same industry in another country.

If the price of carbon is internalized through an allowance program involving every firm in all countries and firms are able to trade allowances freely, the price of an allowance and hence the marginal cost of emitting carbon (or GHGs in carbon equivalents) will be equal across all firms. No competitiveness problems will arise from differences in marginal cost. The allocation of AAUs within countries has no effect on the marginal cost of regulation to each firm. If, however, some firms are exempted from the allowance program and do not face equally stringent alternative regulation, some firms will face a competitive disadvantage relative to others.

In a comprehensive, unrestricted tradable allowance program the following is true in every country. The allowance price will be the same in all countries.

marginal cost with regulation = marginal cost without regulation +
*GHGs produced * AAU price*

Kyoto has some impacts on the relative ability to compete of different countries and sectors. This chapter outlines four basic sources of changes in ability to compete, the exclusion of developing countries from Kyoto commitments, differences in stringency of targets across countries in Annex

---

[1] For more general discussions of environmental regulation and competitiveness see Barker and Köhler (1998), Adams (1998), Boltho (1996), Christiansen and Tietenberg (1985).

B, differences in stringency of regulation across sectors within countries, and domestic regulation methods that provide lump-sum compensation to sectors. These are ordered according to their likely impact on relative abilities to compete. The chapter begins by considering how trading in AAUs generally affects fair competition. Then it considers each of the different sources changes relative ability to compete and discusses how Annex B trading affects these changes. Then it considers how limiting or redesigning trading might affect relative abilities to compete.

2   WHAT DRIVES COMPETITION?

A firm can sell products if their cost is lower than the price they are able to receive in the market. As long as there are no trade barriers, the firm that will have the most success selling products will be the firm with the lowest costs. Two different types of cost are relevant. The first and most important is the cost of producing extra units, or marginal cost. This determines what a firm can sell more output for without making a loss. It determines their ability to expand into new markets. The second is the average cost which determines the overall profitability of the firm and the sustainability of their production and sales. By profitability we mean a return on capital above the normal return or cost of capital. The asset position of the firm, or their wealth, may affect their profitability indirectly. A firm needs to make a normal return on all its capital whether it owns it as assets or has borrowed it, so having more assets does not necessarily make it more profitable. (For example, a small Internet firm might be much more profitable than IBM.) Marginal and average cost and wealth vary significantly across firms for many reasons. They are primarily determined by factors other than regulation such as the skill of their management, the quality and cost of labor, the cost of land, energy and natural resources, access to transportation networks and historical factors that determine the physical and financial capital structure of the firm.

Every country has some comparative advantages – i.e. ability to compete in production of some goods. Government policies that subsidize industries can lower their costs and make them more able to compete. However, these subsidies are costly to the rest of the economy so what increases competitiveness in one industry lowers it in others.

2.1   Effects of Regulation on Marginal and Average Cost and on Wealth

This section considers the general ways that regulation can affect marginal and average cost and the wealth of firms and the effects of trading on these.

With no international trade, MC and AC will vary among countries depending on overall regulatory stringency. Without comprehensive domestic trading, MC and AC will vary also within countries depending on the final emission reductions required across sectors within the country.

2.2 Direct Effects of Regulation

Regulation affects both marginal and average costs of production. In Figure 7.1, two identical firms in the same sector but in different countries are regulated differently.[2] Firm A faces relatively lenient regulation and has low marginal costs of emission reduction MC_A while Firm B faces stringent regulation and has high marginal costs MC_B. If a firm wishes to produce one more unit, to meet its emissions target any extra emissions from extra production must be offset by reductions elsewhere. If one unit of output produces one unit of emissions, the effect on marginal production cost will be roughly the level of marginal cost of emission reductions at the firm's target. Firm B's marginal production costs will rise much more than A's.

Figure 7.1 Regulation and costs

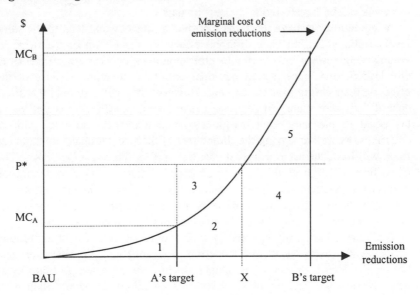

---

[2] In the figure emission reductions are defined relative to business as usual. The firm faces a fixed emission target.

Firm A will also have much lower total costs of abatement and hence less impact on average costs and overall profitability. While marginal costs are key for competition on the margin, overall profitability can affect long run stability of the firm and access to capital. The extent to which access to capital matters for fair competition depends on the differences in cost among sources of finance. Overall profitability and wealth also affects the firm's ability to withstand shocks. Regulation will also affect the wealth of firms.[3] First, regulation reduces the value of the existing physical assets of firms if they are no longer optimal assets given the need to reduce emissions. This reduces firms' wealth. This fall in asset value is often referred to as 'stranded assets'. For example an inefficient coal-fired utility may have broken even with no climate regulation and hence have had positive value, but may make an operating loss after regulation so the firm will close it. A firm that is leniently regulated or exempted from regulation will not suffer the same loss of wealth.

Second, if firms receive grandfathered allowances or make other special deals with government that entitle their firm to more lenient regulatory treatment, their net wealth will rise. If the firm were sold, it would have a higher value than without the special treatment as long as the special treatment can be transferred to the new owners.

A regulation can have the same marginal stringency and lead to the same level of abatement but have different effects on the wealth of the firm. A voluntary agreement by a sector to limit emissions to a certain efficient cap will lead them to face a high marginal cost of production because of the effect on their ability to meet the cap. However they will pay only the direct cost of their abatement. In contrast, a firm facing an efficient tax will pay a tax equal to the same high marginal cost of abatement on every unit of emissions, as well as paying the direct cost of their actual abatement. These firms will have the same marginal cost but very different average cost. The taxed firm will lose wealth because of stranded assets. The firm facing the voluntary agreement also loses stranded assets. If the voluntary agreement only applies to existing firms these firms gain wealth equal to the future value of the implicit output subsidy involved in the voluntary agreement.

If all firms have sufficient access to low cost sources of debt and equity financing, the extra wealth (or reduction in wealth) will not alter their real behavior, which is driven by marginal costs and the expected profitability of new investment. One possible exception is small firms, which often have limited access to cheap finance; the wealth transfer could significantly affect

---

[3] Regulation also affects the wealth of countries. Countries with less stringent targets and hence large numbers of AAUs are made relatively wealthier than those who are allocated few AAUs.

some of them. However, they may have many options for increasing their access to capital such as merging with a larger firm. A good small firm will generally find the capital they need. The additional wealth gained through grandfathering or special deals will reduce a firm's borrowing or allow them to invest elsewhere in the economy; it will not alter their capital or output decisions. It affects the wealth of their owners or shareholders but not their ability to compete in competitive markets.

2.3   Effect of Trading on MC, AC and Wealth

In Figure 7.1, if firms A and B are allowed to trade AAUs on the international market and the international AAU price is p*, A will reduce emissions further to X incurring a cost equal to the area 2 but making profit of area 3. A's total net costs fall by 3. In contrast, firm B will reduce emissions by less than without trade, only to X and will pay area 4 for AAUs. This will reduce their total net costs by area 5. Trading equalizes their marginal costs of emission reductions, and hence their marginal cost of production. Trading lowers the average cost of both firms but does not equalize it. At an economy-wide level, trading lowers the marginal and total costs of compliance by AAU buyer countries and provides profits to seller countries while raising their marginal greenhouse gas abatement costs. Sellers are implicitly those who were given less stringent emissions reduction targets in the agreement. Both the buyer and the seller country gain through trade. The buyer country lowers its cost of emissions abatement and its cost of production allowing it to expand its production of energy intensive output. The seller country will reduce its production of energy intensive output but will gain by selling AAUs for more than the cost of emission abatement and will expand production in other areas of its economy.

Trading moves comparative advantage in energy efficient production from the seller toward the buyer. It lowers the cost of energy use by buyers and raises it for sellers.

Both firms and both countries will face lower net costs of compliance after trade, but what happens to relative costs of compliance? Who wins the most, the buyer or the seller? This depends on how steep the demand and supply curves are (i.e. the relative elasticities). If a buyer has a steep demand curve, they would be willing to pay rapidly decreasing amounts for allowances as they buy more. Given that the price is the value to them of the last unit they buy, they were willing to pay a lot more for earlier units and hence benefited greatly from them. In Figure 7.1, gains were roughly equal (area 3 is almost the same as area 5). Figure 7.2 shows a situation where the buyer and seller both win but the buyer, country A, gains more. The demand curve of buyer A is a reflection of their marginal cost curve around their Kyoto allocation.

The change in firm wealth as a result of regulation depends first on the marginal abatement cost the firm faces and on the emission efficiency of their capital. Trading will equalize these marginal abatement costs, reducing the total 'stranded assets' for firms that face stringent regulation and increasing 'stranded assets' for firms facing lenient regulation (these firms will gain more through trading than they lose through the loss in value of existing capital assets). The ability to trade will raise the wealth of leniently regulated firms because it raises the value of their implicit allocation of allowances.

Figure 7.2 Relative gains to buyers and sellers

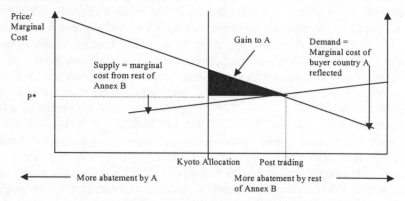

The change in firm wealth depends on whether they are given 'lump-sum' benefits during the negotiations. If the existing firms are grandfathered allowance they gain wealth equal to the value of the allowances times the number of allowances. Without international trading the value of these allowances will vary across countries. Trading will equalize the value of allowances and hence alter the size of wealth transfers. Firms receiving grandfathered allowance or facing voluntary caps (or other forms of tradable non-allowance regulation (see Chapter 6) in countries with high allowance prices will lose wealth as a result of international trading.

3   EFFECTS OF THE EXCLUSION OF DEVELOPING COUNTRIES FROM KYOTO COMMITMENTS

Perhaps the most important effect of the Kyoto Protocol on fair competition arises from the exclusion of all developing countries from the regulatory requirements. Countries that are uninvolved in the agreement face no carbon price when they use fossil fuel energy. They may in fact face lower fossil fuel prices because of reduced fossil fuel demand from countries in the agreement. As the price of carbon intensive production, e.g. steel and aluminum, rises in Annex B countries, developing countries will gain a comparative advantage in their production. This will lead to economic shifts in production and will undermine the agreement as a whole. Energy intensive industries will shift toward non-Kyoto countries because they will face higher output prices and lower fuel prices.[4] This will tend to lead to an exacerbated decline in energy-intensive industries in Annex B countries.

Increased supply of these goods by developing countries will partially offset reductions in production in Annex B. The extent of displacement is a matter of empirical debate.[5] The extent of displacement will clearly depend on the stringency of the Kyoto Protocol and the resulting rise in marginal cost of energy use. If Kyoto has a small effect on costs, it will have small displacement effect. Annex B countries have other advantages in production that may offset much of the disadvantage due to carbon prices.

As an example of empirical results, Tulpulé et al. (1999) suggest that leakage will be low. Their model suggests small changes in iron and steel output in Annex B countries as a result of leakage of production to developing countries.[6] For example US production is predicted to fall 9.3 percent with leakage and 8.2 percent without. Japanese production is expected to fall 12.5 percent with leakage and 11.6 percent without. These changes have infinitesimal effects on GDP. In the same volume, Bernstein et al. (1999) suggest that leakage could be around 18 percent of Annex B reductions, i.e. for every 100 units reduced in Annex B, non-Annex B countries could increase emissions by 18 units. Some of this leakage would be a result of lower fuel prices. The rest can be attributed to shifts in production of energy intensive products.

More generally, empirical evidence seems to suggest that production location decisions are mostly driven by other factors such as the quality of the local labor force, infrastructure such as transportation and local amenities and political stability (for a survey see Jaffe et al. (1995)). Studies generally find no identifiable effect from differences in environmental regulation. In any case, global leakage in energy-intensive production results from the effects of the basic emissions targets rather than of the design of any trading program that allows flexibility within them.

---

[4] In theory, with perfectly flexible trade in goods, this could replace the need for emissions trading (Copeland and Taylor, 1999).
[5] These issues are analyzed in detail in Weyant and Hill (1999).
[6] Tulpulé et al. (1999), p. 278.

3.1   Effects of Trading on Global Competition Issues

Trading does not exacerbate global leakage to developing countries or their increased comparative advantage in energy intensive production. In fact, any country that is actively involved in the Clean Development Mechanism (CDM) will face a domestic carbon price and, if the CDM system achieves reasonable compliance levels, will not gain comparative advantage relative to a world with no regulation. A developing country that uses energy will face the same opportunity cost as an Annex B country. They could take the place of firm A in Figure 7.1 or of the 'rest of Annex B' in Figure 7.2. They will have less comparative advantage in energy intensive production but will make sufficient profit from the sale of allowances to more than compensate. If their baseline is defined for a particular project or sector as business as usual, it will allow for some expansion of energy intensive production due to leakage. If they reduce their carbon-based energy use relative to this they will be rewarded through certified emission credits. They receive the international AAU price as a reward for each ton of carbon saved. An Annex B firm has to spend the international AAU price for each ton used. The effect on marginal cost is identical.

The empirical evidence on this is clear. With no trading, Bernstein et al. (1999) suggest that China's output of energy intensive products will rise 1.94 percent under Kyoto and South East Asia's by 4.69 percent while Europe's will fall by 0.17 percent, Japan's by 1.06 percent and the US by 7.87 percent. In contrast, with global trading, China's output falls by 0.57 percent, South East Asia's rises by only 0.07 percent and Europe, Japan and the US output rises 0.44 percent, 0.18 percent and falls 0.59 percent respectively.[7] Global trading of emissions almost totally removes the effect of Kyoto on energy intensive production patterns (see Table 7.1). These estimates are based on all countries behaving competitively. Some large countries may choose to build their industrial sectors based on their comparative advantage of lower carbon prices rather than participating fully in CDM. Mainstream economics would suggest that this is a bad strategy if the CDM is operational and they cannot affect the world price.[8] The arguments for and against this are presented in Section 3. Trading can only reduce any problems this creates because it reduces the shift in comparative advantage.

---

[7] These results are from one specific model and thus have a high degree of uncertainty but other work is supportive of the overall effects.

[8] If they can affect the world price, as China could, the developed world may have to pay them an additional part of the global gains from Chinese participation to get them to join the trading system, Ellerman et al. (1998).

Table 7.1 Percentage changes in 2010 output of energy intensive products as a result of Kyoto

Country/Region	No trading	Global trading	Annex B trading
China	+1.94	-0.57	+0.89
South East Asia	+4.69	+0.07	+2.01
Former Soviet Union	+5.87	-2.98	-10.22
Europe	-0.17	+0.44	+0.50
Japan	-1.06	+0.18	+0.10
United States	-7.87	-0.59	-2.43

(Estimates from Bernstein et al., 1999)

Box 7.1 Illustration: Steel production in Korea

Suppose, purely for purposes of illustration, that each unit of steel produced in Korea currently leads to 1 ton of CO_2 emissions and they produce 1000 units of steel per year. Without the CDM, the Korean firm faces no cost from CO_2 emissions. Under the CDM they might have baseline emissions of 1000 tons of CO_2. If the firm changes its production process and reduces emissions to 0.9 tons per unit of steel it can gain 100 units of CO_2 as certified emission reduction units which it can then sell. If it reduces its production without reducing the rate of emissions per unit it can sell one certified emission reduction unit for each unit of steel reduced. Producing the last unit of steel not only costs them the normal production cost but they also give up the opportunity to sell a unit of certified emission reductions. Their marginal cost of production rises by the cost of an AAU which is the same as the rise in production cost in an efficiently regulated firm in an Annex B country.

3.2   Annex B Trading and Global Competition

Annex B trading lowers marginal costs of abatement for many countries and hence will reduce the differential between pre-and post-regulation costs and the shift in comparative advantage. Overall Annex B trading will have a small effect on leakage because it will not affect global energy costs significantly.

It will have a significant effect on the production of energy efficient industries in some countries though. Bernstein et al. (1999) project that Annex B trading alone would raise US energy intensive production from a fall of 7.87 percent (Kyoto with no trading), to a fall of only 2.43 percent. They also project that production of energy intensive products in the Former Soviet Union would rise 5.87 percent with no trading but fall 10.22 percent with Annex B trading. Outside of Annex B, Bernstein et al. (1999) predict that Annex B trading would reduce China's expansion of energy intensive production from 1.94 percent with no trading to 0.89 percent with trading, and South East Asia's expansion of energy intensive production from 4.69 percent with no trading to 2.01 percent with trading.

Fair competition with countries outside of Annex B depends primarily on the level of regulation other countries face, and the freedom of international AAU trading. We could try to use border adjustments to improve directly the fairness of competition. For any good other than fossil fuels, however, global leakage may be difficult to address through border adjustments because of WTO rules that do not allow trade restrictions based on the production process rather than the product itself.

With comprehensive and active CDM, even if levels of commitment vary, marginal costs of GHG abatement, and hence the costs of using fossil fuels in production, will be equalized across countries. The only way the design of the Annex B trading system can affect the fairness of external competition favorably is by making the system as efficient as possible within Annex B and facilitating trade with countries outside of Annex B.

4   DIFFERENCE IN STRINGENCY OF TARGETS ACROSS COUNTRIES WITHIN ANNEX B

Countries that have accepted more stringent targets will face higher average costs to their economies. Who is likely to face the highest marginal costs in the absence of trading? Modeling suggests Japan will have the highest costs followed by Europe and then the US. With no trading, Japan would face a carbon price of between $100 and $1,100 (US$ per metric ton), and the EU would be very similar, while the US would face a price of between $75 and $400.[9]

Without marginal costs of production trading, divergences in marginal cost will affect countries' abilities to compete. They will definitely exacerbate the difficulties of global leakage. Differences in targets will affect average and marginal costs of production.

4.1   How Does Trading Affect This?

If trade among countries is unlimited (i.e., no binding quantitative limits on trade) and if countries choose equally efficient abatement policies where source level trading is not possible (gases and sources not covered by allowance systems – see below), then the allocation among countries has no direct implications for efficiency. All marginal costs will be equalized.

---

[9] Weyant and Hill (1999), pp. xxxi–xxxii.

If trade is limited, then the allocation of responsibilities also determines the ultimate distribution of emissions and is critical for efficiency and competitive equality. In Figure 7.3 allocation of emissions will depend only on the allocations along the solid lines and will be very different across similar firms. Marginal costs will vary significantly.

It is empirically unclear whether limitations will cause more overall damage to sellers or buyers, and which buyers will be most affected within Annex B. It is clear, however, that potential buyers will face the largest competitive disadvantage . from limitations. Among buyers, without allowance trading or with limited allowance trading, models suggest that Kyoto will lead to significantly higher marginal costs of production in energy-intensive industry in Japan and Europe than in the US. In fact some models suggest that the US could actually gain from limits on Annex B trading because reduced demand by Japan and Europe for AAUs will lower the price more than enough to compensate for the limit on US purchases.[10]

Figure 7.3 Allocation and trading of allowances

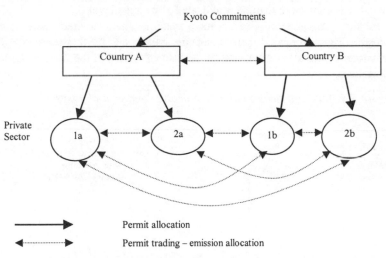

The initial allocation of emission reduction obligations does, however, have major effects on the distribution of cost bearing across countries even with trading. Average costs are not equalized by trading. The initial allocation of AAUs to countries creates a wealth effect. This directly affects the incomes of people in different countries and can also have some macroeconomic effects. These distribution effects depend, however, on the

[10]See Bernstein et al. (1999), p. 246.

already agreed allocation of AAUs among countries and not on the specific form of Annex B trading design chosen.

5 DIFFERENCE IN STRINGENCY OF REGULATION ACROSS SECTORS WITHIN COUNTRIES

Within each country, the total amount of AAUs must be allocated across gases and sources – see Figure 7.4. Because total GHG emissions are capped, the allocation to one gas or set of sources affects those available for others. If some sectors are exempt from regulation or only have policies and measures (PAMs) applying to them, they are not capped; the government, however, still faces an effective cap on emissions from those sectors within its own AAU budget. It could ease this constraint by purchasing AAUs externally. This would change the size of the circle. Trading within the country will affect the relative sizes of the wedges. Sectors covered by PAMs are allocated AAU allowances in the same way that sectors covered by trading are. The government simply bears the compliance risk that PAMs sectors will emit more than their allocated allowance level.

In the EU generally, allowance systems that covered only energy industries and allocated across sectors based on 1990 shares of GHG emissions would allocate around 28 percent of AAUs in the form of tradable allowances.

Figure 7.4 Initial allocation of AAUs among sources and gases

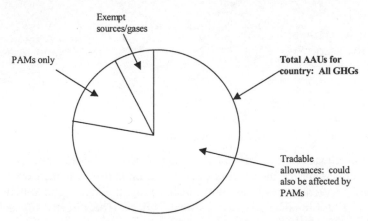

An allowance system that covered all CO_2 emissions and allocated based on 1990 shares (excluding land-use and forestry) would allocate around 79 percent of AAUs as tradable allowances.

Any domestic trading system is unlikely to cover all sources and gases, at least initially. This limitation raises the issue of how countries allocate assigned amounts between sources covered by the trading system and those covered through PAMs, and among those covered by PAMs, and whether a competitive advantage can be derived through this allocation. A country cannot give a marginal competitive advantage to one of its industries by allocating that industry a disproportionate share of allowances with a trading system, because doing so would not change the industry's marginal costs when allowances are tradable. Marginal cost is always determined by the international AAU price. It is possible, however, that a country could provide a competitive advantage to an emissions sector covered by policies and measures (PAMs) other than trading. The domestic allocation of allowances determines the marginal cost of sectors faced by PAMs.

Box 7.2 Illustration: Danish electricity quota

The Danes have recently announced an intention to create a quota system for the electricity sector (Danish Energy Agency, 1999). Suppose, for illustration only, that this was their post 2008 position. They would have a tradable quota system that covers 28 percent of their 1990 emissions (20.4m tons). They plan to allocate 23m tons per year reducing to 20m tons from 2000 to 2003. twenty million tons would be 35 percent of their AAUs and is close to 0 percent reduction from 1990. The Danes have committed to reduce GHGs by 21 percent overall. If this were their 2008 policy they would have to reduce emissions from other sectors and of other gases by nearly 29 percent or purchase external AAUs through Annex B trading or CDM. (In fact, they are planning to ramp up targets as 2008 approaches.) Of course if other sectors are included in the trading system, and/or quota are internationally tradable, the electricity sector may elect to reduce emissions rather than simply returning to 1990 levels if the cost of doing so is lower than the AAU price.

The following section will discuss the effects of different domestic instruments on marginal and average costs of different sectors, on wealth and ultimately on competition. It will give numerical illustrations to clarify the similarities and differences in the effects of different instruments.

5.1   Non-economic Instruments: Emissions Allocation within Country Largely Determined by Regulatory Allocation

A plethora of non-economic instruments to encourage emission reductions exists and more have been proposed. These include efficiency or technology standards, product standards, labeling requirements, voluntary agreements, infrastructure investments and recycling requirements among others. These approaches implicitly allocate GHG abatement responsibility among sectors and actors. They will lead to a pattern of reductions and cost bearing though these may be hard to predict or even monitor *ex post*. They will lead to marginal costs of abatement that vary within and among sectors and are different from the international allowance price. For an illustration see Box 7.3.

Many countries will choose to use non-allowance forms of regulation, especially for those gases and sources that are difficult to directly monitor at a sub-state level. For example, countries may choose to regulate small sources of N_2O through equipment standards rather than directly controlling emissions.

Box 7.3 Illustration: steel industry

Suppose, for simplicity, that all firms in the steel industry have the same emissions per unit of output and the same marginal cost of steel production. 1 unit of output produces one ton of CO_2 and costs $100.

Marginal Cost Differences from PAMs

Suppose that Country A exempts their steel industry from CO_2 regulation. The total marginal cost of steel production is $100.

If country B requires the use of a technology that reduces CO_2 emissions by 8 percent per unit (or 0.08 tons) and costs $8.00 for each unit produced ($100 per ton of emissions reduced) the marginal cost of production for their steel firms is $108.

If country C imposes very stringent technological controls or has a voluntary agreement with the steel industry that limits their total emissions below a cap, their marginal cost of abatement may be brought up to or even beyond the social cost of emissions. If the marginal cost to the firm of reducing the extra emissions produced through an extra unit of output is equal to $150, the firm's marginal cost is equal to their normal production cost of $100 plus the extra abatement cost of $150. Their total marginal cost will be $250.

Clearly, country C will have difficulty competing with country A and even country B. Only country C is making its firms bear the full cost of additional emissions. Country A is making no effort, country B is requiring an efficient level of reduction through technology but making no effort to reflect the social cost of emissions in the price of the product and hence lead to efficient use of steel. These differences are a serious problem for fair competition.

Similarly governments will probably find it infeasible to monitor agricultural sources of methane from individual farms so may subsidize feed additives or try to directly change farming practices. For more discussion of these issues see Chapter 6.

Some governments will simply prefer direct regulation to allowances for historical or political reasons. Governments will need to estimate the number of AAUs necessary to cover the emissions from these non-allowance activities and either the government or a body that represents the sector will trade on their behalf if the sector falls short or has excess.

A country could provide a competitive advantage to an emissions sector covered by PAMs by imposing very lenient regulation on the sector; they would then compensate by placing very strict PAMs on other sectors, by allocating few allowances to trading sectors and hence forcing them to buy more internationally, or by buying external AAUs out of general revenue. For instance, a country that decided not to control methane emissions from livestock might provide a cost advantage to its farms over farms in other countries.

One key situation where many sources may be regulated (or not) outside of the allowance system would be where the allowance system was defined downstream (i.e. at the energy user level not the fossil-fuel producer level). Because of the administrative complexity of such a system many small sources are likely to be excluded from the system.

5.2   Could PAMs be Made Tradable?

One way to reduce the impact of PAMs on competitiveness would be to allow firms to opt out of their PAM if they buy an amount of allowances of AAUs equivalent to the required reduction. This requires clear definition of the expected effect of the PAMs on actual reductions, i.e. specification of a path of emissions under the PAMs regulation. Allowances would have to offset the difference between actual emissions and the projected path under PAMs. For example if annual emissions under PAMs were projected to be 80 tons while actual emissions are 100 tons, the firm would need to buy 20 tons of allowances.

The tools needed to do this are similar to those needed to specify baseline emissions paths for Joint Implementation. The drawbacks, high uncertainty and high transaction costs are also similar. The benefits and costs will vary depending on the PAM.[11] A cap on emissions can easily be made tradable; a labeling requirement could not be made tradable because reliable projections of its impact could not be made. Below we discuss the benefits of tradability for fair competition.

5.3   Economic Instruments: Emissions Allocated by Market within Economy to Equalize MC

Within either a domestic tradable allowance system, or with a tax system, all sources covered will have the same marginal costs of abatement. If the tradable allowances can be internationally traded, or the tax is set and updated to match the international AAU price, this marginal cost will be the same across countries for all firms facing tradable allowances or flexible tax.

---

[11]See Chapter 6 on the interaction between domestic regulation and international trading.

The initial allocation of AAUs to the sector will have no influence on this marginal cost. The marginal cost is defined by actual emission reductions.

If a country limits international sales it will be effectively subsidizing its energy-intensive sector and giving it a competitive advantage because it would have more allowances to use domestically and hence a lower domestic carbon price. Similarly for a country that sets a tax below the international carbon price and buys extra AAUs with taxpayer funds.[12] Conversely a country that limits purchases of AAUs will effectively tax energy-efficient production and give it a competitive disadvantage.

Box 7.4 Illustration continued: marginal costs in steel industry under economic instruments

---

If country D imposes a tax on CO_2 emissions of \$150 per unit of CO_2 their steel firms will face marginal costs equal to their normal production cost of \$100 plus the extra tax of \$150. They will almost certainly reduce emissions to avoid some of this tax but on the margin the cost of reducing emissions further will be equal to the tax. Their total marginal cost will be \$250. They will compete on equal terms with country C but not countries A and B.

They may have an advantage over the firm in country C if they are able to find more efficient ways to reduce emissions than the technology controls. If their government allows them to purchase allowances in lieu of paying the tax they may be better off than country C if the international allowance price falls below \$150.

Suppose country E imposes a tradable allowance system on its steel industry and allows companies to purchase allowances domestically and internationally. The firm's marginal cost will be \$100 plus the allowance price. A firm that holds allowances either through grandfathering or previous purchases faces an opportunity cost because they are unable to sell this allowance; a firm that does not hold allowances must buy an additional allowance.

If the allowance price is \$100 they will compete on better than equal terms with firms in country C and equal terms with D if D can also trade, but will not be able to compete with firms that are exempt from regulation or who face only technology standards that do not control total emissions but only emissions per unit of output.

Another superficially attractive domestic instrument that could lead to unfair competitive advantage even within an allowance system is output-based allocation.

---

[12]Of course the higher taxes required to fund these purchases would reduce the competitive advantage and possibly more than offset it.

5.4   Output-based Allocation

Output-based allocation is similar to grandfathering of allowances with the key difference that the allocation is based on current activity or activity the year before. It is not a lump-sum payment. Over time as activity patterns change, so does the allocation of allowances. Once allocated, the allowances are tradable on the secondary market in absolute amounts – i.e. tons of CO_2 equivalent. Any program that regulates the rate of emissions per unit activity rather the absolute level of emissions is allocating on an output basis. Output-based allocation is essentially an output subsidy.

If a grandfathering program is going to continue for a long time, output-based allocation can address the perceived inequity of allocations based on historical data that exclude new firms and do not take changes in industry structure into account. Note that this inequity is only perceived, because in a competitive industry, the owners of new firms do not bear any costs from regulation when they enter an industry that is already regulated. They have no 'stranded assets'. New firms will have appropriate technology and will enter only if it is profitable to do so. The costs are incurred because of existing assets at the time of regulation.

An example of output-based allocation was the trading program used in the phasedown of lead in gasoline in the United States (1982–1987). In this program, during 1983 and 1984 a refinery that produced another gallon of leaded gasoline received 1.1 grams of additional allowances to use lead additive. The new covenant between industry and the Dutch government can be thought of as a loose form of output-based allocation though allowances are not clearly defined and are not tradable. The industry has agreed to be as efficient in terms of emissions as the highest world standards. They have not agreed to limit total emissions.

Box 7.5   Illustration continued: marginal costs in steel industry with output-based allocation

Suppose Country F uses a tradable allowance system with output-based allocation. Suppose that the firm receives 0.92 allowances for each unit of output (an 8 percent reduction from business as usual). A firm that produces one more unit will need to buy an extra allowance for $100 but they will also receive 0.92 more allowances valued at $92. Thus their marginal cost will only rise by $8 to $108. They are in the same situation as country B. The firm has a lower marginal cost of production than those facing a normal tradable allowance system, a tax or stringent PAMs.

5.4.1   Inefficiency of output-based allocation

The most efficient strategy to control emissions involves a combination of reduced emissions per unit output and reduced output of goods that involve emissions.   Output-based allocation creates an allowance system that encourages emissions reductions per unit output but creates a perverse incentive for output; extra output is rewarded with extra allowances.   By saying that increased output should not be encouraged we are not anti growth.   Output needs to move toward less GHG intensive goods.   Increased output of GHG intensive goods means that, for a given target, greater reductions have to be achieved through reductions per unit output – this is inefficient especially as these rate reductions become more and more expensive to achieve (Fischer, 1997).   The quantitative importance of not providing adequate incentives to alter the output mix will vary by place and time period.

In the short run, output-based allocation may lead to lower consumer prices; in the long run the increased inefficiency will lead to higher consumer prices as well as greater overall cost of emissions reduction.   In the short run this gives a marginal cost advantage to firms receiving the subsidy and downstream firms that face lower prices, but a disadvantage to other sectors that face more stringent regulation as a result.   In the long run it raises the costs overall because of the inefficiency; which agents bear the increased cost depends on the extent of international trading allowed and allocation of obligations within a country.

One very simple and often ignored case of output-based regulation is where allowances are grandfathered based on historical emissions but are only received each year by firms if they continue to operate.   The government claims 'Shutdown' credits.   This has inefficient implications for entry and exit discussed below.

In summary, exemptions or special treatment for some sectors may give those sectors marginal cost advantages relative to their competitors in other countries.   Marginal production costs will be lower for those with exemptions or lenient PAMs.

5.5   Average Costs under PAMs and Economic Instruments

The average cost of abatement varies with variations in regulatory stringency. It varies even when economic instruments are used and the marginal cost is equalized.   Firms that face less stringent initial targets or who receive some form of output-based allocation (possibly based simply on continuing to operate) will have lower average costs.

Regulation will make average costs vary across countries but not as much as marginal costs. Trading will reduce average costs for each firm but will not necessarily make them converge. Average costs do not affect competitiveness directly but they do directly affect profitability. In a non-competitive market a firm with lower average costs is able to subsidize its marginal units in order to capture a greater share of the market. While this is not profitable in the short run it may lead to the collapse of competitors and have longer run advantages. Firms that are more profitable, and that have larger assets or access to capital are more able to oppose and deter such non-competitive practices.

Box 7.6 Illustration continued: average costs in the steel industry

Suppose that steel producers face fixed costs of $1m per year. Suppose each firm produces 100,000 units of steel prior to the regulation. Prior to the regulation each firm faces a marginal cost of $100. In a competitive market the average cost will be equal to the marginal cost and the price.

Post regulation average cost will not rise in country A. Suppose that in Country C when marginal cost rises to $250, average cost rises to $175. [For the example I assume that emission reduction costs are linear and that each country has marginal cost of emission reduction of $100 after their trade.] Suppose also that the firm in country A henceforth firm A, sells firm C 50, 000 allowances at the international allowance price of $100. Firm A receives $5m in allowance revenue from firm C and incurs emission reduction costs of say $2.5m. Its average costs net of allowance revenue fall from $100 to $50 but its marginal cost rises to $200. If it produced one more unit it would either need to sell one fewer allowance to firm C and lose $100 or reduce emissions one more unit, which would cost it $100. Firm A is much more profitable but has the same marginal cost as Firm C.

Firm C would pay $5m for allowances but saves $6.25m in abatement costs so its average costs would fall from $175 to $162.50. Its marginal cost falls to $200. The price of output will rise until enough products are produced to meet demand and all firms that remain in production are profitable. The level of output in the industry as a whole will reduce as the product price rises. Current output levels would require a price of $200 per unit to cover marginal cost.

5.6 Social Costs to Countries

Exemptions for some industries will hurt the economy as a whole and lead to competitive disadvantage in the sectors that are not exempted. Overall, less efficient domestic regulation will tend to hurt the economy more. Once the macroeconomic effects of inefficiency are included, the policies may even end up hurting the sectors the differential policies were intended to help.

The cost to the economy as a whole is the cost of the extra emissions that the steel industry is not covering. Each extra unit of emission has to be matched by a reduction elsewhere or the purchase of an AAU from another country. When a firm is not facing the full cost of the extra emissions someone else must pay to reduce those emissions. In a non-trading system this is likely to cost more than the international allowance price because more reductions will be required in other sectors or the government will use tax dollars to purchase foreign AAUs.

Some of this inefficiency will feed back to the firm that was given the subsidy. They may face higher input or labor costs and may have to pay higher taxes. This will raise their marginal cost. (see Table 7.2.)

Table 7.2 Social and firm costs from different instruments

Instrument	Firm's direct cost for each extra unit of emissions	Cost to rest of country
Exemption	0	More than $100
Technology standard	$8	More than $92
Tax	$100	$0
Tradable allowances	$100	$0
Output-based allocation or voluntary efficiency standards	$8	More than $92

5.7   Can Annex B Trading Reduce the Adverse Effects of Uneven Domestic Regulations?

The freer is AAU trade generally, the less likely it is that any one country's policies will have a large effect on the global AAU market. Free AAU trade will tend also to lower carbon prices in many countries. The lower the international allowance price is the more pressure there will be on government from non-subsidized sectors to allow them to trade freely and the weaker the arguments for subsidies will be from sectors that could be subsidized. Lower AAU prices will also reduce the impact of any non-competitive regulatory practices that would affect production on other countries by simply limiting the effect of regulation on production costs.

Exclusions and subsidies to specific sectors should be discouraged in the usual ways including pressure from WTO. However, we should not fall into the trap of requiring comprehensiveness or even harmonization of regulation as a prerequisite of trading. This would fall into the hands of those who want to undermine trading and the treaty as a whole. This would directly limit trading and would be damaging to all parties. These problems are caused as much or more by the use of PAMs.

6 DOMESTIC REGULATION METHODS THAT PROVIDE LUMP-SUM COMPENSATION TO SECTORS

The effect of regulation through product prices, wages and returns to capital (e.g. dividends) changes marginal costs in the same way as an auctioned allowance program as in a grandfathered program. All efficient forms of regulation lead to a series of marginal costs across industries and individuals that are determined by the way the owners of firms are able to pass on costs to other firms, workers and consumers. The changes in the distribution of wealth that result from grandfathering and the use of tax/auction revenue determine how the ultimate distribution of wealth varies among the options.

6.1 Grandfathering and Voluntary Agreements

Some people believe that if firms are grandfathered allowances rather than having to buy them in auctions, they will have a competitive advantage *vis-à-vis* those who must buy allowances or pay carbon taxes. This would imply that firms involved in voluntary agreements would also have a competitive advantage even if they set absolute caps on emissions. This is generally based on a misunderstanding of allowance markets and grandfathering.

Well designed grandfathering gives allowances to firms based on past behavior, not current or future behavior. It is a lump-sum payment. If a firm increases its production to export more, and emits more greenhouse gases in doing so, it requires more allowances. If allowances were auctioned, the expanding firm would need to buy more or draw down banked reserves. If allowances were grandfathered, it would need to use up some of the stock it holds and would have fewer to sell or use in the future. In every case, the opportunity cost of increasing output is the production cost plus the cost of the additional allowances necessary. If the firm reduces production, it saves the opportunity cost of the allowance price; it avoids the need to buy allowances, or can sell the allowances it was grandfathered. The grandfathering of allowances makes the owners of the firm wealthier, but does not directly alter their marginal production costs.

Grandfathering will have no direct adverse efficiency effects through marginal costs if it is based on previous, non-manipulable data. If allowances are allocated on the basis of things that cannot be altered they have no effects on the costs of production; they are simply a transfer of wealth. The reallocation of wealth across and within industries could affect efficiency if there is imperfect capital mobility. Firms that receive allowances will be wealthier and therefore may have a cheaper more liquid source of finance available than firms that must rely on their usual sources of finance. Of course, grandfathering will have a major effect on the wealth of the current shareholders and owners so firms have a strong interest to fight for it.

Whether the wealth transfer is efficiency improving depends on the value of the capital to the firms that receive it and what would have happened to the resources if they had not been given away in grandfathering (see revenue recycling). Grandfathering could give resources to relatively less efficient firms, or to firms in industries that are declining and do not need new capital. The firms that receive the resources will not necessarily invest them in the same industry; they will invest them wherever they can get the best return.

Box 7.7 Use of lump-sum payments

> There is an old joke about a farmer who wins $1m in the lottery. When asked what he will do with the money, he says that he will keep farming until it runs out. If firms are run by profit maximizers they will not behave in this way. They certainly would not gain economic advantage by doing so. A coal mine that receives a large allocation of allowances through grandfathering will not spend the money the allowances represent subsidizing the coal price when they can see that their mine will never be profitable. Maybe they will invest it in Internet companies.

Grandfathering can occur in a number of ways. The cleanest form is where the existing firms are given allowance rights in perpetuity. This is a simple wealth transfer. However, in practice, grandfathering is often done on an annual basis where a firm that closes down ceases to receive allowances. This can affect a firm's decision to exit an industry. A firm may have average costs that exceed the price of the product so be making a loss but that loss may be offset by the value of the allowances they receive each year. Thus an inefficient firm may stay in business.[13] If the allowances were grandfathered lump-sum, an uneconomic firm would simply sell the future allowances and make their exit decision on the basis of economic profitability.

---

[13]This has not been a key issue in past allowance programs because the value of the allowances was very small relative to the size of the firms involved. In some industries, such as for coal utilities, carbon allowances may be extremely valuable relative to overall capital.

Box 7.8 Illustration continued: grandfathering of emission allowances

Suppose country E has a tradable allowance system and auctions all allowances to its firms. The firm will face a marginal cost of production of $200 and will have average costs of say $175 and will lose some wealth through stranded assets. If country 2 uses lump-sum grandfathering (where all allowances are allocated at the beginning of the program), its operating costs are not changed so marginal costs are still $200 and average costs are $175. However, although the firm loses some stranded assets it also receives a large wealth transfer of say $10m if grandfathering is established for 10 years.

If a firm is grandfathered allowances annually, as long as it is in existence its marginal costs are still $200 but its average costs depend on its output at the time of grandfathering and now. If it were grandfathered based on output of 10,000 p.a. (10,000 permits p.a) it receives $1m per year, which could lower its average costs dramatically (see later discussion of entry and exit). In contrast, a firm that receives allowances through output-based allocation faces a marginal cost of only $108. Its average costs are very low but it receives no wealth transfer.

	Marginal Cost	Average Cost	Wealth
Auctioned permits or tax	$200	$175	$0
Grandfathered permits-lump sum	$200	$175	$10m
Grandfathered permits-annual	$200	$175–$1m/output	$0
Output-based allocation	$108	$104	$0

6.2 Output-based Allocation and Voluntary Agreements

If the grandfathering is done on the basis of output it is more like an output subsidy than grandfathering and has very different effects on costs and wealth. A firm with output-based allocation does not face the full opportunity cost of emitting. If they reduce output, they do not have excess allowances to sell. They do not receive a wealth transfer. However, a large number of firms receive similar output-based allocations (or are exempt), the price of the product will fall to reflect their marginal cost and they will take over the entire market.

Box 7.9 Illustration: Voluntary agreements and wealth transfer

---

A voluntary industry cap that is actually enforced and where the firms are allowed to trade above and below the cap is equivalent to a grandfathered tradable allowance system. If the firms emit at the cap they do not need to buy allowances and have none to sell but if they change their output or emissions they face the true opportunity cost of emissions. Relative to a firm that needs to pay for every allowance, or pay tax on every unit, they have received an implicit wealth transfer equivalent to that under grandfathering.

A voluntary agreement that limits emissions per unit output (such as the Dutch agreement) and that are enforced is equivalent to output-based allocation in a allowance system if firms can trade if they exceed or fall below the standards. No wealth is transferred because the allocation only continues if they produce output, but their marginal and average costs are very low.

Output-based allocation is a problem for competition as are many voluntary agreements and any other rate-of-emission-based forms of regulation as it directly lowers marginal production costs. Lump-sum grandfathering is not a problem for competition. It makes the owners of companies richer but does not give companies a competitive advantage.

In fact, the economy of the country as a whole will be disadvantaged if grandfathering is used because of the loss of efficiency gains that could have been achieved through revenue recycling if the allowances were auctioned (see discussion below). Grandfathering would lower that country's overall productivity and make it harder for their firms to compete. Some firms will be wealthier, but all will face higher production costs because general tax levels (e.g. on capital and labor) will be higher than they would have been if the auction revenue had been recycled into tax cuts. Even firms that are grandfathered allowances will face higher marginal production costs and hence will find it harder to compete with other countries.

6.3   Revenue Recycling

Auction revenue can replace distortionary taxes.[14] Distortionary taxation creates a dead-weight efficiency loss by inserting a wedge between marginal cost and price. By lowering taxes and reducing these distortions auction revenue can offset part of the cost of the GHG regulations (dead-weight loss).[15]

Careful use of this scarcity rent can significantly lower total costs. Ballard et al. (1985) estimate that each additional $1.00 of government revenue,

---

[14]See Cramton and Kerr (1998) for a detailed discussion of how and why to auction permits.
[15]See Bovenberg and Goulder (1996) and Parry (1995). Those who believe in a double dividend believe that it can more than offset the cost.

raised through distortionary taxation, costs society $1.30. These estimates are for the US tax system and economy. Tax distortions in Europe are almost certainly greater, implying even higher potential gains from revenue recycling.

Revenue can be recycled in a large number of ways. Three considerations could affect the choice of recycling method: efficiency, equity and politics. The most efficient way to recycle revenue is to cut the most distortionary taxes. In Europe this may be labor and capital taxes. Alternatively revenue could also be used to pay off government debt and hence reduce pressure on interest rates. The estimates of efficiency gains given above depend on the most efficient options being chosen.

Lump sum payments to consumers or workers (e.g. through increasing the income level below which income is tax-free) do not create efficiency benefits. Returning the equivalent amount to these groups through a reduction in their marginal tax rate, and the rate at which welfare payments are reduced as welfare recipients begin to work, will not only give them more income but also a greater return from extra work. Some of the revenue could be used to create a fund for pensions in future years when demographics mean that the ratio of retired people to workers is high. Auctions create revenue that can improve equity.

In contrast, grandfathering allowances redistributes wealth only to shareholders. Only those who directly receive allowances gain because it produces a pure wealth effect. Voluntary agreements with industry essentially provide free allowances to those industries and hence are similar to grandfathering.

7   WHY WOULD COUNTRIES SUBSIDIZE SOME INDUSTRIES AT THE EXPENSE OF OTHERS?

Do the advantages to some sectors outweigh the macroeconomic disadvantages from limitations on trade, and subsidies to specific sectors through exemptions or grandfathering? There are two basic schools of thought on this: the strategic trade school (e.g. Tyson 1992, or Thurow 1992) and the productivity school (e.g. Krugman 1996). This is essentially an argument that has been going since the 1700s (Adam Smith vs. the Mercantilists) so is unlikely to be resolved in this context.

7.1   Strategic Trade Arguments

If a country can alter its long-term comparative advantage through short–run subsidies to some sectors, the short-run economic costs could be outweighed by long-run economic advantages.

If international trade is seen as a zero sum game where everyone wants to specialize in energy intensive industries and countries have to fight for market share, subsidies will help energy-intensive industries gain market share. But is market share worth it? Are the countries that subsidize their industries and gain market share really winning relative to the countries that lose market share in this industry? Five basic arguments are put forward for subsidizing some sectors at the expense of others.

The first argument is the 'infant industry argument' whose proponents argue that industries need a certain amount of help to get started possibly because there are initial learning costs or minimum economies of scale, combined with limits on capital availability. Others would argue that some industries have greater potential to generate growth in the economy as a whole through technological or skills leakage and hence should be subsidized. Alternatively it might be argued that some industries are so large that they cannot be allowed to fail because they would have significant macroeconomic effects. Fourth, countries have historically argued that some industries are essential for national security and must be maintained at all cost. Finally, if trade negotiations are seen as a game, countries may believe that they should maintain protection even if it is costly so that they have concessions to offer other protectionist countries in order to get them to lower their trade barriers. This works only if the other barriers are eventually lowered in response.

7.2   Productivity Arguments

This argument is built on basic neoclassical economics. What matters for competitiveness, i.e. the ability to sell products, is being able to produce high quality products at lower cost than your competitors. Unless there is some sort of market failure, the benefits of subsidies to one sector do not outweigh the increased costs to other sectors from the higher tax burden. While there may be technological spillovers and minimum economies of scale, governments are not good at 'picking winners' i.e. emerging sectors, or providing effective support. Empirical evidence suggests that decisions on which industries to support tend to be based on political economy rather than any objective assessment of potential efficiency gains to the economy (Grossman and Helpman 1994). The government is probably better to focus on running an efficient economy across all sectors and treating all equally.

While mainstream economists generally believe the productivity arguments, it is clear that governments are still persuaded to create regulatory and trade policies that protect some sectors. Hence it seems likely that governments will choose to exempt some sectors from regulation and provide more lenient regulation to others. It seems unlikely that this will benefit the country as a whole but it almost certainly benefits the sectors that receive preferential treatment.

7.3   How Does This Affect Other Countries?

If one country subsidizes its exporting sector, the importing countries gain overall through purchasing products that are subsidized by a foreign government. For example if Japan subsidizes steel production by imposing lenient carbon regulation on their steel sector, New Zealand as a whole benefits from cheaper steel imports. The New Zealand steel industry cannot compete with lower steel prices but resources can be moved from this industry to other more productive areas in the economy.[16] New Zealand and other countries lose to a certain extent because the Japanese economy is less efficient and hence they demand fewer imports. New Zealand could also lose if Japanese protection is inconsistent, e.g. dumping, so that steel prices fall enough to destroy the New Zealand steel industry but then rise again so that New Zealand does not reap the benefits of lower steel prices.

The equivalent destructive trade practice in Annex B trading might be unstable regulation (e.g. suddenly allowing a very stringently or very leniently regulated major sector to trade or suddenly disallowing it from trading AAUs) that destabilizes the allowance market and makes it difficult for other countries to make good long-term decisions in energy intensive industries.[17]

In summary, some sectors will face some comparative disadvantage if another country treats those sectors in a preferential way. It is not clear that this leads to disadvantage in the economy as a whole; however, it will benefit the other sectors who receive cheaper imports and whose competitors in the other country are being forced to subsidize their preferred sector. The net effect on importing countries, contentiously argued though the mainstream economic consensus, is that the global effect of freer trade is positive for all.

---

[16]This argument has come out clearly in the recent US debate over the demand for protection of the US steel industry against cheap Asian imports. The automobile industry, for one, has argued against steel import restrictions because they gain from the cheaper steel.

[17]Because the AAU market deals with homogeneous goods it will tend to be more liquid and competitive than product markets so the ability of individual countries to influence the AAU market itself as a whole will be lessened.

In any case, if the importing country retaliates with its own protection it is generally agreed that this will not help the importing country; it will impose punishment on the original protectionists but also hurt domestic importers.

8   CONCLUSION

Although economic theory (and empirical evidence) suggests that comprehensive non-preferential regulation is preferable for each individual country and hence that no fair competition issues should arise within Annex B if all sectors and countries trade freely, some countries are likely to exempt or subsidize some sectors at the expense of others. This will lower global gains from trade and raise overall costs. It will harm these sectors in other countries though it will probably benefit others. Even though the net effect on the countries that do not engage in differential domestic regulation is probably negative, restricting trade among Annex B countries will not improve the situation. Free trade combined with pressure to avoid distorting forms of regulation is probably the most effective approach.

Common policies on whether allowances are auctioned or grandfathered within domestic trading programs are probably not critical for encouraging fair competition. Poor design of CDM, limitations on international trade, the use of PAMs and voluntary agreements, and the possibility of exemptions for some groups pose much more danger for fair competition. To date, discussion on fair competition within Annex B has focused on the minor issue of allowance allocation and may be missing the main risks. Pressure to eliminate limitations on tradability of allowances both domestically and internationally and to increase the comprehensiveness of the regulation would enhance competitive equality. In all cases it is probably in each country's macroeconomic interest to choose the policies that are in the international interest but for political economy reasons they may not.

8   Market Power and Annex B Trading

Suzi Kerr[1]

1   INTRODUCTION

Market power in the emissions trading market could create unfair advantage
for some actors and increase the overall cost of compliance. Will market
power be a major issue in Annex B trading and what could we do to avoid it
and/or ameliorate its effects?

We consider two forms of market power. The first is the traditional form
where an actor or a small group of actors tries to influence the market price.
When sellers exert market power they are behaving as monopolists. When
buyers exert market power they are behaving as monopsonists. It is
uncommon that any one actor has complete control over one side of the
market, i.e. pure monopoly or monopsony. Even without this, however,
actors may still be able to have some individual influence on prices.
Alternatively they may form a cartel with others on their side of the market to
jointly influence prices. A second form of market power is the power to
bring non-market pressures to bear on particular trades. In an ideal market
trade is purely voluntary. When trade involves bilateral negotiations among
governments it is possible that a more powerful state could try to force
another player to make a certain deal. This could damage the interests of the
weaker player and could negatively affect other players that might have
wanted to trade with the weaker player.

One key point is that even if market power is exerted in important ways,
there is no environmental effect. The total amount of emissions in Annex B
is fixed. Those who want to exert monopsony power by restricting their
buying to lower the price, have to do additional abatement to replace the
AAUs they would have bought. Those who exert monopoly power by selling
less do less abatement but the buyers have to do more. The environment is

[1] The author, and the Center for Clean Air Policy are grateful to the Dutch Ministry of Housing,
Spatial Planning and Environment for its support of the International Emissions Trading
Dialogue project. We would also like to thank Mike Toman for general support, and Andrew
Muller for references on experimental economics.

unaffected in the short run. In the long run if market power affects compliance or long-term willingness to accept stringent targets market power could indirectly affect environmental outcomes. This chapter discusses the general issues relating to market power in tradable permit markets. It looks at the effects and sources of market power. It then presents empirical evidence and illustrations showing how these issues may apply in the case of Annex B emissions trading. Finally we discuss possible approaches to minimizing market power and reducing its adverse effects.

2 EFFECTS OF MARKET POWER

Market power can have several deleterious effects in terms of both efficiency and distribution. It can be exercised in two ways. First, a large player can attempt to alter the market price. Second, a powerful actor could use its political power to influence market transactions. These forms of market power affect efficiency of abatement, the distribution of gains from trade and potentially treaty compliance.

2.1 Efficiency Effects

Figure 8.1 illustrates the effects of perfect monopoly. This is extremely unlikely to arise in Annex B trading because several Eastern European states and the Former Soviet Union are all likely to be sellers and are unlikely to behave as a united cartel.[2] The effects on the overall market are, however, qualitatively the same with monopolistic competition, the effects are simply muted. The effects of monopsony power would be very similar in effect so are not discussed separately.

The first effect of monopoly power is to raise the price of AAUs beyond their social optimum. The marginal revenue curve that reflects the additional returns to the monopolist from selling extra units is much steeper (more inelastic) than the competitive demand curve. The monopolist recognizes that every additional unit that it sells lowers the price on all the other units that it sells. Thus their net return on additional units is much lower than the price they receive. The price will rise from P^* to P_m. The high price means that sellers will be abating less than is efficient (only until their marginal cost $= MC_m$), while buyers will abate more than is efficient. The net quantity of AAUs transferred will be lower than it should be. It will fall from Q^* to Q_m.

---

[2] Also, they could still be competing with Clean Development Mechanism (CDM) credits.

Monopsony (buyer market power) will lower market prices but will also reduce the quantity traded and lead to inefficiency.

The high price and restricted trade will reduce efficiency of the market but the loss of efficiency (increase in global abatement costs) will not generally be as great as the effects on price or quantity traded. The loss of efficiency is area B + area C.

Figure 8.1 Effects of monopoly power

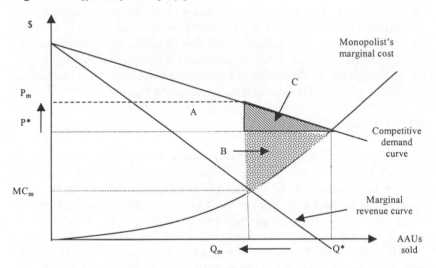

These effects on prices will not only affect AAU trade but will also affect production costs of energy-intensive goods. The monopolist will face a much lower marginal abatement cost which will give their traded goods a competitive advantage. For a country that favors its energy-intensive sector anyway (for reasons discussed in Chapter 7) this could be an additional benefit from exercising monopoly power. In contrast, a monopsonist will gain profits in the AAU market but their abatement costs will be higher than otherwise and they will face a competitive disadvantage in terms of production costs.

The price distortions created by market power will not only affect static efficiency but also dynamic efficiency. If a monopolist raises AAU prices, the incentive to innovate and adopt new technologies will be inefficiently high in buyer countries and inefficiently low in the seller countries. The marginal return to the seller is well below the market price. A monopolist also may want to limit the diffusion of its own technology because diffusion would lower global prices.[3]　This would lead to unbalanced and costly technology development.

These distortions of prices also affect the flow of information in the market. The market price does not reflect the true abatement cost of sellers, or the globally efficient marginal abatement cost. If the market power is exercised through an unstable cartel, or a change in government in the monopoly state leads to a change in policy, the global price could change rapidly. Witness, for example, the instability in global oil prices as a result of OPEC. This will add to existing uncertainty about the path of AAU prices. The exercise of market power is also likely to be associated with government trading and private bilateral deals so the flow of public information could be restricted. On the other hand, to maintain a cartel the cartel may require transparent trading so that no cartel member can trade secretly and undermine the cartel's power. This could increase information flows.

2.2　Distributional Effects

The obvious distributional effect of monopoly power is that buyers lose by paying higher prices and the seller wins. The size of the gains and losses depends on the elasticity of demand and supply. If demand is quite elastic (flat), which is likely in the case of the AAU market, buyers will not lose too much even though the quantity they buy will fall significantly. They lose areas A + C in Figure 8.1. The seller gains area A and loses area B.

The less obvious distribution effect is that when there are several sellers and one large one uses its power to set the price, the other sellers benefit proportionately more than the one that actually has market power. For example, if Russia acted alone by reducing its sales to raise AAU prices, other Eastern European states would benefit from the price rise without having to cut their own sales to induce it. Similarly, if the European Union restricted purchases of AAUs, the US would benefit from the lower AAU price.

If states that exert monopoly power compete in energy-intensive goods markets, their competitors will lose because the firms in the monopoly state will face lower marginal abatement costs and hence lower marginal production costs. If states exert monopsony power, their competitors will benefit because the firms in the monopsony state will face higher production costs.

---

[3] See discussion of this effect in Fischer et al. (1998b).

2.2.1 Manipulation of bilateral trading

The second form of market power is more hidden and could occur with many states. If governments trade bilaterally on a large scale, their motives for trade may be political as well as economic. Trade may not be completely voluntary. A state with military or economic power over another may require that the weaker state sell AAUs on favorable terms (or buy on unfavorable terms) in exchange for continuation of military protection or trade privileges. For example, the US could make a deal with Russia where Russia sells a large quantity of AAUs on favorable terms to the US in exchange for US support with the IMF and maybe US loans to help with economic restructuring. The EU could put explicit or implicit limitations on its members, or potential members' trading to benefit other member states. This form of market power will not affect international prices. It could have a small effect on the efficiency of abatement in the weaker state because they see a low price of AAUs. It would have significant effects on distribution of gains from the market and on efficiency. Strong states would win relative to weak states.

2.3 Potential Effects on Treaty Compliance

Market power raises global compliance costs, creates inequity, reduces the liquidity of the AAU market, leads to effects on fair competition and increases uncertainty in AAU prices. All of these things will make it harder for many states to comply and may reduce their commitment to the agreement. The states that benefit may be more committed as a result of their market power but this will probably be outweighed by the negative perceptions of other states.

3 SOURCES OF MARKET POWER

Market power is a potential problem. How does it come about? What are the conditions that make it likely to be significant? We first look at the conditions required to make exerting market power profitable for any agent.[4] We then discuss the actors that could possibly face these conditions and how that depends on the form of trading, that is, legal-entity vs. government trading. We also discuss the problems of sustaining a cartel. We then discuss the effects of AAUs being a durable (i.e. long lasting) good on the chances of market power being significant.

---

[4] These are discussed in detail in Hahn (1984).

3.1 Static Market Power

A price-setting buyer (monopsonist) would understate its demand thus lowering the price on the AAUs it does buy. This under buying means that it has to control its emissions more than is efficient. Thus exerting market power is costly to the monopsonist. It is more costly the more inelastic is the buyer's demand. If additional abatement is rapidly more expensive, cutting AAU purchases will raise control costs rapidly. The buyer needs to have elastic demand.

The monopsonist must take into account the fact that other buyers will respond to the lower price by increasing their demand thus dampening the effect of the monopsonist's actions on price. If other buyers respond too much the monopsonist would lose. To be effective, the monopsonist must control a large share of the buying side of the market and other buyers must have relative inelastic, unresponsive demand.

The monopsonist must also take into account the fact that as the price falls because of their demand reduction, supply will also fall leading the price to fall more slowly. If supply is too elastic, the monopsonist would have to reduce demand too far to make the price fall and would lose.

More indirectly, given the importance of energy in the overall economy, the potential monopsonist would want to take into account the effect of changes in the AAU price on the price of energy-intensive goods (which they may import or compete with) and on the demand of other states for their exports.

The requirements for an effective monopoly are similar. They must control a large percentage of aggregate supply. They must have elastic supply so that the loss in profits from not selling marginal units is not too great. Other suppliers must have inelastic supply and buyers must have relatively inelastic demand.

3.1.1 Effects of allocation on market power

The ability of a state to exert market power will depend heavily on its initial allocation of AAUs. Market power depends not on total emissions or abatement relative to business-as-usual but on emissions net of AAU allocations, i.e. the cost of abating toward and beyond the allocation of AAUs. An obvious case where this is important is with the 'hot air' allocated to Eastern Europe and the Former Soviet Union. Hot air essentially provides zero cost abatement opportunities and makes these nations large net sellers with initially very elastic supply curves. In contrast, the US may produce a large share of emissions and hence have a large share of the AAU allocation but they do not necessarily have a very elastic supply of net AAUs to the market.

3.2   Exclusionary Manipulation of the AAU Market

A second form of manipulation that regulators are traditionally concerned about is 'exclusionary manipulation'.[5] This occurs when a seller or buyer deliberately reduces the available supply of AAUs in an attempt to stop their competitors getting access to AAUs. In this pure form this will not occur in AAU markets because too many AAUs are already distributed across countries. Domestically it is a potential problem for new firms but unless there are new countries, all countries have access to AAUs and no country can destroy that access. It could be a problem in domestic markets but is not an international problem.

States or large actors could, however, attempt to influence product markets through the AAU market in a different way. Powerful industries could try to influence their governments to limit sales of AAUs, or use more lenient regulation on their sector, implicitly making AAUs available to the industry at lower than the international price.[6] This would give them a price advantage relative to their competitors and may give them the ability to fight more effectively for market share. It would not directly exclude competitors. If their state was also a potential monopolist, the incentives would operate in the same direction and the state would have stronger reasons to limit sales.

3.3   Who Could Exert Market Power within Annex B?

The potential for market power depends critically on the way countries carry out their trading. We will consider two forms of trading, legal-entity trading and government level trading and then discuss the conditions under which a cartel of governments could exert power.

3.3.1   Legal-entities
If all states carried out a large percentage of their trade through legal-entity trading, no one actor could affect the international price. It would also be more difficult for powerful governments to impose trades on their weaker counterparts.

As an example, we consider the US. Even if the US used a comprehensive upstream market for CO_2 regulation there would be more than

---

[5] See Misiolek and Elder (1989) for the seminal discussion of this in permit markets.

[6] Companies would prefer even more to be allocated excess allowance that they can trade. This wouldn't give them a competitive advantage but would directly increase shareholder wealth.

1,700 traders. Even the largest US traders would constitute just a tiny fraction of the US market let alone the international market, as is seen in Table 8.1. Table 8.1 shows the shares of permits each part of the US energy sector would have demanded if an upstream permit market had been introduced in 1995.[7] No one firm would control more than 6 percent of the market. In addition, in the active secondary market many more buyers will participate as speculators. It is inconceivable that any party would be successful in exercising substantial market power in the US market for carbon permits. If all these entities could trade internationally, the US would be unable to exercise any market power.

Table 8.1 Carbon permit needs across US firms – direct permit market players

Carbon user	Total carbon produced in 1995 (million metric tons)	% of permit market
Oil industry[8] (175 refineries)	**436**	**31.1**
Largest oil company (Chevron)	31.1	2.3
Second largest (Exxon)	28.7	2.0
Largest 10 oil companies	226.7	16.2
Coal industry[9] (550 coal preparation plants)	**610**	**43.5**
Largest coal producer (Peabody Holdings)	79.3	5.6
Largest 3 companies	158.6	11.2
Natural gas industry[10] (250 natural gas pipeline companies and 725 natural gas processing plants)	**356**	**25.4**
Total	**1402**	**100**

If the US and other big states or potential groups, e.g. the EU and the FSU allowed their legal-entities to trade AAUs derived from CO_2, market power

---

[7] This is based on actual 1995 carbon use not the reduced carbon use that would result from regulation. Of course, different sectors will reduce carbon usage by different percentages. The table is taken from Cramton and Kerr (1999).

[8] U.S. Department of Energy, Energy Information Administration (1996).

[9] U.S. Department of Energy, Energy Information Administration (1997a).

[10] U.S. Department of Energy, Energy Information Administration (1997b).

through non-price-taking behavior would not be a problem.   Even large multinationals are not large enough in the overall market.   If governments hold a large percentage of the ability to trade themselves it may be a different story.

3.3.2   Government trading

As reported by Richard Baron, 'The IEA World Energy Outlook projects that under business-as-usual projections, emissions from countries with economies in transition would already be some 150 million tons of carbon below their 1990 levels, whereas OECD emissions would be more than 880 million tons higher than their Kyoto objective.' This 150 million tons of 'hot air' will be a large share of the AAUs available to sell.   It is perfectly elastic supply.   In addition, economies in transition are expected to be able to abate quite cheaply at least at first.   They could meet the conditions for an effective monopolist if they acted together.   Russia alone could potentially wield market power.   The scale of this effect is an empirical question discussed below.

The United States and the European Union acting together could similarly dominate the buying side of the market.   Their increased control costs would be very high from any restrictions in supply.   Exerting market power would be economically costly to them unless they can lower AAU prices significantly with relatively little restriction in supply.   Alternatively, either the EU or the US could also influence individual trades by using their economic and political power to coerce sellers to provide AAUs in bulk at below market prices.

If governments trade, they may also take into account their effect on the competitiveness of their energy-intensive industries.   Sellers could see the increased competitiveness as offsetting reduced profits from AAU sales. Although this would be unlikely to help their economy as a whole (see Chapter 7 and Westkog (1996)) it could help politically powerful, concentrated interest groups.

If governments trade, they may also take into account other political motives such as the European environmentalists and renewable industries' lobbying to carry out more domestic action.   Desire to be perceived to be carrying your own weight internationally and to be self sufficient in meeting commitments may also reinforce the desire to reduce demand.   Even if buyer states do not meet the economic conditions for being effective monopsonists and may be unlikely to exert market power explicitly, they may do it indirectly by putting conditions on the sale of 'hot air' or by imposing 'supplementarity' restrictions (Ellerman and Wing, 2000). 'Supplementarity' defined as limits on buying, would have the same effects as monopsony power. In contrast, a country that wants to subsidize energy-intensive industries may be able to limit abatement in these sectors and raise AAU prices credibly. An economy in transition that wants to improve its energy efficiency, decrease pollution and maximize capital inflow for these purposes is less likely to limit its abatement efforts and the sales of AAUs.

3.3.3   Cartels
The effectiveness of economies in transition as monopolists would probably depend on their ability to create an effective cartel. Russia may be able to exert some market power on its own but no others are large enough. Cartels are inherently unstable because every member of the cartel has an incentive to cheat by selling more (in a monopoly cartel) or buying more (in a monopsony cartel). Each country has a marginal abatement cost that is not equal to the market price. Another problem cartels face is how to distribute the gains from market power within the cartel. Disagreements over this often lead to cartel breakdown.

If countries can trade without being observed, a cartel would be impossible to sustain. Even if trades are all observable, given that there would be international pressure against the cartel, many states would choose to break the cartel or not join in the first place. Eastern European countries that are hoping to join the EU are particularly unlikely to join a cartel that directly opposes European interests and also restricts trade with Europe.

3.3.4   Effects of poor domestic policies
The discussion above, and the empirical evidence given below, assumes that countries know their marginal abatement curves and enact domestic policies to efficiently abate. As we discuss in Chapter 6 countries are unlikely to use domestic trading for all sources of GHGs and many will not use them at all at least initially.[11] This means that many sectors in many countries will not face marginal abatement costs equal to the market price even without market power. It makes government trading more likely. On the other hand, because of the wide range of likely domestic policies and the possibly serious efficiency, competitiveness and distributional effects they will have, any effects of market power may pale in comparison.

3.3.5   Effects of uncertainty about future of Kyoto, about compliance and about AAU prices
Similarly, concerns about market power within Annex B may be dominated by more serious concerns about the credibility and sustainability of Kyoto as

[11]See also, Hahn and Stavins (1999).

a whole. Perceptions of market power could undermine Kyoto further. At the same time, if Kyoto is not credible, the effect of lack of credibility on market prices would be far greater than any effect of market power. Credibility problems may interact negatively with market power. If Russia believed that Kyoto will collapse it would want to sell its excess AAUs quickly while there was a market. Because Russia is so large it could affect market prices, especially when other states realized that Russia would be unlikely to comply given its high rate of sales. One large state could change all other states' perceptions of Kyoto's sustainability. Uncertainty about future AAU prices will also make cartels unstable as the gains of belonging to the cartel are largely in the uncertain future while present opportunities are being given up.

3.3.6 Effects of the Clean Development Mechanism

The Clean Development Mechanism introduces new sources of AAU supply (assuming that certified emission reductions (CERs) produced under the CDM can substitute for AAUs). This reduces the chance that the countries in transition could exert monopoly power. The effectiveness of the CDM in offsetting market power will depend on the substitutability of CERs for AAUs and the transactions costs involved in CDM. If CDM is complex and bureaucratic the supply of CERs may be limited and would not affect the Annex B market.

If CDM is effective, a new market power problem could arise. China and/or India are large enough suppliers that they could easily dominate the market and exert substantial market power.[12]

3.4 Dynamic AAU market power

The discussion so far has been totally static. What is likely to happen to market power when we recognize that the market is long term and that AAUs are durable bankable commodities that last until they are surrendered? The basic point here is that monopoly (or monopsony) is harder to sustain with a durable good. AAUs can be used at any point in the five-year commitment period and can be banked for future commitment periods. Any state exercising market power not only has to decide how many to buy or sell but also when.

If a monopolist restricts supply in one year, to affect prices it has to credibly commit to continue to restrict supply in the rest of the commitment

---

[12]See for example Ellerman et al. (1998).

period (and beyond if other states are planning to bank).[13] Otherwise other states will simply wait for future periods when the AAUs are released on the market. They would incur some cost because they might prefer the certainty of purchasing AAUs as their emissions happen but the cost would not be high. Few would agree to pay the high monopoly prices unless they really believed that the AAUs would never be sold. With perfect information and continuous trading the monopoly profit would go to zero.

Without deliberately destroying AAUs (by voluntarily surrendering them) it is very difficult to commit not to sell hot air because those AAUs are always excess. A state could commit to not sell excess abatement by not enacting domestic regulation that will lead to abatement. Each year they would use more of their AAUs and have less available to sell. This would not commit them not to enact policies in the future but would steadily contract the available AAU supply.

It might be more efficient for the state to actually do the abatement but then commit to bank the AAUs rather than selling them in the first commitment period. If the second commitment period is uncertain or not too stringent this may lead to a real restriction in supply because other states would not plan to bank. The state would, however, have to find a way to force themselves not to withdraw the banked AAUs before the next period. They will always be tempted to sell them at the last moment in the first commitment period for the much higher prices available then. If other countries think they will do this, they will not be willing to pay high prices earlier in the period.

As we can easily see, market power is diminished due to the durable nature of the good but strategic behavior could easily lead to considerable instability in the market.[14] It could even lead to a gross shortfall at the end of the commitment period and widespread non-compliance if other states call the monopolists bluff by not purchasing (they would be assuming they will be able to buy later at lower prices) and then the monopolist continues to refuse to sell the banked AAUs.

---

[13]The theory behind this starts with the Coase conjecture (Coase (1972)). It is discussed in some detail in Chapter 10, Fudenberg and Tirole (1991). I am indebted to discussions with Sushenjit Bandyopadhay, Peter Cramton and Larry Ausubel for the discussion in this section.

[14]For a discussion of the effects of private information, and ability to write long term contracts on this market see the literature discussed in Fudenberg and Tirole (1991), Chapter 10.

4 EMPIRICAL EVIDENCE ON MARKET POWER IN ANNEX B TRADING

Empirical evidence comes from three sources. First, global integrated models allow simulations that compare competitive markets to markets where key players use their potential monopoly power or impose restrictions on buying. These models assume that domestic and international markets operate efficiently in all other ways and usually assume that those who exert market power are forward looking, have perfect information, and face no time consistency or commitment problems. The second source is experimental economics, which attempts to look at how individuals behave when faced with situations in a controlled laboratory environment. The third source is historical evidence on previous permit markets.

4.1 General Equilibrium Modeling

Bernstein et al. (1999) use the MS-MRT global model. They include banking and fully rational forward-looking expectations about the effects of market power on energy markets and trade. Their model predicts that Eastern Europe and the Former Soviet Union (EE–FSU) are the only net sellers. They calculate the optimal mark-up over domestic marginal abatement costs to maximize EE–FSU welfare. The find that this is 180 percent in 2010 but declines to only 18 percent by 2030 as marginal costs converge and hot air disappears. This mark-up would imply that the international AAU price would rise from US$90 to US$129 in 2010. Thus the cartel could use its monopoly power to raise prices by up to 43 percent.

Bernstein et al. (1999) also model restrictions on trade. They model varying degrees of restriction ranging from buying limits of 10 percent of assigned amount up to 30 percent and also look at limits on selling: 30 percent of assigned amount and no 'hot air' sales. As an illustration of the effects of these limitations, they all raise the US domestic AAU price: from $90 to $104 with 30 percent trading allowed and to $230 with 10 percent trading allowed. Prices rise to $130 with a ban on hot air sales. The effects on domestic prices vary across countries depending on how much they demand or sell with no restrictions. Ellerman and Wing (2000) use MIT's EPPA model to consider the effects of different forms of supplementarity based on the EU's June 1999 proposal. Their results indicate large potential efficiency losses and redistribution of gains but these vary significantly across scenarios.

MacCracken et al. (1999) model market power without modeling banking. They find that an EE–FSU cartel could raise prices by 44 percent to $105 from $73 and restrict sales to 62 percent of the competitive level. The sellers would be able to make profits that are 10 percent higher with this strategy than behaving competitively. The effects on energy markets are not that great. For example, Japanese energy consumption, which they predict to be most affected by Kyoto, will rise by 20 percent between 1990 and 2010 with competitive trading; this will only decrease to 16 percent growth with monopoly power. In contrast, with no trading at all, Japanese energy consumption is predicted to fall. If the FSU formed a cartel on its own it could still raise prices to $99 and make 7 percent higher profits than with competition. To consider the effects of supplementarity or limits on purchases they model the effects of allowing purchases only equal to 10 percent of assigned amounts. They also limit countries in transition's sales to actual abatement. This causes prices to diverge from the common price of $73 and range up to $304 (Japan).

Manne and Richels (1999) look at the effects on the US of various levels of permit market restrictions that could arise from market power or from supplementarity; they do not model the likelihood of market power being exercised or its extent. They find that limiting purchases to 30 percent of abatement in the US would raise the total cost by two and one-half to three times.

Burniaux (1999) uses the OECD GREEN model. He predicts that if Russia and Ukraine collude and trade in a centralized way, and others behave competitively, and they ignore effects on energy prices and terms of trade, they could raise permit prices by 20 percent. Gains from trade would fall by around 20 percent. This means that costs of control would rise considerably less than 20 percent.

4.2   Experimental Evidence

Experimental work on tradable permit markets has been done by Plott (1989), Muller and Mestelman (1998), Carlén (1998), Godby (1997 and 1999) and Hizen and Saijo (1998) among others. At present the results with respect to international trading are ambiguous. The strength of experimental work is that conditions can be controlled to isolate the effect of one aspect of market trading. For example, Hizen and Saijo (1998) have looked at the effects of making prices transparent on trading efficiency. They find that transparent trading does not affect efficiency though it does affect the pattern of trading. The weakness of experimental work is that it abstracts from many real world realities. Hizen and Saijo's results may not hold up in a world where traders are representing the interests of states and where transactions costs are positive.

4.3   Historical Experience in other Tradable Permit Markets

The earliest relevant historical evidence is summarized in Tietenberg (1985). Various US studies show that the conditions for market power were not generally prevalent in actual permit markets. Evidence from the US lead phasedown suggests that in a bilateral market trade does not occur solely on the basis of price (Kerr and Maré, 1999). Large companies tended to heavily bias toward trading among firms within the same company. This reduced transaction costs and also kept information about trading confidential. They also biased toward trading with other large companies rather than small traders. However, no one company was able to dominate trading or affect the price, though the large companies admitted that they would have liked to.

More recently, evidence from the US Acid Rain market, which is the closest current model to a CO_2 market, suggest that market power is not a significant issue in that market. In the early Environmental Protection Agency auctions of allowances some market power was probably exercised; this was due to poor auction design and was a tiny fraction of total market trading. Market prices are now publicly available from a variety of brokers and have tended to converge (Joskow et al. 1998). The number of transactions is enormous and no one player dominates the market.

5   INSTRUMENTS TO MINIMIZE AND ADDRESS THE EFFECTS OF MARKET POWER

Market power can be most effectively addressed by looking at the sources of market power and finding ways to make conditions less favorable for market power. To recap, the conditions required are that one actor, or a small group, controls a large percentage of supply (or demand), that they have elastic supply (or demand), that their competitors have inelastic supply (demand) and that buyers have inelastic demand (sellers have inelastic supply).

The first approach is to avoid market power by allocating AAUs as closely as possible on the basis of need, i.e. to equalize marginal cost across countries. This will reduce the need to trade and make it less likely that one country controls one side of the market. In particular, by this argument, we should try to avoid 'hot air'. A problem with this argument is that one major advantage of using tradable permits internationally is precisely that there is flexibility to allocate AAUs on the basis of equity and political necessity not efficiency. This has been essential to induce participation by less committed countries and is likely to be even more important when negotiating the participation of developing countries.

Increasing the elasticity of supply and demand in the market as a whole, i.e. market liquidity, makes market power less likely. Restrictions by any one actor will be compensated by increases in supply or demand by others. It also increases access to AAUs and reduces the power of strong countries in making deals with weaker ones.

A first step to having a liquid market is to make the goods traded as homogeneous as possible. Making AAUs, CERs and ERUs close substitutes in the market means that no one can exert market power in any of the sub-markets. Banking will gradually build up a pool of AAUs that can be released onto the market to smooth prices. Avoiding restrictions on trading such as supplementarity, permanent reserves and 'surplus trading' and avoiding buyer liability will increase general liquidity and avoid times in the market when countries have hit international trading limits and the market size shrinks dramatically.[15] Supplementarity type restrictions or 'surplus trading' mean that AAUs within states subject to these constraints are not equivalent to other AAUs in the open market.

Perhaps the single most effective way to reduce market power would be to have all large countries (and regional groupings) institute legal-entity trading systems for a significant percentage of their greenhouse gas emissions. If these legal-entities were able to trade freely, their governments would be unable to exert market power. Even if Russia devolved only the selling of all hot air AAUs to private brokers that operated independently they would not be able to exercise market power. Buyers would also not be able to influence them politically. In general, a small state's best defense against unfavorable political deals may be to devolve the right to trade to a large number of legal-entities.

Reducing the transactions costs of trading will encourage more actors to be involved in international trading. Creating efficient registry systems, putting no constraints on private traders of AAUs, and creating domestic systems that directly use AAUs as currency with no restriction on international trading will lower transaction costs. Without restrictions, private brokers can be expected rapidly to provide market-making services. Permit brokers already exist and are competing to position themselves to serve this market. No broker is likely to be able to dominate the market because of the relatively low costs of providing brokerage services in a homogeneous durable good.

To make it harder for cartels to develop, we should allow anonymous trades. These trades would still be recorded in registries but with the use of non-national accounts it would not be clear who had traded with whom.

---

[15]For more discussion of these restrictions see Chapters 3 and 4 on compliance issues.

Anonymous trading will probably be impossible to avoid with legal-entity trading in any case. The counter argument is that requiring all trades to be visible will avoid trades based on non-economic reasons. If two countries trade significantly below the market price others may argue that they have been excluded from this trading opportunity or that the seller was subject to undue pressure. On the other hand, if all trades are visible, it would be possible for a government to put pressure on their legal-entities and on other governments to trade or not trade with certain countries on non-economic grounds. Requiring all trades to go through visible registered brokers also has the disadvantage that it might limit entry to brokerage. Limited entry would not only reduce efficiency in the market but also allow brokers to wield market power themselves.

Finally, if all else fails and some countries are seen to be behaving non-competitively the usual mechanisms for encouraging free trade could be applied here also. If the WTO would recognize permits as a good, the powers of the WTO could be invoked to reduce restrictions on trade and practices such as 'dumping' of permits. This is very different from trying to get the WTO to help enforce international environmental agreements by allowing border adjustments and trade limits in environmentally sensitive goods. It is standard WTO business.

6   CONCLUSION

Market power would reduce efficiency, lead to inequitable outcomes and increase instability in the market. Empirical evidence suggests that if Eastern Europe and the Former Soviet Union could form a cartel to control the sale of their AAUs they could raise AAU prices significantly. This would not have a large impact on total GHG control costs or energy intensive production patterns. It would significantly increase their benefits from the market at the expense of all other nations.

These empirical models assume that all states have efficient domestic policies, have perfect information about international abatement costs and behave as though compliance with Kyoto is certain. Inefficient domestic policies, international uncertainty about abatement costs, and lack of certainty about compliance are likely to swamp any effects of market power in Annex B. Market power when the CDM is active, however, may be a different story.

To reduce the effects of market power we need to increase the liquidity of the market. We can do this by directly avoiding restrictions on international trade in AAUs. We can make the units traded, AAUs, ERUs, and CERs as homogeneous as possible. We can encourage domestic regulations that allow legal-entity participation in the market. We can reduce the transaction costs of trading by having efficient registries, and not limiting private trading and brokers. By allowing anonymous trading we can weaken cartels. As a last resort we could invoke the powers of the WTO that favor free trade.

9 Developing Rules and Guidelines for Joint Implementation

Cathleen Kelly and Catherine Leining[1]

1   INTRODUCTION

Both the 1992 United Nations Framework Convention on Climate Change (UNFCCC) and the 1997 Kyoto Protocol allow Parties to implement joint measures to reduce atmospheric greenhouse gas (GHG) concentrations. The underlying rationale for joint measures is that they enable Parties to direct their resources toward the GHG mitigation opportunities that achieve the greatest benefits at the lowest cost. Whereas the Framework Convention contains one provision for joint measures, the Kyoto Protocol contains three: International Emissions Trading (IET), the focus of this book, Annex B Joint Implementation (Annex B JI), and the Clean Development Mechanism (CDM). This chapter focuses on the relationship between Annex B JI and IET, which involve only Annex B Parties (industrialized countries and countries with economies in transition) and the distinctions between the rules required for Annex B JI and the CDM. What are the differences between these mechanisms, and why are both IET and Annex B JI needed? How should a Party choose whether to participate in one or both of these mechanisms? What kinds of rules and guidelines will be needed in order to successfully implement these mechanisms? Should the Annex B JI rules be different from the CDM rules?

The chapter begins with a brief history of joint implementation under the Framework Convention, and describes the legal differences between Annex B JI and IET under the Kyoto Protocol. The chapter then analyzes one of the

[1] Cathleen Kelly is the principal author of this chapter and Catherine Leining made important substantive contributions to the final version. The authors wish to thank Ned Helme, Executive Director, Center for Clean Air Policy, for contributing some of the original ideas for this chapter and commenting on early drafts, Tim Denne, Deputy Director, Tim Hargrave, Senior Policy Analyst, and Ellina Levina, Policy Analyst for their comments and suggestions.

key issues that needs to be addressed when developing rules and guidelines for Annex B JI in view of its relationship with IET: determining the emissions additionality of Annex B JI projects and the associated role of national GHG inventories and project baselines. The term 'additionality' refers to the requirement under the Kyoto Protocol that emission reductions credited to Annex B JI projects be 'additional to any that would otherwise occur'.

The chapter concludes with recommendations for developing the essential rules for ensuring additionality under Annex B JI that avoid creating unnecessary administrative barriers for JI investors or countries hosting JI projects. In order to accomplish this goal, the authors conclude that two sets of rules and guidelines for evaluating the additionality of Annex B JI projects are needed:

- For Parties where national GHG inventories are sufficient to safeguard against the undetected export of non-additional emission reduction units (ERUs), the additionality rules need not be stringent. In these cases, countries should be allowed to determine project additionality based on their own internal criteria and procedures. In addition, it is not necessary to require that the additionality of each project in such countries be evaluated by independent entities designated by the appropriate body under the Protocol.

- For Parties where there *is* a risk that the export of non-additional ERUs will not be detected based on their national GHG emissions inventories because their GHG accounting systems or data collection procedures are not in compliance with the requirements of under the Kyoto Protocol, then more stringent additionality rules are required. The conditions for evaluating project additionality for such Parties would be similar to those in non-Annex B Parties participating in the CDM. Thus, the rules and guidelines for evaluating the additionality of Annex B JI projects without adequate GHG accounting systems and emissions inventories should be the same as those established for the CDM. In these cases, project additionality would need to be validated by independent entities designated by the appropriate body under the Protocol.

One advantage of establishing two sets of rules and guidelines for evaluating the additionality of Annex B JI projects is that it would allow Parties without adequate GHG inventories to participate in Annex B JI without damaging the environmental integrity of the Kyoto commitments. Providing the opportunity for Parties without adequate inventories to participate in Annex B JI is important since it is likely that such Parties will not be eligible to participate in IET. Potential eligibility requirements for participation in IET are discussed in more detail in Chapter 3. If such Parties are also prohibited from participating in Annex B JI, they could miss out on important opportunities to implement projects that attract foreign investments, install new technologies, and have local environmental benefits. Lastly, subjecting Parties to different Annex B JI additionality rules based on the quality of their inventories would avoid creating bureaucratic hurdles and unduly high transaction costs for those Parties with adequate inventories. However, it is likely that Parties that have reliable inventories will opt not to participate in Annex B JI and will instead favor the relatively less burdensome requirements that are likely to be established for IET.

2   THE EVOLUTION AND CHARACTERISTICS OF JOINT IMPLEMENTATION AND INTERNATIONAL EMISSIONS TRADING

The use of cooperative efforts to achieve GHG mitigation goals was introduced in 1992 in the Framework Convention, which states that Annex I Parties may implement GHG mitigation policies and measures 'jointly with other Parties'.[2] In 1995, the First Conference of the Parties to the Framework Convention advanced the concept of joint implementation by initiating the Activities Implemented Jointly (AIJ) pilot phase.[3] This decision enabled Annex I Parties to undertake voluntary greenhouse gas mitigation projects jointly with other Annex I Parties or non-Annex I Parties (developing countries). Such projects had to produce greenhouse gas benefits that would not have occurred in the absence of the projects, and had to be funded outside of the financial mechanism of the Framework Convention and official development assistance flows. However, Annex I Parties cannot use the GHG benefits achieved by these projects during the pilot phase to meet their UNFCCC commitment to reduce their anthropogenic emissions of GHGs to 1990 levels by 2000. At the time of writing, the Parties had yet to determine the future course of the AIJ pilot phase.

The concept of joint implementation in the Framework Convention has evolved into three mechanisms in the Kyoto Protocol: International Emissions Trading (IET), the main focus of this book, Annex B Joint Implementation (Annex B JI), and the Clean Development Mechanism (CDM).[4] Unlike the AIJ pilot phase of joint implementation under the Framework Convention, these three mechanisms enable Annex B Parties to

---

[2] Article 4.2(a), UNFCCC (1992).
[3] Decision 5/CP.1, UNFCCC (1995c).
[4] IET is outlined in Article 17, Annex I JI in Article 6 and the CDM in Article 12. See UNFCCC (1995c).

achieve a portion of their quantified emission reduction or limitation commitment through cooperative efforts with other Parties.

- Annex B JI: provides for the transfer of emission reduction units (ERUs) tied to the implementation of specified projects. These projects can be implemented by Annex B Parties, or by 'legal-entities' within those countries. When ERUs are generated by one Party and sold to another Party, the seller Party subtracts the ERUs from its assigned amount, and the buyer Party adds the ERUs to its assigned amount. [5] Although this mechanism is commonly referred to as Annex B JI, this term does not appear in the Protocol and should not be confused with joint implementation under the Framework Convention.

- The CDM: enables non-Annex B Parties to host projects that contribute to their sustainable development goals and reduce greenhouse gas emissions, and Annex B Parties to use the resulting certified emission reductions (CERs) to meet part of their commitment.

- IET: allows for transfers of assigned amount units (AAUs) among Annex B Parties. Both Annex B JI and the CDM essentially are project-based forms of emissions trading, while IET is budget-based and allows Parties to trade portions of their emissions budgets (assigned amounts).

There are important benefits to Parties that choose to participate in these mechanisms. By participating as sellers, Parties can benefit from an increased flow of investment capital, access to new technology, the transfer of skills, new partnerships with foreign companies, and increases in government and/or private-sector revenue. Through participation as buyers, Annex B Parties can reduce the overall costs of meeting their Kyoto commitments and thus improve the chances of compliance.

A preliminary assessment of the legal differences between Annex B JI and IET can be conducted on the basis of the language in the Kyoto Protocol. The Protocol places the following restrictions on Annex B JI transactions:

- These transactions must be linked to projects that reduce anthropogenic emissions by sources or enhance anthropogenic removals by sinks.
- The projects must have the approval of the Parties involved.
- Emission reductions and sink enhancements must be 'additional to any that would otherwise occur'.
- A buyer may not apply ERUs toward meeting its commitment if there is a question about seller compliance with Annex B JI requirements.

---

[5] A Party's assigned amount is its net GHG emission budget based on its commitment under the Kyoto Protocol.

- Parties may not buy ERUs unless they have met their requirements under Articles 5 and 7.[6]
- The acquisition of ERUs must be supplemental to domestic actions undertaken by the buyer, and therefore can only be used to meet a portion of the buyer's commitment.

In contrast, the Protocol only places a single restriction on the acquisition of AAUs through IET transactions: such acquisitions must be supplemental to domestic actions undertaken by the buyer.

Parties will need to consider the implications of these differences when deciding whether to participate in one or both of these mechanisms. In the Protocol's current form, IET clearly offers more flexibility than Annex B JI and, therefore, may lure Annex B Parties away from participation in Annex B JI. Although it is not explicitly stated in the Protocol, it is widely assumed that legal-entities will be allowed to directly participate as buyers and sellers of AAUs in IET. Entity-level trading offers the greatest flexibility to sources that might face domestic targets because it provides entities the option to buy AAUs to comply with their targets or to sell AAUs if they are able to reduce emissions below their targets. Several Parties have submitted proposals for legal language to the UNFCCC that would authorize legal-entities to participate in IET.[7]

Some Annex B Parties lack experience with emissions trading and have not yet developed the legal framework or capacity to manage legal-entity transactions. For example, if the government allows legal-entities to participate directly in IET, then the government needs to be able to set legal-entity level emission reduction targets, distribute emission allowances to emissions sources either through auctioning or grandfathering, and monitor and enforce compliance with these targets.

Parties that do not yet have the capacity to allow entity-level trading may choose to restrict IET to transactions undertaken at the government level. Government-level trading would allow a Party to maintain more control over each transaction and to protect against overselling of AAUs needed for compliance with their Kyoto commitments. This option is also appealing to

---

[6] Articles 5 and 7 outline requirements for the preparation and submission of national inventories of GHG emissions and sinks by Annex I Parties. Interestingly, the Protocol does not require Parties that sell ERUs to meet the national GHG inventory requirements under Articles 5 and 7. This limitation on buyers and not sellers of ERUs is intriguing given that it would be of greater consequence to the international community if Parties *selling* ERUs were not in compliance with Article 5 and 7 because it would be impossible to determine if such Parties were in compliance with their Kyoto commitments and thus, whether they were exporting non-additional ERUs.

[7] UNFCCC (1999e).

some Parties because it allows governments to maintain control over revenues earned from AAU sales.

Under either government-level or entity-level IET, Parties could also undertake project-based transactions similar to those envisioned under Annex B JI. For example, a Party might tie the transfer of AAUs to the emission reductions anticipated from a specific project. To avoid the additionality requirements and potentially higher transaction costs associated with Annex B JI, it is likely that Parties will simply choose to implement project-based transactions through IET rather than through Annex B JI.[8] However, some policy makers have proposed that Parties whose inventories do not meet the requirements of Articles 5 and 7 of the Protocol should not be allowed to participate in IET, since it would not be possible to verify whether such Parties were exporting AAUs needed to comply with their emission reduction commitments. This proposal is discussed in more detail in Chapter 3. Parties that are disqualified from participating in IET would need to rely on the Annex B JI framework to sell ERUs to other Parties.

Ultimately, the participation requirements and level of flexibility associated with participation in Annex B JI and IET will depend on how the rules and guidelines for these mechanisms are defined. The remainder of this chapter focuses on options for defining the guidelines for Annex B JI in view of a key difference between Annex B JI and IET: the additionality requirement for Annex B JI projects.

- Section 3 addresses the linkages between the need for assessing the emissions additionality of Annex B JI projects and the adequacy of national GHG emissions inventories.
- Section 4 presents several methods for simplifying the development of baselines that may be used to determine the additionality of Annex B JI projects. These methods include benchmarking and the use of top-down baselines.
- Section 5 discusses two approaches for defining the additionality rules for Annex B JI. Under the first approach, the Annex B JI additionality rules would be the same as those established for the CDM. The second

---

[8] There is a possibility that some Parties may actually prefer the more restricted transactions under Annex I JI relative to IET because the more stringent requirements associated with Annex I JI transactions could serve to protect Parties from exposure to risks of domestic corruption and political pressure from strong domestic actors that could result in the export of AAUs needed for compliance with its Kyoto commitments. Since IET has no additionality requirement, it unlikely that IET transactions will be subjected to review and approval by independent entities designated by appropriate bodies under the UNFCCC. While it has not yet been determined whether Annex I JI transactions will be subjected to this kind of review and approval process, this is an option currently under negotiation by Parties. UNFCCC (1999e).

approach involves a two-tiered system for testing project additionality. The Tier One rules would apply to countries that have adequate GHG inventories and that are in compliance with Articles 5 and 7. The Tier Two rules, which are more stringent, would apply to countries with inadequate inventories.

3   LINKAGES BETWEEN ADDITIONALITY AND ADEQUACY OF NATIONAL GHG INVENTORIES

As discussed above, the Kyoto Protocol requires that emission reductions credited to an Annex B JI project must be additional to those that would have occurred in the absence of the project. However, the Protocol does not define the term 'additional', nor does it require the certification of project additionality by an international compliance authority. In practical terms, the purpose of the additionality requirement is to prevent an Annex B Party from exporting project-based emission reductions that are needed by that Party to meet its commitments. In other words, an Annex B JI project can be considered additional if it is not part of the domestic activities that must be undertaken by the host Party in order to meet its emission reduction commitments. Ultimately, the ERUs generated by an Annex B JI project will be proven additional when the host Party that exports the ERUs is still able to meet its emission reduction commitments under the Protocol. This determination can be made on the basis of the host Party's national GHG inventory, assuming the Party is in compliance with Article 5 and 7 and thus, has an adequate inventory.

If a Party sells non-additional ERUs, it will fail to meet its commitment on the basis of its national inventory. In this case, the Party will have to find another means to achieve compliance such as undertaking further domestic reductions or purchasing emission reductions from another Party through one of the Kyoto mechanisms or incur penalties for noncompliance. This should provide a strong disincentive for Parties to sell non-additional ERUs.

If Parties maintain adequate national data collection and inventory reporting systems and if they face meaningful penalties for noncompliance with their emission reduction commitments, then it should be feasible to verify the additionality of ERUs on the basis of the seller Party's national GHG inventory. In this case, a separate evaluation of project additionality should not be necessary from the perspective of the international community. However, if the additionality of Annex B JI projects is determined on the basis of inadequate national inventories, then the environmental integrity of the Protocol could be undermined. For example, if a Party exporting ERUs under-reports its actual GHG emissions in its inventory and this error is not detected, the ERUs will not represent real reductions in GHGs. Because the buyer party will be able to use the ERUs to increase its emissions beyond its target, the actual combined emissions by both the seller and buyer Parties will exceed the sum of their assigned amounts. The conditions for evaluating project additionality for Parties without adequate inventories are similar to those in non-Annex B Parties participating in the CDM. Since non-Annex B Parties have not agreed to national emission reduction targets, there is no process whereby the export of non-additional credits is captured other than through an evaluation of the additionality of each project and project-level monitoring.

Therefore, when designing guidelines for determining project additionality for Annex B JI, it may be necessary to distinguish between host (seller) Parties that have adequate national inventory systems, and those that do not. Whereas host Parties with adequate national inventory systems can rely on GHG accounting systems to demonstrate the additionality of their Annex B JI projects, host Parties without adequate national inventory systems should be subject to a more stringent test for additionality that extends beyond the consideration of national inventories. More specifically, for Parties without adequate inventories, project additionality and baselines would need to be validated by independent entities based on the same criteria and rules for evaluating project additionality as established under the CDM. This idea is further discussed in Section 5. To lay the groundwork for this discussion, Section 4 discusses different baseline methods for determining project additionality with an emphasis on options for simplifying the baseline setting process.

4   OPTIONS FOR SIMPLIFYING ANNEX B JI PROJECT BASELINE

One method for evaluating the additionality of Annex B JI projects is the comparison of emissions for those projects against an emission baseline. An emission baseline is the annual stream of net GHG emissions that would be expected to occur without the project (i.e., under business-as-usual conditions). If the stream of net emissions with a project were less than the stream of net emissions without the project (i.e., the baseline), then the project could be considered additional, and the credits awarded to the project would be equal to the difference between the two emission streams.

Parties have gained experience with the use of baselines for this purpose under the AIJ pilot phase of joint implementation under the UNFCCC. Under the AIJ pilot phase, project baseline setting and additionality determination have taken place on an ad hoc, case-by-case basis because formal rules do not yet exist. This 'bottom-up' approach has required project developers to expend significant time and resources in preparing the paperwork related to projects, and both host and investor countries to devote substantial resources to reviewing project applications. The high transaction costs associated with project preparation and review have discouraged investment by buyer Parties in AIJ projects, which in turn has meant less fresh capital, less new technology, and few local environmental and other project benefits for host countries.[9]

To improve the efficiency of project development and approval under the Kyoto Protocol, policy makers have proposed a number of methods to standardize and thus simplify the baseline-setting process. The goal of these methods is to reduce transaction costs without compromising the quality of the estimates of projects' GHG impacts. Two of the methods under discussion by international policy makers are summarized below.[10]

4.1   Benchmarks

Under this approach, baselines would be derived from emission benchmarks: performance standards for the emission intensity of technologies, products, management practices, or sectors under business-as-usual circumstances (i.e., in the absence of the project). Benchmarks could be expressed in units of GHGs emitted per unit of output or operation (e.g., tons of CO_2 per kWh or tons of CO_2 per ton of cement). Benchmarks could be calculated in reference to historic, current, or projected emission intensity trends for a given sector, technology, or mix of technologies. For instance, the baseline emission rate for new power generation projects in a region could be set at the weighted-average emission rate for new clean coal and combined cycle natural gas plants (rather than in reference to one or the other). Basing benchmarks on a mix of technologies would be especially appropriate for projects that may offset emissions from a range of facilities using different technologies or fuel types. To test project additionality using a benchmark, a project's emission intensity would be compared against the benchmark for that project type or sector. To establish an annual emission baseline using a benchmark, the benchmark would be multiplied by the number of units of output or operation (e.g. kWh or tons of cement) associated with business as usual.[11]

---

[9] For an overview of experiences and lessons learned from the AIJ pilot phase, see Dixon (1999). For a discussion of factors influencing AIJ transaction costs see, Carter (1997), Dudek and Wiener (1996), and Lile et al. (1998).

[10] For a further discussion of methods for setting baselines, see Hargrave et al. (1998), Pape and Rich (1998), Hamwey and Szekely (1998), Puhl and Hargrave (1998), and Puhl (1998).

[11] For a more detailed discussion of emissions benchmarks, see Hagler (1998) and Lazarus et al. (1999).

4.2   Top-down Baselines

The development of top-down baselines would involve the projection of annual emissions under business-as-usual at the national or regional level and the allocation of those emissions first by sector and then by project. Under a top-down baseline approach for Annex B JI projects, a Party's GHG emission reduction target under the Kyoto Protocol would serve as the basis for the national or regional emission baseline from which project baselines would be derived. The national government's approach to disaggregating the baseline by sector would need to account for the anticipated growth in emissions in each sector as well as the reductions that would be needed by each sector in order to meet the overall national target. For this reason, this approach is best applied in countries that have committed to national emission reduction targets and have adequate inventory and projected emissions data available. If this approach is used by Parties that have adequate data for the sectors in which the top-down approach is applied, but are not in full compliance with the GHG inventory requirements under Article 5 and 7, top-down baselines would need to be validated by independent third-party entities. This issue is discussed in more detail in Section 5.

Project baselines derived from the aggregate baseline could either be set in terms of absolute emissions or based on GHG emissions per unit of output (e.g., carbon emissions per C/kWh for power sector or C/TJ for district heating sub-sector, etc). To determine project additionality, a project's emission stream would be compared against the top-down baseline. Top-down baselines developed in this manner would allow a country to assess project additionality in the context of its overall planning effort to meet its Kyoto target.

The following example illustrates how a top-down baseline could be developed for an Annex B JI project. An Annex B Party with a national emission reduction target of eight percent below 1990 levels could establish sub-targets for key sectors. Given differences in emission reduction potential and costs associated with different sectors, a country might set more stringent targets in the sectors where emission reductions could be achieved most cost effectively. For instance, a country could set a target of 12 percent below 1990 levels in the power generation sector in order to limit the emission reduction required in sectors where emission reductions are harder to measure or more costly to achieve (e.g., transportation).

Policy makers evaluating the potential use of both benchmarking and top-down baselines need to consider the level of environmental accuracy associated with these more standardized baseline approaches. Standardized approaches may not necessarily be less accurate than project-specific approaches, since many of the same challenges (such as projecting future trends and quantifying emission impacts beyond the project boundary) apply to both approaches. In the case of Annex B JI projects, standardized baselines developed using high-quality sectoral data and consideration of business-as-usual trends in new technology penetration could reduce project transaction costs without reducing Parties' abilities to determine project additionality. However, standardized approaches may not be appropriate for some sectors (e.g., non-homogeneous sectors such as the chemical sector) and for some countries (e.g., those without adequate data collection and institutional capacity, or those not anticipating many projects). Standardized approaches are most easily applied to sectors with fairly homogeneous processes of production, technologies, and outputs (e.g., electricity, cement, steel).

Further research is needed to test the environmental accuracy of standardized approaches in different sectors. The next section discusses the application of the benchmarking and top-down baseline approaches in the context of two approaches for defining the additionality rules for Annex B JI that are currently under consideration by international policy makers. The following section also raises the issue of the importance of linking the stringency of additionality rules applied to Parties participating in Annex B JI to the adequacy of their national inventories.

5   TWO APPROACHES TO DEFINING THE ADDITIONALITY RULES FOR ANNEX B JI

International negotiators are currently discussing rules for defining and assessing the additionality of Annex B JI projects. Two approaches for defining these rules are under consideration:[12]

- Approach 1: Apply the same additionality criteria and rules to Annex B JI and CDM projects.

---

[12]UNFCCC (1999e) and CCAP (1999). Several developing countries and countries within the EU have submitted proposals to the UNFCCC along the lines of Approach 1. Countries in the Umbrella Group (which includes Australia, Canada, Iceland, Japan, New Zealand, Norway, the Russian Federation, Ukraine and the US) have submitted proposals that outline less stringent requirements for evaluating the additionality or Annex I JI projects than those they propose for the CDM. For example, the Umbrella Group proposal does not require the review of the additionality of Annex I JI projects by independent entities appointed by the appropriate UNFCCC body. The proposal to develop two sets of rules to evaluate the additionality of Annex I JI projects, as outlined in Approach 2, is based on a Center for Clean Air Policy proposal submitted to the UNFCCC in October 1999.

- Approach 2: Establish two sets of additionality rules for Annex B JI projects that are tied to the adequacy of the host Party's national GHG inventory.

The merits of both approaches are discussed below.

5.1   Approach 1: Apply the Same Additionality Rules to Annex B JI and CDM Projects

Although both Annex B JI and CDM projects are subject to an additionality requirement under the Kyoto Protocol, the additionality requirement operates in a different context for each mechanism. Since the Parties hosting CDM projects do not have emission limitation or reduction commitments under the Kyoto Protocol, it is more difficult to judge whether the CERs generated by these projects and used to modify the target of the Annex B buyer are tied to real and additional emission reductions. Furthermore, in the absence of targets, both project developers and host countries have an incentive to inflate baseline estimates to maximize project CERs and associated revenue. Thus, the additionality tests for CDM projects cannot be conducted on the basis of the host country's inventory, and must be stringent in order to preserve the environmental integrity of the Protocol.

As discussed in Section 3, the additionality of Annex B JI projects can be determined on the basis of the host Party's commitment and national inventory, assuming the inventory is sufficiently rigorous and is in compliance with Article 5 and 7 requirements. In this case, gaming is less of a risk because selling Parties have an incentive to use conservative baselines to stay in compliance with their Kyoto targets.

Establishing identical additionality rules for Annex B JI and CDM projects is appealing to some negotiators not because of issues associated with environmental integrity, but those linked to competitiveness. Some negotiators believe that establishing the same additionality rules for Annex B JI and CDM would help to equalize the standards for both mechanisms and would addresses the concern among G77 countries that different and less burdensome rules for Annex B JI will divert resources away from the CDM. Thus, this approach may be more politically acceptable because it appears to level the playing field between Annex B JI and the CDM.

Identical rules for Annex B JI and the CDM may not be necessary to ensure that Annex B JI does not overshadow the CDM because the Kyoto Protocol allows the CDM to be operational by 2000 and implies a later starting date of 2008 for Annex B JI. However, some Annex B countries are considering the possibility of developing 'early Annex B JI' projects (i.e., prior to 2008). Under an 'early Annex B JI' program, sellers would encourage early emission reduction activity by setting aside a portion of their

AAUs for the first commitment period (2008 to 2012) to award to emission reduction projects implemented prior to 2008. Switzerland has outlined a proposal that would link 'hot air' sales to Annex B JI projects developed prior to 2008.[13] Under this approach, sellers with 'hot air' would set a portion of it aside to guarantee investors in early Annex B JI projects that ERUs equivalent to the anticipated project emission reductions would be delivered during the first commitment period. If an early Annex B JI project actually achieved its anticipated emission reductions, the AAUs used to guarantee that project would be retired from the market. The Swiss proposal requires that sellers invest their early Annex B JI revenues in improving national data collection systems or financing additional projects.

Because the additionality rules have not yet been developed for the CDM, it is difficult to predict the implications of requiring identical additionality rules for the CDM and Annex B JI. On the basis of submissions from Parties to the UNFCCC, it appears increasingly likely that the Parties will include some kind of baseline assessment in the additionality test for CDM projects, and that Parties may have some flexibility in the choice between project-specific baselines and more standardized baselines such as benchmarks and top-down baselines.[14] While project-specific and benchmark baseline methods could be applied to both CDM and Annex B JI projects, top-down baseline methods may be more appropriate for Annex B JI projects than CDM projects because top-down baselines require sectoral targets and strong inventory data.

The Protocol establishes some criteria for the CDM that are not specified for Annex B JI. For example, CDM projects are required to meet host country sustainable development goals, and project emission reductions must be certified by operational entities. In addition, the eligibility of carbon sequestration projects (e.g., forestry conservation and reforestation) has not yet been determined under the CDM. Furthermore, the development of the rules for Annex B JI and the CDM may take place within slightly different timeframes. Another important consideration is that some policy makers have proposed including a criterion in the rules for the CDM that would prevent the diversion of funds from official development assistance to CDM project development. This criterion would not be appropriate in the context of Annex B JI. Therefore, tying the additionality rules for Annex B JI to

---

[13]'Hot air' refers to emission reductions achieved by some Annex I Parties with economies in transition because of a decline in economic productivity since 1990 (or their base year or base period under the Protocol), rather than because of the implementation of GHG mitigation measures. For this reason, annual emissions for some of these Parties are currently below the target for the 2008–2012 commitment period. These countries could potentially trade the excess emission reductions to other Annex I Parties under Article 6 or Article 17.

[14]UNFCCC (1999e).

those developed for the CDM could unnecessarily increase the bureaucratic hurdles for Annex B JI projects and could delay implementation of either or both of these mechanisms.

Although it is technically feasible to require that all Annex B JI projects be subjected to the same additionality rules as those established for the CDM, it may not be expedient to do so. This approach may unnecessarily complicate the additionality test for Annex B Parties that otherwise could prove the additionality of their JI projects using rigorous national inventories. Increasing the administrative burden and the transaction costs associated with developing Annex B JI projects will simply lead investors to select IET transactions instead of Annex B JI projects. Since IET does not restrict the activities that may be used to produce tradable AAUs, it is conceivable that Annex B Parties could easily establish a domestic project-based system tied to exports of AAUs using IET instead of exports of ERUs under Annex B JI in order to avoid the additionality requirement under JI. This would not be a problem from an environmental perspective. Regardless of whether Parties choose to participate in Annex B JI or IET, they will still be required to demonstrate that they are in compliance with their Kyoto commitments on the basis of their national inventories.

If the additionality rules for Annex B JI projects were identical to those established for the CDM, it is likely that the only Parties that would opt to participate in Annex B JI would be those that did not have adequate inventories and were thus prohibited from participating in IET. This is not a problem from the perspective of the international community. However, some Annex B Parties may want to have the flexibility to participate in both Annex B JI and IET, and thus may want to ensure that transactions are not burdened with requirements other than those necessary to ensure the environmental integrity to the Protocol. These countries would likely prefer Approach 2 presented below, which only establishes stringent additionality requirements in those cases where they are necessary – in countries that do not have adequate GHG emissions inventories.

5.2   Approach 2: Apply a Two-tier Additionality Rule to Annex B JI Projects Based on the Adequacy of National GHG Inventories

Another approach to defining the additionality rules for Annex B JI would be to apply two different sets of additionality criteria based on the adequacy of a Party's national GHG inventory. This approach would allow Parties with inadequate inventories to participate in Annex B JI without jeopardizing the environmental integrity of the Kyoto emission reduction commitments. In addition, this approach avoids creating unnecessary administrative barriers for Annex B JI transactions in countries that have adequate GHG inventories.

These two sets of criteria are discussed below.

(a) Additionality criteria for countries with adequate GHG inventories

For those Parties that can demonstrate that they had adequate data systems and GHG inventories and were thus in compliance with the monitoring and reporting requirements of the Kyoto Protocol under Articles 5 and 7, separate international rules for demonstrating the additionality of Annex B JI projects would not be necessary. The evaluation of the Parties' national greenhouse gas inventories against their commitments and the imposition of penalties for noncompliance with the Kyoto targets would serve as a safeguard against the transfer of non-additional ERUs. The host country would still need to make its own internal determination of a project's additionality in order to protect itself against the liability of noncompliance. However, this internal determination would not have to be evaluated against an international standard, and could be conducted in the context of a country's overall planning effort to meet its Kyoto obligations. For instance, additionality could be assessed using an aggregate or 'top-down' baseline set equal to a country's Kyoto target. From the aggregate target or baseline, the national government could allocate baselines (i.e., targets) to projects, and emission reductions below these baselines would be defined as additional. As discussed in the previous section, this approach would allow a country to use Annex B JI to transition to full legal-entity trading because it would involve the same type of sectoral planning necessary for legal-entity IET participation.

(b) Additionality criteria for countries with inadequate GHG inventories

If Annex B Parties participating in Annex B JI did not have rigorous national inventories and monitoring and verification systems, then transfers of non-additional credits might not be captured by comparing their inventories to their commitment under the Protocol. Such Parties would be out of compliance with the monitoring and reporting requirements of the Protocol, and likely would be prohibited from participation in IET. However, Parties without adequate inventories could still be allowed to participate in Annex B JI on the condition that project additionality be reviewed by independent entities designated by the appropriate UNFCCC body based on the same criteria and rules established for reviewing additionality under the CDM. As long as the baseline was approved by independent entities, the additionality of Annex B JI projects for such Parties could be determined using benchmarking, top-down baselines, or project-specific baselines.

It is important to note that under this option, the only rules for Annex B JI projects that would need to be identical to those established for the CDM are those associated with determining project emissions additionality. Although it is essential to establish more stringent additionality rules for Annex B Parties without adequate inventories, these rules should not establish requirements beyond those needed to ensure the environmental integrity of the Protocol. As is discussed above, the Protocol defines requirements and characteristics for the CDM that are not specified for Annex B JI, such as the CDM sustainable development objective. Because of these additional goals, the Protocol has defined a more extensive administrative structure (e.g., the CDM Executive Board, Operational Entities, etc.). Tying CDM rules and requirements and administrative processes other than those associated with the evaluation of project additionality to Annex B JI could unnecessarily increase the bureaucratic hurdles for Annex B JI projects and could delay implementation of either or both of these mechanisms.

6   CONCLUSIONS

Both Annex B JI and IET enable Annex B Parties to achieve a portion of their commitment under the Kyoto Protocol through the acquisition of emission reductions generated by other Annex B Parties. Two key factors that distinguish Annex B JI from IET as currently defined in the Protocol are (1) Annex B JI transactions must be linked to specific projects that have the approval of the Parties involved, and (2) Annex B JI projects are subject to an additionality requirement. Since the Protocol does not apply these restrictions to Article 17, IET offers more flexibility than Annex B JI and may be selected as the mechanism of choice among Annex B Parties with the capacity to participate in IET. Ultimately, the level of flexibility associated with participation in Annex B JI and IET will depend on how the rules and guidelines for these mechanisms are defined.

International negotiators have proposed two approaches for establishing the additionality rules for Article 6. Under the *first* approach, the same additionality rules would apply to both Annex B JI and CDM projects. However, the additionality requirement does not operate in the same context under Article 6 and Article 12. Annex B JI projects can be considered additional if the transfer of ERUs from the host Party to another Party does not prevent the host Party from meeting its emission reduction commitment. Therefore, project additionality can be assessed on the basis of the host Party's commitment and national GHG inventory, assuming the national GHG inventory meets the requirements in Articles 5 and 7. Since non-Annex B Parties have not agreed to emission reduction targets, there is no process whereby the export of non-additional credits is detected other than by evaluating the additionality of each project and project-level monitoring.

If the rule for evaluating project additionality is the same for both Annex B JI and CDM projects, Annex B investors would have little incentive to participate in Annex B JI and would likely favor investment in IET to avoid the additionality rules and associated transaction costs. This is not a problem from the perspective of the international community. However, some Annex B Parties may want to have the flexibility to participate in both Annex B JI and IET, and thus may want to ensure that Annex B JI transactions are not burdened with requirements other than those necessary to ensure the environmental integrity to the Protocol. These countries would likely prefer the second approach for defining the Annex B JI. The second approach would establish a two-tiered system for testing project additionality.

- For Parties with adequate inventories, project baselines and additionality would be determined by the Parties involved in the project, based on their own internal criteria and evaluation process. Such Parties would have an incentive to conduct an internal assessment of the additionality of Annex B JI projects to ensure compliance with their Kyoto commitment. However, review and validation of project additionality by independent entities would not be necessary.
- For Parties without adequate inventories, project additionality and baselines would need to be validated by independent entities. In these cases, the criteria and rules for evaluating project additionality would be the same as those established under the CDM.

The two-tiered approach would offer the advantage of ensuring that the level of stringency of the additionality requirement for Parties without adequate GHG inventories remains consistent with what is needed to preserve the integrity of the Kyoto commitments without overburdening Parties with adequate inventories.

10 The Way Forward?
Design Principles for Annex B Trading

Suzi Kerr

International trading of assigned amount units among Annex B parties is not only feasible but could be relatively simple and effective. Most of the perceived problems are really related to the Protocol as a whole (e.g. compliance concerns or hot air), or are unlikely to eventuate in a simple flexible market (e.g. market power or limitations on access for some parties). We conclude that the best system would involve a conceptually simple tracking system, similar to an extremely simplified form of the international banking system. The complexities in this system would be technical not political or institutional and are familiar to those who trade currency, bonds or shares. The units traded would be homogeneous; every AAU would be equivalent. The actual organization of exchange mechanisms and market design would be left to the private sector and only regulated in the way commodity or financial markets are regulated. International attention could be focused on the critical area of compliance with the Protocol as a whole.

The ultimate goal of the Kyoto Protocol is to make progress in reaching an environmental objective. Environmental effectiveness requires that countries are accountable for their compliance with the targets they accepted. Compliance is not primarily a trading issue but is the major issue that will determine the success or failure of the international effort. The main policies to promote compliance directly will be independent of trading: monitoring, reporting and compliance procedures. In addition, in every aspect of trading, and design of the institutions for the agreement in general, we need to bear in mind the effects of our decisions on compliance and hence environmental effectiveness.

A second goal is to achieve environmental goals at the lowest economic and social cost possible. This is of direct concern because climate policies involve real resource costs that must be traded against the environmental benefits gained. It is also of indirect concern, as lower costs will facilitate compliance and willingness to cooperate further. Because the Protocol is negotiated and voluntary, the costs of compliance may not only affect current welfare but also the stringency of future environmental targets chosen. Efficiency requires that the private sector be actively engaged in seeking and implementing emission reduction activities. To do this effectively they must face a reasonably stable investment environment with relatively simple and predictable regulatory requirements. This allows them to make long-term investment plans.

In addition, effective international trading can potentially lower costs dramatically by focusing effort on the lowest cost abatement opportunities. For trading to work well, transaction costs must be low, and all actors must have competitive access to the market. Domestic regulations must be defined, as far as possible, to facilitate seamless interaction of legal-entities with the international market. A flexible Annex B emissions market could potentially involve an enormous volume of trade as states and sub-state actors continuously respond to new information and opportunities. An active competitive market will provide useful price signals, will allow the development of derivatives such as futures and options and will allow buyers at the state and sub-state level to comply in a flexible way. Trading can also provide an effective mechanism for the transfer of technology between private actors.

The lower costs that trading brings will facilitate compliance. Lower costs increase buyers' capabilities to comply and reduce their incentives to non-comply. Greater profits and hence lower overall costs of compliance for sellers encourage their continuing participation and make the threat of withdrawing trading rights a powerful penalty. At the same time, trading creates the risk of overselling. In addition, with large uncertainties in measurement of some gases and sources, particularly gases other than CO_2, trading can either help or hinder compliance depending in part on whether these gases are most important in buyer or seller countries. Joint Implementation or project-based trading raises specific issues for compliance when the seller countries do not have adequate inventories. Each project must show that the emission reduction units claimed are 'additional' in the sense that they represent real reductions relative to business as usual. This requires international rules and assessment. Allowing multiple gas and Annex B JI trading, however, can further lower costs. In general, we must be careful not to restrict all actors because of possible concerns with a minority. Unreliable actors or actors with serious capability problems can be dealt with as special cases through Annex B JI, or through rules that apply only voluntarily or in the second commitment period if non-compliance has been egregious.

A direct cost of the Protocol is the cost of administration. Some trading-related compliance regimes, such as buyer liability or compliance reserves, require complex monitoring and tracking. Proposals aimed at forcing domestic action and commitment to the treaty such as 'supplementarity' or aimed at avoiding additional emissions from the 'hot air' created by the collapse of some economies in transition would have limited effectiveness and high cost both directly and in terms of the precedents they create. Some proposals have been put forward to avoid some countries using their political and economic power to affect the market. For example there are proposals that all trades must go through open transparent exchanges. These are well intentioned but may be unnecessary and will almost certainly be ineffective. Other proposals are aimed at controlling domestic policy either by requiring certain policies and measures, such as energy efficiency standards, or banning others, such as grandfathering of AAUs. While they may have value and justification, the costs of the intrusion and reduced flexibility are probably not worth the uncertain gains. Any of these limitations on trading impose high costs on the international community and the monitored states. They tend to raise complexity, which increases uncertainty, reduces transparency, raises trading costs and tends to reduce trading efficiency. To be truly effective, the trading rules need to be as simple as possible without sacrificing integrity.

The dynamics of institutional design are important for the climate effort. In the early years of the program, building confidence that others will participate fairly and that the environmental goals will be reached is critical. The Kyoto Protocol is the most ambitious international environmental treaty ever created. The international emissions trading system is the first on this scale. This means that there is a lot of uncertainty about how countries will comply with the Protocol and how trading will operate. What can we do early? We recommend designing and implementing all components of the agreement as early as possible to reduce uncertainty and gain experience with the mechanisms. In particular early completion of inventories, early establishment of trading registries and clarification of compliance rules would be clearly valuable. Pilot trading programs based on the established international rules could be created for a sub-group of countries before 2008 with voluntary targets that are more generous than the Kyoto allocations. Credits used in these programs would not be bankable for the Kyoto period but the early action would have domestic and international benefits through learning and increased investment certainty.

The potential for trading has created some concerns about fairness. For example some parties are concerned about market power, which could mean that some parties benefit disproportionately from trading. We consider that this is unlikely to be of great significance in Annex B trading though it may be important if global trading ever becomes effective. Trading can actually reduce fairness problems relating to competitiveness in product markets when countries face different levels of regulatory stringency. By experimenting early with trading and by having a simple trading system we will be able to learn which perceived concerns are real concerns either in terms of fairness or compliance. Then, with flexible institutions we can address the real concerns but avoid fighting phantom demons. If we make the system restrictive from the beginning we will never know if the restrictions were justified.

We must trade off increasing confidence in individual trades in the early years through restrictions on trade that risk high costs and an inactive market, against having simple rules that allow development of an active liquid market earlier but trust to overall compliance measures and market pressures to avoid invalid trades or manipulation of the trading system. We would push for a simple market with strong emphasis on overall compliance for traders and non-traders. Concerns about compliance need to be addressed primarily through the overall Protocol mechanisms. We believe that many of the perceived trading risks will not eventuate in a simple but well designed market and that if compliance is a general problem, limiting trading will hurt not help.

Appendix 1: Annex B Countries, Commitments and 1990 Emissions of Key Gases (in Gg of CO_2 equivalent)

	CO_2	CH_4	N_2O	Total	% commit-ment	AAUs[1]
Australia	275,344	112,236	23,216	410,796	108	443,660
Austria[2]	62,042	9,655	2,030	73,727	87	64,142
Belgium	116,090	13,314	9,539	138,943	92.5	128,522
Bulgaria	84,405	29,820	9,207	123,432	92	113,557
Canada	461,250	73,500	55,800	590,550	94	555,117
Croatia[3]					95	
Czech Rep.	165,490	16,349	7,998	189,837	92	174,650
Denmark	52,277	8,841	10,540	71,658	79	56,610
Estonia	37,797	2,209	713	40,719	92	37,461
Finland	59,200	7,520	5,766	72,486	100	72,486
France	395,506	63,489	94,581	553,576	100	553,576
Germany	1,014,501	116,990	69,626	1,201,117	79	948,882
Greece	85,349	9,179	9,269	103,797	125	129,746
Hungary	71,673	11,437	3,519	86,628	94	81,430
Iceland	2,147	294	130	2,571	110	2,828
Ireland	30,719	17,038	9,105	56,861	113	64,253
Italy	432,607	49,319	50,964	532,890	93.5	498,252

[1] AAUs are approximate, they do not include all gases or sinks.
[2] The % commitment for EU states is based on the Burden Sharing Agreement. The total EU commitment is 92%. Source for BSA: Community Strategy on Climate Change–Council Conclusions 3 March 1997.
[3] No data is available for Croatia.
Source: http://www.unfccc.de

(Appendix 1 (continued))

	CO_2	CH_4	N_2O	Total	% commit -ment	AAUs[1]
Japan	1,124,532	32,400	18,090	1,175,022	94	1,104,521
Latvia	24,771	3,913	6,984	35,669	92	32,815
Liechtenstein	208	21	31	260	92	239
Lithuania	39,535	7,937	4,077	51,548	92	47,424
Luxembourg	12,750	502	197	13,448	72	9,683
Monaco	108	1	1	111	92	102
Netherlands	161,360	27,138	19,809	208,307	94	195,809
New Zealand	25,241	35,145	11,503	71,889	100	71,889
Norway	35,202	6,657	5,270	47,129	101	47,600
Poland	380,697	58,821	19,530	459,048	94	431,505
Portugal	47,123	16,979	4,340	68,442	127	86,921
Romania	172,510	41,500	15,096	229,105	92	210,777
Russia	2,372,300	556,500	69,967	2,998,767	100	2,998,767
Slovakia	60,032	8,589	3,875	72,496	92	66,696
Slovenia	13,935	3,701	1,576	19,212	92	17,675
Spain	226,423	45,806	29,203	301,431	115	346,646
Sweden	55,443	5,964	8,060	69,467	104	72,246
Switzerland	45,070	5,114	3,565	53,749	92	49,449
UK	584,171	76,371	66,100	726,642	87.5	635,812
Ukraine	703,792	197,448	17,980	919,220	100	919,220
United States	4,928,900	622,860	351,230	5,902,990	93	5,489,781

[1] AAUs are approximate, they do not include all gases or sinks.
Source: http:www.unfccc.de

Appendix 2:   100-Year Global Warming Potentials for Selected Greenhouse Gases

Gas	GWP
Carbon dioxide (CO_2)	1
Methane (CH_4)	21
Nitrous oxide (N_2O)	310
Hydrofluorocarbon (HFC-23)	11,700
HFC-32	650
HFC-41	150
HFC-43-10mee	1,300
HFC-125	2,800
HFC-134	1,000
HFC-134a	1,300
HFC-143	300
HFC-143a	3,800
HFC-152a	140
HFC-227ea	2,900
HFC-236fa	6,300
HFC-245ea	560
Perfluoromethane (CF_4)	6,500
Perfluoroethane (C_2F_6)	9,200
Perfluoropropane (C_3F_8)	7,000
Perfluorobutane (C_4F_{10})	7,000
Perfluorocyclobutane (c-C_4F_8)	8,700
Perfluoropentane (C_5F_{12})	7,500
Perfluorohexane (C_6F_{14})	7,400
Sulfur hexafluoride (SF_6)	23,900

Source: IPCC (1996a), *Climate Change 1995: The Science of Climate Change – Contribution of Working Group I to the Second Assessment Report of the IPCC*, NY: Cambridge University Press, p. 121.

Appendix 3:   Key Climate Websites

Intergovernmental Panel on Climate Change:
www.ipcc.ch

MIT Joint Program on the Science and Policy of Global Change:
web.mit.edu/globalchange

Organisation for Economic Cooperation and Development:
www.oecd.org/env/cc

Resources for the Future – Weathervane:
www.weathervane.rff.org

United Nations Framework Convention on Climate Change:
www.unfccc.de

United States Environmental Protection Agency:
www.epa.gov/ghginfo

Glossary

Allowance: Any unit that allows one unit of CO_2 equivalent emissions. Commonly used in the context of domestic trading program (e.g., the US Acid Rain Program).

AIJ: Activities Implemented Jointly – This is the Pilot trading program that is evolving into Joint Implementation for Annex B states and the Clean Development Mechanism for developing countries. Confusingly it is often referred to as Joint Implementation.

Annex B Countries: Those that have agreed to quantified emission limitations in Article 3 of the Kyoto Protocol. See Appendix 1. Also often referred to as Annex I because they are almost equivalent groups.

Annex I Countries: These are the same group as Annex B except that they also include Turkey and Belarus and do not include Croatia, Monaco, Liechtenstein or Slovenia. Annex I countries agreed in the Convention to return their emissions to 1990 levels by 2000.

Assigned Amounts: The total amount of greenhouse gas emissions that each Annex B country has agreed that its emissions will not exceed in the first commitment period. This is equal to 1990 emissions multiplied by 5 and then by the percentage agreed to as listed in Annex B of the Kyoto Protocol. This combines all different gases weighted by their greenhouse warming potentials.

AAU: Assigned Amount Unit – Generally defined as one metric ton of CO_2 equivalent emissions. Can be used to meet international emissions reduction obligations.

BAU: Business-As-Usual – What would occur in the absence of any policy action. For example, business-as-usual emissions are projections of the emissions levels that would occur if a country makes no efforts to reduce.

CDM: Clean Development Mechanism – Defined in Article 12 of the Kyoto Protocol. It is intended to promote sustainable development in developing countries while allowing more flexibility in the achievement of Annex B targets. Part of the proceeds is to be used to assist developing countries that are vulnerable to the adverse effects of climate change. It allows a form of trading of emissions reductions between developing countries and Annex B.

CER: Certified Emission Reduction. A unit of CO_2 equivalent created through emission reductions or sequestration in non-Annex B countries and traded through the Clean Development Mechanism.

CO_2 Equivalent: The quantity of a given gas that would cause the same amount of radiative forcing as a given quantity of CO_2. These are calculated by the Intergovernmental Panel on Climate Change (see also Global Warming Potential).

Commitment Period: Time period over which countries' commitments are defined. The first 'commitment period' is 2008–2012. All emissions within this period are treated equally.

Conference of the Parties (COP): The group of states that has ratified or acceded to the FCCC. The subset of these who are also Parties to the Kyoto Protocol will make decisions on Kyoto related issues in the interim. A similar group, the Meeting of Parties (MOP) will be the supreme body of the Kyoto Protocol when it comes into force. Only the MOP can make amendments to the Protocol.

ERU: Emission Reduction Unit – Units created through Joint Implementation. Measured in tons of CO_2 equivalent.

EU: European Union.

'Flex mechs': The three different economic mechanisms available for trading within the Kyoto Protocol: Annex B trading, Joint Implementation and the Clean Development Mechanism. Also known as Kyoto mechanisms.

FSU: Former Soviet Union.

GHG: Greenhouse Gas.

Grandfathering: Allocating allowance within a country for free on the basis of past activity.

GWP: Global Warming Potential – used to translate other gases into CO_2 equivalents. CO_2 has a global warming potential of 1. See Appendix 2.

Hot Air: AAUs allocated to Eastern Europe and the Former Soviet Union that are likely to be in excess relative to their business-as-usual emissions.

IET: International Emissions Trading – refers to trading among Annex B states where trades are based on national assigned amounts rather than being associated with specific abatement projects. Defined in Article 17 of the Kyoto Protocol.

IEA: International Energy Agency.

IPCC: Intergovernmental Panel on Climate Change – A body created by the World Meteorological Organization in 1988. Their charge is to provide high-quality, unbiased, and policy-relevant syntheses of knowledge concerning the science of climate change and its potential impacts and also the socio-economic consequences of climate change and greenhouse gas limitation policies.

ITQ: International Transferable Quota – refers to assigned amount units held and traded by governments.[1] Confusingly, also stands for Individual Transferable Quota in the context of tradable quota in fisheries management.

JI: Joint Implementation – Project-based trading among Annex B states, defined in Article 6 of the Kyoto Protocol.

'Kyoto': The Kyoto Protocol to the Convention on Climate Change, negotiated in Kyoto, Japan in December, 1997.

Legal-entities: Any non-state entity. Usually refers to entities that are devolved the obligation to reduce emissions or the right to trade AAUs by their domestic governments.

MCP: Multilateral Consultative Process – body established to resolve questions regarding implementation of the Convention.

NGO: Non-Governmental Organization. These include environmental and social activist groups and industry/business groups as well as academic groups.

PAA: Parts of Assigned Amounts (see also AAU).

PAMs: Policies And Measures: used here to primarily refer to any mitigation policies other than permit markets. For example, efficiency standards, labeling requirement.

Permits = quotas = allowances.

Sub-state actors: See legal-entities. Sometimes also refers to Non-Governmental Organizations.

Supplementarity: The Kyoto Protocol states that emissions trading is to be supplemental to domestic action. The exact definition of supplementarity is unclear. It refers to ideas that the use of trading to meet commitments should be explicitly limited to ensure a given level of domestic action.

UNCTAD: United National Conference on Trade and Development.

UNDP: United Nations Development Program.

UNEP: United Nations Environment Program.

UNFCCC: United Nations Framework Convention on Climate Change.

USEPA: United States Environmental Protection Agency.

USDOE: United States Department of Energy.

WTO: World Trade Organization.

---

[1] See Stavins (2000), Tietenberg et al. (1998) and Joshua (1998).

References

Ackerman, B. and R. Stewart (1985), 'Reforming Environmental Law', *Stanford Law Review*, **37**, 1333–1365.

Adams, J. (1998), 'Environmental Policy and Competitiveness in a Globalized Economy: Conceptual Issues and a Review of the Empirical Evidence', in *Globalization and Environment: Preliminary Perspectives*, OECD, Paris.

Annala, J. (1996), 'New Zealand's ITQ system: Have the First Eight Years been a Success or a Failure', *Reviews in Fish Biology and Fisheries*, **6**, 43–62.

Ausubel, J. H. and D. G. Victor (1992), 'Verification of International Environmental Agreements', *Annual Review of Energy and Environment*, **17**, 1–43.

Ballard C. L., J. B. Shoven and J. Whalley (1985), 'General Equilibrium Computations of the Marginal Welfare Costs of Taxes in the United States', *American Economic Review*, **75**, 128–138.

Barker, T. and J. Köhler (1998), *International Competitiveness and Environmental Policies*, Cheltenham, UK: Edward Elgar.

Baron, R. (1999a), 'An Assessment of Liability Rules for International GHG Emissions Trading', OECD and IEA Project for the Annex I Expert Group on the UNFCC, IEA, Paris.

Baron, R. (1999b), 'Market Power and Market Access in International GHG Emissions Trading', IEA Information Paper, Energy and Environment Division, IEA, Paris, October.

Becker, G. S. (1968), 'Crime and Punishment: An Economic Analysis', *Journal of Political Economy*, **76** (2), 169–217.

Ben-David, S., D. S. Brookshire, S. Burness, M. McKee and C. Schmidt (1999), 'Heterogeneity, Irreversible Production Choices, and Efficiency in Emission Permit Markets', *Journal of Environmental Economics and Management*, **38** (2), 176–195.

Benedick, R. E. (1991), *Ozone Diplomacy, New Directions in Safeguarding the Planet*, Cambridge, MA: Harvard University Press.

Bernstein, P. M., D. W. Montgomery, T. F. Rutherford and G-F. Yang (1999), 'Effects of Restrictions on International Permit Trading: The MS-MRT Model', in Weyant, J. P. (ed), *The Costs of the Kyoto Protocol: A multi-model evaluation*, The Energy Journal, Kyoto Special Edition, pp. 221–256.

Bohm, P. (1994), 'On the feasibility of joint implementation of carbon emissions reductions', Presented to the IPCC Workshop on Policy Instruments and their Impacts, Tsukuba, Japan, January 17–20.

Bohm, P. (1998), 'Benefits of International Carbon Emissions Trading, Theory and Experimental Evidence', Draft Manuscript, University of Stockholm.

Bohm, P. and B. Carlén (1999), 'Emission Quota Trade Among the Few: Laboratory Evidence of Joint Implementation Among Committed Countries', *Resources and Energy Economics*, **21**, 43–66.

Boltho, A. (1996), 'The Assessment: International Competitiveness', *Oxford Review of Economic Policy*, **12** (3), 1–16.

Bovenberg, A. L. (1997), 'Environmental Policy, Distortionary Labour Taxation and Employment: Pollution Taxes and the Double Dividend', in Carraro, C. and D. Siniscalco (eds), *New Directions in the Economic Theory of the Environment,* Cambridge, UK: Cambridge University Press.

Bovenberg, A. L and L. H Goulder (1996), 'Optimal Environmental Taxation in the Presence of Other Taxes: General Equilibrium Analysis', *American Economic Review*, September.

Braithwaite, J. (1985), *To Punish or Persuade: Enforcement of Coal Mine Safety*, Albany, NY: State University of New York Press.

Brower, M. (1992), *Cool Energy*, Cambridge, MA: MIT Press.

Brown, J. P. (1973), 'Toward an Economic Theory of Liability', *Journal of Legal Studies*, **2** (2), 323–349.

Burniaux, J. M. (1999), 'How Important is Market Power in Achieving Kyoto? An Assessment based on the GREEN Model', Economics directorate, OECD, Paris.

Burtraw, D. (1996), 'The SO_2 Emission Trading Program: Cost Savings without Allowance Trades', *Contemporary Economic Policy*, **14** (April).

Burtraw, D., C. Carlson, M. Cropper and K. Palmer (1996), 'SO_2 Control by Electric Utilities: What are the Gains from Trade?', Presented at the National Bureau of Economic Research Summer Institute, July.

Calabresi, G. (1970), *Costs of Accidents*, New Haven, CT: Yale University Press.

Carlén, B. (1998), 'Effects of Dominant Countries on a Tradable Quota Market for Carbon Emissions: a Laboratory Test', Department of Economics, Stockholm University. Draft.

Carter, L. (1997), 'Modalities for the Operationalization of Additionality', Presentation at the International Workshop on Activities Implemented Jointly, Leipzig, Germany, 5–6 March.

Center for Clean Air Policy (CCAP) (1999), 'Draft Specifications for Language to Implement International Emissions Trading and Realted Compliance Procedures Pursuant to Articles 5, 7, 8, 17 and 18 of the Kyoto Protocol', Submitted to the United Nations Framework Convention on Climate Change, October 1999.

Chayes, A. and A. H. Chayes (1993), 'On Compliance', *International Organization*, **47** (Spring), 175–205.

Chichilnisky, G. (1997), 'Development and Global Finance: The Case for an International Bank for Environmental Settlements', Discussion Paper Series No. 10, Office of Development Studies, United Nations Development Programme (UNDP).

Cline, W. (1992), *The Economics of Global Warming*, Washington, DC: Institute of International Economics.

Christiansen, G. and T. Tietenberg (1985), 'Distributional and Macroeconomic Aspects of Environmental Policy', in Kneese, A. and J. Sweeney (eds), *Handbook of Natural Resources and Energy Economics*, Vol. 1, Amsterdam: Elsevier Science Publishers, pp. 345–393.

Coase, R. H. (1937) 'The Nature of the Firm', *Economica*, **4** (N.S.), 386–405.

Coase, R. H. (1960), 'The Problem of Social Cost', *Journal of Law and Economy*, **3**, 1–44.

Coase, R. H. (1972), 'Durability and Monopoly', *Journal of Law and Economics*, **15**, 143–149.

Connolly, B. and R. O. Keohane (1996), 'Institutions for Environmental Aid: Politics, Lessons and Opportunities', *Environment* 38 (5).

Cooper, R. N. (1998), 'Toward a Real Global Warming Treaty', *Foreign Affairs,* **77** (2), 66–79.

Copeland, B. R. and M. S. Taylor (1999), 'Global Warming and Freer Trade: A Trade Theory View of the Kyoto Protocol', Presented at the NBER Summer Institute, August. Draft.

Corfee-Morlot, J. (1998a), 'Ensuring Compliance With a Global Climate Change Agreement', OECD Information Paper, Paris.

Corfee-Morlot, J. (1998b), 'Monitoring, Reporting and Review of National Performance under the UNFCCC and the Kyoto Protocol', OECD Information Paper, Paris.

Cramton, P. and S. Kerr (1998), 'A Tax-Cut Auction for the Environment: How and Why to Auction CO_2 Emissions Permits', Discussion Paper 98-34, Resources for the Future, Washington, DC.

Cramton, P. and S. Kerr (1999), 'The Distributional Effects of Carbon Regulation: Why Auctioned Carbon Permits are Attractive and Feasible', in T. Sterner (ed), *The Market and the Environment*, Cheltenham, UK: Edward Elgar, pp. 257–273.

Dales, J. (1968), *Pollution, Property and Prices*, Toronto: University Press.

Danish Energy Agency (1999), 'The Electricity Reform: Agreement between the Danish Government, the Liberal Party, the Conservative Party, the Socialist People's Party and the Christian People's Party on a legislative reform of the electricity sector', English Version.

de Mooij, R. A. (1999), 'The Double Dividend of an Environmental Tax Reform', in Bergh J. van den (ed), *Handbook of Environmental Land Resource Economics*, Cheltenham, UK: Edward Elgar.

Denne, T. (1999), 'Implementation issues in international CO_2 trading', in S. Sorrell and J. Skea, *Pollution for Sale: Emissions Trading and Joint Implementation,* Cheltenham, UK: Edward Elgar, pp. 343–353.

Diamond, P. A. (1974a), 'Single Activity Accidents', *Journal of Legal Studies*, **3** (1), 107–164.

Diamond, P. A. (1974b), 'Accident Law and Resource Allocation', *The Bell Journal of Economics and Management Science*, **5** (2), 366–406.

Diamond, P. A. and J. A. Mirrlees (1971), 'Optimal taxation and public production I: Production efficiency and II: Tax rules', *American Economic Review*, **61**, 8–27 and 261–278.

Diamond, P. A. and J. A. Mirrlees (1975), 'On the Assignment of Liability: The Uniform Case', *The Bell Journal of Economics*, **6** (2), 487–516.

Dixon, R. K. (1999), *The U.N. Framework Convention on Climate Change Activities Implemented Jointly (AIJ) Pilot: Experiences and Lessons Learned*, Boston, MA: Kluwer Academic Publishers.

Downs, G. W. (1998), 'Enforcement and the Evolution of Cooperation', *Michigan Journal of International Law*, **19**, 319.

Downs, G. W., D. M. Rocke and P. N. Barsoom (1996), 'Is the good news about compliance good news about cooperation?', *International Organisation*, **50** (3), 379–406.

Dudek, D. J. and J. B. Wiener (1996), *Joint Implementation, Transaction Costs and Climate Change*, Paris: OECD.

Ellerman, A. D., H. D. Jacoby and A. Decaux (1998), 'The Effects on Developing Countries of the Kyoto Protocol and Carbon Dioxide Emissions Trading', Policy Research Working Paper 2019, The World Bank Development Research Group, Infrastructure and Environment, December.

Ellerman, A. D. and I. S. Wing (2000), 'Supplementarity: An Invitation to Monopoly?', Report No. 59, MIT Joint Program on the Science and Policy of Global Change, MA, US, April.

European Commission (2000), 'Greenhouse Gas Emissions Trading Within the European Union', Working Paper COM (2000)87 (http://europa.eu.int/comm/environment/docum/0087_en.htm.)

Fischer, C. (1997), 'An Economic Analysis of Output-Based Allocation of Emissions Allowances', Resources for the Future, Washington, DC. Draft.

Fischer, C., S. Kerr and M. Toman (1998a), 'Using Emissions Trading to Regulate US Greenhouse Gas Emissions: An Overview of Policy Design and Implementation Issues', *National Tax Journal,* **3**, pp. 453–464.

Fischer, C., I. W. H. Parry and W. Pizer (1998b), 'Instrument Choice for Environmental Protection When Technological Innovation is Endogenous', Discussion Paper 99-04, Resources for the Future, Washington, DC.

Fischer, C., S. Kerr and M. Toman (1998c), 'Emissions Trading to Regulate U.S. Greenhouse Gas Emissions: Basic Policy Design and Implementation Issues: Parts 1 and 2', Climate Issue Briefs #10 and #11, Resources for the Future (http://www.rff.org/enviroment/climate.htm).

Fudenberg, D. and J. Tirole (1991), *Game Theory*, Cambridge, MA: MIT Press.

Fullerton, D. and S. West (1999), 'Tax and Subsidy Combinations for the Control of Car Pollution', Working Paper prepared for the Public Policy Institute of California, September.

Fullerton, D. and G. Metcalfe (2000), 'Environmental Controls, Scarcity Rents, and Pre-Existing Distortions', *Journal of Public Economics*, Forthcoming.

Godby, R. (1997), *The Effect of Market Power in Emission Permit Markets*, Ph.D. Thesis, McMaster University.

Godby, R. (1999), 'Market Power in Emission Permit Double Auctions', in R. M. Issac and C. Holt (eds), *Emission Permit Experiments: Research in Experimental Economics*, Vol. 7, Stanford, CA: JAI Press, pp. 121–162.

Godby, R., S. Mestelman and R. A. Muller (1999) 'Experimental Tests of Market Power in Emission Trading Markets', in E. Petrakis, E. Sartzetakis and A. Xepapadeas (eds), *Environmental Regulation and Market Power*, Cheltenham, UK: Edward Elgar.

Green, J. R. (1976), 'On the Optimal Structure of Liability Laws', *The Bell Journal of Economics*, **7** (2), 553–574.

Grossman, S. and O. Hart (1983), 'An Analysis of the Principal–Agent Problem', *Econometrica*, **51**, 7–45.

Grossman, G. M. and E. Helpman (1994), 'Protection for Sale', *American Economic Review*, September.

Grubb, M. (1998), 'International Emissions Trading Under the Kyoto Protocol: Core Issues in Implementation', Royal Institute of International Affairs, London.

Haas, P. M. (1989), 'Do regimes matter? Epistemic communities and Mediterranean pollution', *International Organization*, **43**, 377–403.

Haas, P. M. (1992), 'Banning chlorofluorocarbons: epistemic community efforts to protect stratospheric ozone', *International Organization*, **46**, 187–224.

Haas, P. M., R. O. Keohane and M. A. Levy (1993), *Institutions for the Earth: Sources of Effective International Environmental Protection*, Cambridge, MA: MIT Press.

Hagler, B. (1998), *Evaluation of Using Benchmarks to Satisfy the Additionality Criterion for Joint Implementation Projects*, Boulder, CO: Hagler Bailly.

Hahn, R. W. (1984), 'Market Power and Transferable Property Rights', *Quarterly Journal of Economics*, **99**, 753–765.

Hahn, R. W. (1989), 'Economic Prescriptions for Environmental Problems: How the Patient Followed the Doctor's Orders', *Journal of Economic Perspectives*, **3**, 95–114.

Hahn, R. W. (1998), *Climate Change: Economics, Politics and Policy*, Washington, D.C: American Enterprise Institute.

Hahn, R. W and G. Hester (1989), 'Where Did All the Markets Go? An Analysis of EPA's Emissions Trading Program', *Yale Journal on Regulation*, **6**, 109–153.

Hahn, R. W. and G. L. Hester (1989), 'Marketable Permits: Lessons for Theory and Practice', *Ecology Law Quarterly,* **16**, 380–391.

Hahn, R. W. and R. N. Stavins (1992), 'Economic Incentives for Environmental Protection: Integrating Theory and Practice', *American Economic Review*, **82** (2), 464–468.

Hahn, R. W. and R. N. Stavins (1995), 'Trading in Greenhouse Permits: A Critical Examination of Design and Implementation Issues,' in H. Lee, (ed), *Shaping National Responses to Climate Change: A Post-Rio Policy Guide*, Cambridge, MA : Island Press, pp. 177–217.

Hahn, R. W. and R. N. Stavins (1999), 'The Real Architecture of International Tradable Allowance Markets', Discussion Paper 99-30, Resources for the Future, Washington, DC.

Haites, E. (1998), 'International Emissions Trading and Compliance with Greenhouse Gas Emissions Limitation Commitments', Working Paper for IAE Policy Dialogue, *International Emissions Trading under the Kyoto Protocol: Rules, Procedures and the Participation of Domestic Entities*, International Academy of the Environment, Geneva, 6–7 September 1998.

Hamwey, R. and F. Szekely (1998), 'Practical approaches in the energy sector', in Goldemberg, J. (ed), *Issues & Options: The Clean Development Mechanism*, United Nations Development Programme, New York.

Hanley, N., J. F. Shogren and B. White (1997), *Environmental Economics In Theory and Practice*, New York: Oxford University Press.

Hargrave, T. (1997), 'U.S. Greenhouse Gas Emissions Trading: Description of an Upstream Approach', Airlie Papers, Centre for Clean Air Policy, Washington, DC, September.

Hargrave, T. (1998), 'Preconditions for Participation in International Greenhouse Gas Emissions Trading', Center for Clean Air Policy, Washington, DC. Draft.

Hargrave, T., N. Helme, and I. Puhl (1998), 'Options for Simplifying Baseline Setting for Joint Implementation and Clean Development Mechanism Projects', Center for Clean Air Policy, Washington, DC.

Hargrave, T., N. Helme, T. Denne, S. Kerr and J. Lefevere (1999a), 'Design of a Practical Approach to Greenhouse Gas Emissions Trading Combined with Policies and Measures in the EC', Centre for Clean Air Policy, Washington, DC. (http://www.ccap.org/pdf/Ectrading.pdf.)

Hargrave, T., S. Kerr, N. Helme, and T. Denne (1999b), 'Defining Kyoto Protocol Non-Compliance Procedures and Mechanisms', Leiden International Emissions Trading Papers, Center for Clean Air Policy, Washington, DC.

Harvey, R. de la Chesnaye, F. and S. Laitner (1999), 'The Cost-Effective Emission Reduction Potential of Non-Carbon Dioxide Greenhouse Gases within the United States and Abroad', Presented at IEA International Workshop on Technologies to Reduce Greenhouse Gas Emissions: Engineering-Economic Analysis of Conserved Energy and Carbon, 5–7 May, 1999, Washington, DC, USA.

Harrington, W. (1988), 'Enforcement Leverage When Penalties are Restricted', *Journal of Public Economics*, **37**, 29–53.

Harrison, D. (1997), *Considerations in Designing and Implementing an Effective International Greenhouse Gas Trading Program*, Cambridge, MA: National Economic Research Associates.

Hawkins, K. (1984), *Environment and Enforcement: Regulation and the Social Definition of Pollution*, Oxford, UK: Clarendon Press.

Hayhoe, K., A. Jain, H. Pitcher, C. MacCracken, M. Gibbs, D. Wuebbles, R. Harvey and D. Kruger (1999), 'Costs of Multigreenhouse Gas Reduction Targets for the USA', *Science*, **286**, 905–906.

Herold, A. and R. Juelich (1998), *Monitoring and Verification Under the Kyoto Protocol*, Freiburg, Germany: Öko-Institut.

Hizen, Y. and T. Saijo (1998), 'Designing GHG Emissions Trading Institutions in the Kyoto Protocol: An Experimental Approach', Graduate School of Economics, Osaka University.

Holmström, B. (1982), 'Moral Hazard in Teams', *Bell Journal of Economics* **13**, 324–340.

Holmström, B. and P. Milgrom (1990), 'Regulating Trade Among Agents', *Journal of Institutional and Theoretical Economics*, **146**, 85–105.

Houghton, J. T., L. G. M. Filho, B. Callander and N. Harris (1996), *Climate Change 1995: The Science of Climate Change*, Cambridge, UK: Cambridge University Press.

Houghton, J. T., L. G. M. Filho, B. Lim, K. Treanton, I. Mamaty, Y. Bonduki, D. J. Griggs and B. A. Callender (1999), 'Intergovernmental Panel on Climate Change (IPCC)/Organisation for Economic Co-operation and Development (OECD)/International Energy Agency (IEA), Revised IPCC Guidelines for National Greenhouse Gas Inventories', Bracknell, UK: UK Meteorological Office (available from IPCC Secretariat).

Intergovernmental Negotiating Committee (INC) (1994), 'Consideration of the Establishment of a Multilateral Consultative Process for the Resolution of Questions Regarding Implementation (Article 13): Note by the Interim Secretariat', IPCC Secretariate, Montreal, Canada, 26 July.

IPCC (1996a), 'Climate Change 1995: The Science of Climate Change', in J. P. Houghton, L. G. M. Filho, B. A. Callendar, A. Kattenberg and K. Maskell (eds), *The Contribution of Working Group I to the Second Assessment Report of the Intergovernmental Panel on Climate Change*, New York: Cambridge University Press.

IPCC (1996b), 'Climate Change 1995: Impacts, Adaptations and Mitigation of Climate Change: Scientific-Technical Analyses', in Watson, R. T. M. C. Zinyowera, R. H. Moss and D. J. Dokken, *Contribution of Working Group II to the Second Assessment Report of the Intergovernmental Panel on Climate Change*, New York: Cambridge University Press.

IPCC (1996c), 'Climate Change 1995: Economic and Social Dimensions of Climate Change' in J. P. Bruce, H. Lee and E. F. Haites (eds), *Contribution of Working Group III to the Second Assessment Report of the IPCC*, New York: Cambridge University Press.

IPCC (1999), 'Good Practice Guidance and Uncertainty Management in National Greenhouse Gas Inventories', For Government/Expert Review, Intergovernmental Panel on Climate Change (IPCC), IPCC Secretariate, Montreal, Canada, December. Draft.

Isaac, R. M. and C. Holt (1999), *Emission Permit Experiments: Research in Experimental Economics*, Vol. 7, Stanford, CA: JAI Press

Jackson, T. (1995), 'Joint Implementation and Cost-effectiveness under the Framework Convention on Climate Change', *Energy Policy*, **23** (2), 117–138.

Jacobson, H. K. and E. B. Weiss (1995), 'Strengthening Compliance with International Environmental Accords: Preliminary Observations from a Collaborative Project', *Global Governance,* **1** (2), 119–148.

Jacoby, H. D., R. G. Prinn and R. Schmalensee (1998), 'Kyoto's Unfinished Business', *Foreign Affairs,* **77** (4), 54–66.

Jaffe, A. B. and R. N. Stavins (1995), 'Dynamic Incentives of Environmental Regulations: the Effects of Alternative Policy Instruments on Technology Diffusion', *Journal of Environmental Economics and Management,* **29** (3), 43–63.

Jaffe, A. B., S. Peterson, P. Portney and R. Stavins (1995), 'Environmental Regulation and the Competitiveness of US Manufacturing: What Does the Evidence Tell Us?', *Journal of Economic Literature,* **XXXIII**, 132–163.

Jepma, C. (1999), 'Planned and Ongoing AIJ Pilot Projects', *Joint Implementation Quarterly,* **5** (3).

Jol, A. (1997), *Methods, Results and Current State-of-Play of the European CORINAIR Programme,* Copenhagen, Denmark: European Environment Agency.

Joshua, F. T. (1998), *International Greenhouse Gas Emissions Trading-Structure and Organisation of the Emissions market (Implications for Developing Countries),* Geneva: OECD.

Joskow, P. L. and R. Schmalensee (1998), 'The Political Economy of Market-Based Environmental Policy: The U.S. Acid Rain Program', *Journal of Law and Economics,* **41**, 81–135.

Joskow, P. L., R. Schmalensee and E. M. Bailey (1998), 'The Market for Sulfur Dioxide Emissions', *American Economic Review,* **88** (4).

Keohane, R. O. (1984), *After Hegemony: Cooperation and Discord in the World Political Economy,* Princeton, NJ: Princeton University Press.

Keohane, R. O. and M. A. Levy (1996), *Institutions for Environmental Aid,* Cambridge, MA: MIT Press.

Keohane, N. O., R. L. Revesz and R. N. Stavins (1999), 'The Positive Political Economy of Instrument Choice in Environmental Policy', in A. Panagariya, P. Portney and R. Schwab (eds), *Environmental and Public Economics,* Cheltenham, UK: Edward Elgar.

Kerr, S. (1995), 'Markets versus International Funds for Implementing International Environmental Agreements. Ozone Depletion and the Montreal Protocol', Working Paper No. 95-12, Center for International Affairs, Harvard University.

Kerr, S. and D. Maré (1999), 'Transaction Costs and Tradable Permit Markets: The United States Lead Phasedown', Motu Economic Research, New Zealand. Draft.

Kerr, S. (1996), 'Towards a Theory of Compliance Institutions in International Tradable Permit Markets: Joint Implementation of the Framework Convention on Climate Change', Working Paper 96-25, Department of Agricultural and Resource Economics, University of Maryland at College Park.

Kerr, S. (1998a), 'Enforcing Emissions Reductions: Allocating Liability in International Greenhouse Gas Emissions Trading and the Clean Development Mechanism', Climate Issues Brief No. 15, Resources for the Future, Washington, DC.

Kerr, S. (1998b), 'Enforcing Compliance, The Allocation of Liability in International GHG Emissions Trading and the Clean Development Mechanism', Climate Issue Brief No. 15, Resources for the Future, Washington, DC. (http://www.rff.org/environment/climate.htm).

Kerr, S. (1998c), 'Buyer vs. Seller Liability, Improving the Credibility of Clean Development Mechanism Credits', Resources for the Future, Washington, DC. Draft.

Kerr, S, T. Hargrave and N. Helme (1998), 'Policy Options For Addressing Compliance Issues Raised By Emissions Trading', Center for Clean Air Policy, Washington, DC. (http://www.ccap.org).

Kerr, S. and R. Newell (2000), 'Policy-Induced Technology Adoption: Evidence from the U.S. Lead Phasedown', Resources for the Future, Washington, DC. Draft.

Kerr, S. and A. Pfaff (2000), 'Measuring Carbon Sequestration Offsets: How Accurate Should We Be?', Columbia University, NY. Draft.

Klaasen, G. (1999), 'Emissions Trading in the European Union, Practice and Prospects', in S. Sorrell and J. Skea (eds), *Pollution for Sale: Emissions Trading and Joint Implementation*, Cheltenham, UK: Edward Elgar, pp. 83–100.

Klaasen, G. and A. Nentjes. (1997), 'Creating Markets for Air Pollution control in Europe and the USA', *Environmental and Resource Economics*, **10**, pp. 125–146.

Kopp, R., R. Morgenstern, W. Pizer and M. Toman (1999), 'A Proposal for Credible Early Action in US Climate Policy', Resources for the Future, Washington, DC.
(http://www.weathervane.rff.org/features/feature060.html).

Kreps, D. and R. Wilson (1982), 'Reputation and Imperfect Information', *Journal of Economic Theory*, **27**, 253–279.

Krugman, P. (1996), *Pop Internationalism*, Cambridge, MA: MIT Press.

Kuik, O. P. P. and N. Schrijver (1994), *Joint Implementation to Curb Climate Change: Legal and Economic Aspects*, Dordrecht, The Netherlands: Kluwer Academic Publishers.

Laffont, J-J. and J. Tirole (1993), *A Theory of Incentives in Procurement and Regulation*, Cambridge MA: MIT Press.

Lazarus, M., S. Kartha, M. Ruth, S. Bernow and C. Dunmire (1999), *Evaluation of Benchmarking as an Approach for Establishing Clean Development Mechanism Baselines*, Boston, MA: Tellus Institute.

Ledyard, J. O. and K. Szakaly-Moore (1994), 'Designing Organizations for Trading Pollution Rights', *Journal of Economic Behavior and Organization*, **25**, pp. 167–196.

Lile, R., M. Powell and M. Toman (1998), 'Implementing the Clean Development Mechanism: Lessons from U.S. Private-Sector Participation in Activities Implemented Jointly, Discussion Paper 99-08, Resources for the Future, Washington, DC.

Lind, R. C. and R. Schuler (1998), 'Equity and Discounting in Climate-Change Decisions', in W. D. Nordhaus (ed), *Economics and Policy Issues in Climate Change*, Washington, DC: Resources for the Future.

MacCracken, C. N., J. A. Edmonds, S. H. Kim and R. D. Sands (1999), 'The Economics of the Kyoto Protocol', in Weyant, J. P. (ed), *The Costs of the Kyoto Protocol: A multi-model evaluation*, The Energy Journal, Kyoto Special Edition, pp. 25–71.

Manne, A. S. and R. Richels (1999), 'The Kyoto Protocol: A Cost-Effective Strategy for Meeting Environmental Objectives?', in Weyant, J. P. (ed), *The Costs of the Kyoto Protocol: A multi-model evaluation*, The Energy Journal, Kyoto Special Edition, pp. 1–23.

Martin, L. L. (1993), 'Credibility, Costs, and Institutions: Cooperation on Economic Sanctions', *World Politics*, **45** (3), 406–432.

Matsuo, N. (1997), 'Key Elements Related to Emissions Trading for the Kyoto Protocol', The Institute of Energy Economics, Japan.

Mendelsohn, R. (1998), 'Climate-Change Damages', in W. D. Nordhaus (ed), *Economics and Policy Issues in Climate Change*, Washington, DC: Resources for the Future, pp. 219–236.

Milgrom, P. and J. Roberts (1982), 'Predation, Reputation and Entry Deterrence', *Journal of Economic Theory*, **27**, 280–312.

Misiolek, W. S. and H. W. Elder (1989), 'Exclusionary Manipulation of Markets for Pollution Rights', *Journal of Environmental Economics and Management*, **16**, 156–166.

Mitchell, R. B. (1994a), 'Regime Design Matters: Intentional Oil Pollution and Treaty Compliance', *International Organization*, **48** (3), 425–458.

Mitchell, R. B. (1994b), *Intentional Oil Pollution at Sea*, Cambridge, MA: MIT Press.

Mitchell, R. B. and A. Chayes (1995), 'Improving Compliance with the Climate Change Treaty', in Lee, H. (ed), *Shaping National Responses to Climate Change: A Post Rio Guide*, Washington, DC: Island Press.

Mitchell, R. B. (1996), 'Compliance Theory: an Overview', in Cameron, J., C. J. Werksman and P. Roderick (eds), *Improving Compliance with International Environmental Law*, London: Earthscan Publications.

Montero, J. P. (1997), 'Volunteering for Market-based Regulation: The Substitution Provision of the SO_2 Emissions Trading Program', Working Paper 97-001, MIT Centre for Energy and Environmental Policy Research, US.

Montero, J. P. and J. M. Sánchez (1999), 'A Market-Based Environmental Policy Experiment in Chile', Department of Industrial Engineering, Catholic University of Chile.

Montgomery, D. W. (1972), 'Markets in Licenses and Efficient Pollution Control Programs', *Journal of Economy Theory*, **5**, 395–418.

Moran, A. and J. E. Salt (1996), *Greenhouse Gas Inventories: National Reporting Processes and Implementation Review Mechanisms in the EU: CORINAIR and the IPCC*, Jülich, Germany: Forschungszentrum Jülich GmbH.

Morlot, J. C. (1998), 'Monitoring, Reporting and Review of National Performance under the UNFCCC and the Kyoto Protocol', OECD, Paris, 3 September. Draft.

Moulin, Hervé (1988), *Axioms of Cooperative Decision Making*, Econometric Society Monographs No. 15, New York: Cambridge University Press.

Moulton, R. and K. Richards (1990), 'Costs of Sequestering Carbon Through Tree Planting and Forest Management in the United States', General Technical Report WO58, US Department of Agriculture.

Muller, R. A. and S. Mestelman (1998), 'What have we Learned From Emissions Trading Experiments?', *Managerial and Decision Economics*, **19**, 225–238.

Mullins, F. (1998), 'Lessons from Existing Trading Systems for International Greenhouse Gas Emission Trading', Annex I Expert Group on UNFCCC Information Paper (http://www.oecd.org/env/cc/mechanisms.htm).

Mullins, F. and R. Baron (1997), 'International Greenhouse Gas Emission Trading', Annex I Expert Group on the UNFCCC Working paper No. 9 (OCDE/GD (97) 76), OECD, Paris.

New Zealand Ministry for the Environment (1997), *Climate Change and CO_2 Policy A Durable Response*, Discussion Paper of the Working Group on CO_2 Policy.

New Zealand Ministry for the Environment (1999), 'Climate Change: Domestic Policy Options Statement', Ministry of the Environment, New Zealand. Draft.

Newell, R. G., A. B. Jaffe and R. N. Stavins (1999), 'The Induced Innovation Hypothesis and Energy-Saving Technological Change', *Quarterly Journal of Economics*, **114** (3), 941–975.

Nordhaus, W. D. (1994), *Managing the Global Commons: The Economics of Climate Change*, Cambridge, MA and London: MIT Press.

Nordhaus, W. D. (1998), *Economics and Policy Issues in Climate Change*, Washington, DC: Resources for the Future.

OECD (1998), 'Reporting and Review of National Performance under the UNGCCC and the Kyoto Protocol: A Scoping Paper', OECD, Paris.

Ostrom, E. (1990), *Governing the Commons: The Evolution of Institutions for Collective Action*, Cambridge, UK: Cambridge University Press.

Palmisano, J. (1998), 'Buyer Liability for Greenhouse Gas Trading is Good for the Environment and Good for Emissions Trading', Enron International, Washington, DC.

Pape, A. and J. Rich (1998), 'Options for Guiding Greenhouse Gas Emission Baseline Determination', CERI Alberta Offset Development Workshop, Canada, 2–3 February.

Parry, I. W. (1995), 'Pollution Taxes and Revenue Recycling', *Journal of Environmental Economics and Management*, **29** (3), 64–77.

Parry, I. W. H., R. C. Williams and L. H. Goulder (1998), 'When Can Carbon Abatement Policies Increase Welfare? The Fundamental Role of Distorted Factor Markets', *Journal of Environmental Economics and Management*, **37** (1), 52-84.

Parson, E. A. and O. Greene (1995), 'The Complex Chemistry of the International Ozone Agreements', *Environment*, **37** (2), 16–43.

Parson, E. A. and D. W. Keith (1998), 'Fossil Fuels Without CO_2 Emissions', *Science*, **282**, 1053–1054.

Pearce, D. W. and R. K. Turner (1990), *Economics of Natural Resources and the Environment*, Baltimore, MA: Johns Hopkins.

Petrakis, E. and A. Xepapadeas (1996), 'Environmental Consciousness and Moral Hazard in International Agreements to Protect the Environment', *Journal of Public Economics*, **60**, 95–110.

Petricone, S., C. Figueres and R. Bradley (1995), 'Discussion White Paper: Joint Implementation', Presented at Hemispheric Energy Symposium, October 29–31.

Pizer, W. (1999), 'Choosing Price or Quantity Controls for Greenhouse Gases', Climate Issues Brief, Resources for the Future, Washington, DC. (http://www.rff.org/issue_briefs/PDF_files/ccbrf17.pdf).

Plott, C. R. (1989), 'An Updated Review of Industrial Organization: Applications of Experimental Methods', In Schmalensee, R. and R. D. Willig (eds), *Handbook of Industrial Organization*, Volume II, Amsterdam: North Holland, pp. 1109—1176.

Portney, P. (1998), 'Applicability of Cost-Benefit Analysis to Climate Change' in W. D. Nordhaus (ed), *Economics and Policy Issues in Climate Change*, Washington, DC: Resources for the Future.

Princen, T. and M. Finger (1994), *Environmental NGOs in World Politics: Linking the Local and the Global*, London: Routledge.

Puhl, I. (1998), 'Status of Research on Project Baselines under the UNFCCC and the Kyoto Protocol', OECD, Paris, France.

Puhl, I. and T. Hargrave (1998), 'Top-Down Baselines to Simplify the Setting of Project Emission Baselines for JI and CDM', Center for Clean Air Policy, Washington, DC.

Radunsky, K. and M. Ritter (1996), *CORINAIR 1990 Summary Report 3: Large Point Sources. Topic Report 20/96*, European Environment Agency, November, 2 (http://themes.eea.eu.int/showpage.php/state/air?pg=39781).

Raustiala, K., E. Skolnikoff and D. G. Victor (1998), *The Implementation and Effectiveness of International Environmental Commitments*, Cambridge, MA: MIT Press.

Rawls, J. (1971), *A Theory of Justice*, Cambridge, MA: Harvard University Press.

Reilly, J., R. Prinn, J. Harnisch, J. Fitzmaurice, H. Jacoby, D. Kicklighter, J. Melillo, P. Stone, A. Sokolov and C. Wang (1999), 'Multi-Gas Assessment of the Kyoto Protocol', *Nature*, **401**, 549–555.

Sandor, R. L., J. B. Cole and M. E. Kelly (1994), 'Model Rules and Regulations for a Global CO_2 Emissions Credit Market', in UNCTD, *Controlling Global Warming: Possible Rules, Regulations and Administrative Arrangements for a Global Market in CO_2 Emission Entitlements*, Part 2, United Nations Conference on Trade and Development (UNCTD), Geneva.

Schelling, T. C. (1980), *The Strategy of Conflict*, Cambridge, MA: Harvard University.

Schelling, T. C. (1998), 'The Cost of Combating Global Warming – Facing the Tradeoffs', *Foreign Affairs*, **76** (6), 8–14.

Schmalensee, R. (1998), 'Greenhouse Policy Architectures and Institutions', in W. D. Nordhaus (ed), *Economics and Policy Issues in Climate Change*, Washington, DC: Resources for the Future.

Schmalensee, R., P. L. Joskow, A. D. Ellerman, J. P. Montero and E. M. Bailey (1998), 'An Interim Evaluation of Sulfur Dioxide Emissions Trading', *Journal of Economic Perspectives*, **12** (3), 53–68.

Schmutzler, A. and L. H. Goulder (1997), 'The Choice between Emission Taxes and Output Taxes under Imperfect Monitoring', *Journal of Environmental Economics and Management*, **32** (1), 51–64.

Schwarze, R. (1999), 'Trading Emissions Among Nations: Are Governments Efficient Marketeers? Lessons from the AIJ-Pilotphase', Stanford University.

Sebenius, J. K. (1993), *Negotiating the Law of the Sea: Lessons in the Art and Science of Reaching Agreement*, Cambridge, MA: Harvard University Press.

Sebenius, J. K. (1995), 'Overcoming Obstacles to a Successful Climate Convention', in Henry Lee (ed), *Shaping National Responses to Climate Change*, Washington, DC: Island Press.

Shärer, B. (1994), 'Economic Incentives in Air Pollution Control: The Case of Germany', *European Environment*, **4** (3), 3–8.

Sierra Club (1995), 'Risky Business: Why Joint Implementation is the Wrong Approach to Global Warming Policy', Sierra Club, Washington, DC and Sierra Club of Canada, Ottawa, Ontario, Canada.

Smith, A. E., A. R Gjerde, L. I. DeLain and R. R. Zhang (1992), 'CO$_2$ Trading Issues: Volume 2: Choosing the Market Level for Trading', Decision Focus Incorporated, Report prepared for US EPA Office of Policy, Planning and Evaluation.

Stavins, R. N (1995), 'Transaction Costs and Tradable Permit Markets', *Journal of Environmental Economics and Management*, **29** (2), 133–148.

Stavins, R. N. (1997a), 'Policy Instruments for Climate Change: How Can National Governments Address a Global Problem', in *The University of Chicago Legal Forum*, pp. 293–329.

Stavins, R. N. (1998), 'What Can We Learn from the Grand Policy Experiment? Positive and Normative Lessons from SO$_2$ Allowance Trading,' *Journal of Economic Perspectives*, **12** (3), 69–88.

Stavins R. N. (1999), 'The Costs of Carbon Sequestration: A Revealed Preference Approach', *American Economic Review*, **89** (4), 994–1009.

Stavins, R. N. (2000), 'Experience with Market-based Environmental Policy Instruments', in K. Mäler and J. Vincent (eds), *The Handbook of Environmental Economics*, Amsterdam: Elsevier. Draft.

Susskind, L. E. (1994), *Environmental Diplomacy: Negotiating More Effective Global Agreements*, New York: Oxford University Press.

Thurow, L. C. (1992), *Head to Head: The Coming Economic Battle Among Japan, Europe and America*, New York: Morrow.

Tietenberg, T. (1985), *Emissions Trading: An Exercise in Reforming Pollution Policy*, Resources for the Future: Washington, DC.

Tietenberg, T. (1992), *Environmental and Natural Resource Economics*, 3rd ed, New York: Harper Collins.

Tietenberg, T. and D. G. Victor (1994), 'Possible Administrative Structures and Procedures (For Implementing a Tradable Entitlement Approach to Controlling Global Warming)', in UNCTD, *Controlling Global Warming: Possible Rules, Regulations and Administrative Arrangements for a Global Market in CO_2 Emission Entitlements*, Part 1, United Nations Conference on Trade and Development (UNCTD), Geneva.

Tietenberg, T. (1995), *Environmental and Natural Resource Economics*, 4th Edition, New York: Harper Collins.

Tietenberg, T., M. Grubb, B. Swift. A. Michaelowa, Z. X. Zhang and F. T. Joshua (1998), *Greenhouse Gas Emissions Trading: Defining the Principles, Modalities, Rules and Guidelines for Verification, Reporting and Accountability*, United Nations Conference on Trade and Development, Geneva.

Tietenberg, T. (1999), 'Disclosure Strategies for Pollution Control', in Sterner, T. (ed), *The Market and the Environment*, Cheltenham, UK: Edward Elgar.

Tirole, J. (1992), 'Collusion and the Theory of Organizations', in Laffont J-J. (ed), *Advances in Economic Theory: Sixth World Congress*, Vol. 2 Econometric Society Monograph 21, Cambridge, UK: Cambridge University Press.

Tol, R. S. J. (1999), 'Kyoto, Efficiency, and Cost-Effectiveness: Applications of FUND', in Weyant, J. P. (ed), *The Costs of the Kyoto Protocol: A multi-model evaluation*, The Energy Journal, Kyoto Special Edition, pp. 131–156.

Toman, M. A. and S. M. Gardiner (1991), 'The Limits of Economic Instruments for International Greenhouse Gas Control', Discussion Paper ENR92-06, Resources for the Future, Energy and Natural Resources Division, Washington, DC.

Tulpulé, V., S. Brown, J. Lim, C. Polidano, H. Pant and B. S. Fisher (1999), 'The Kyoto Protocol: An Economic Analysis Using GTEM', in Weyant, J. P. (ed), *The Costs of the Kyoto Protocol: A multi-model evaluation*, The Energy Journal, Kyoto Special Edition.

Tyson, L. (1992), *Who's Bashing Whom: Trade Conflict in High-Technology Industries*, Washington, DC: Institute for International Economics.

United Nations Environment Programme (UNEP), Organization for Co-Operation and Development (OECD), International Energy Agency (IEA), Intergovernmental Panel on Climate Change (IPCC) (1997), *Revised 1996*

Guidelines for National Greenhouse Gas Inventories. Bracknell, UK: IPCC.

UNFCCC (1992), 'United Nations Framework Convention on Climate Change', UNFCCC Secretariat, Bonn, Germany.

UNFCCC (1995a), 'Review of First Communications from the Parties Included in Annex I to the Convention (Decision 2/CP.1)', UNFCC Secretariat, Bonn, Germany.

UNFCCC (1995b), 'Report on the Conference of the Parties on its First Session, Berlin, 28 March–7 April 1995. Addendum, Part II, Action Taken by the Conference of the Parities at its First Session', (FCCC/CP/1995/7/Add.1), UNFCCC Secretariat, Bonn, Germany.

UNFCCC (1995c), Decision 5/CP.1: Activities Implemented Jointly under the Pilot Phase, FCCC/CP/1995/7/Add.1, UNFCCC Secretariat, Bonn, Germany.

UNFCCC (1996a), 'Communications from Parties Included in Annex I to the Convention: Guidelines, Schedule and Process for Consideration (Decision 9/CP.2)', UNFCCC Secretariat, Bonn, Germany.

UNFCCC (1996b), 'Review of the Implementation of the Convention and of Decisions of the First Conference of the Parties, Commitments in Article 4: Second compilation and synthesis of the first national communications from Annex I Parties: Executive Summary' (FCCC/CP/1996/12/Add.2), UNFCCC Secretariat, Bonn, Germany.

UNFCCC (1997), 'The Kyoto Protocol to the United Nations Framework Convention on Climate Change', UNFCCC Secretariat, Bonn, Germany.

UNFCCC (1998), 'Kyoto Protocol to the United Nations Framework Convention on Climate Change', UNFCCC Secretariat, Bonn, Germany.

UNFCCC (1999a), 'National Communications from Parties Included in Annex I to the Convention: Work Programme on Methodological Issues Related to Articles 5, 7 and 8 of the Kyoto Protocol. April 16' (FCCC/SB/1999/2), UNFCCC Secretariat, Bonn, Germany.

UNFCCC (1999b), 'National Communications from Parties Included in Annex I to the Convention: Guidelines for the Preparation of National Communications: Draft Conclusions by the Chairman. June 8' (FCCC/SBSTA/1999/L.5), UNFCCC Secretariat, Bonn, Germany.

UNFCCC (1999c), 'National Communications from Parties Included in Annex I to the Convention: Guidelines for the Technical Review of Greenhouse Gas Inventories: Draft Guidelines for the Technical Review of Annex I Parties' Greenhouse Gas Inventories (Greenhouse Gas Review Guidelines): Note by the Secretariat. September 1', (FCCC/SBI/1999/13), UNFCCC Secretariat, Bonn, Germany.

UNFCCC (1999d), 'Methodological Issues: Characteristics of National Systems and Issues Relating to Adjustments Referred to in Article 5 of the Kyoto Protocol: Submissions from Parties: Note by the Secretariat. September 8' (FCCC/SBSTA/1999/MISC.9), UNFCCC Secretariat, Bonn, Germany.

UNFCCC (1999e), 'Mechanisms Pursuant to Articles 6, 12 and 17 of the Kyoto Protocol. Synthesis of proposals by Parties on principles, modalities, rules and guidelines', Note by the Chairman, FCCC/SB/1999/8, UNFCCC Secretariat, Bonn, Germany.

US Congress (1992), *Energy Policy Act of 1992*, P.L. 102-486, Section 1605(b), October 24.

United States Department of Energy, Energy Information Administration (1997), *Emissions of Greenhouse Gases in the United States 1996*, Pittsburgh, PA: US Government Printing Office.

United States Department of Energy (1998), *Emissions of Greenhouse Gases in the United States 1997*, Pittsburgh, PA: US Government Printing Office.

United States Department of Energy, Energy Information Administration (1996), *Petroleum Supply Annual.*

United States Department of Energy, Energy Information Administration (1997a), 'Coal Production Industry Profile', Unpublished Report.

United States Department of Energy, Energy Information Administration (1997b), 'Oil and Gas Production Industry Profile', Unpublished Report.

United States Environment Protection Agency (1994a), 'The Allowance Tracking System: Accounting for SO_2 Allowances under the Acid Rain Program', EPA 430-F-94-002, United States Environmental Protection Agency.

United States Environmental Protection Agency (1994b), 'The Allowance Tracking System: An Introduction for Authorized Account Representatives', EPA 430-F-94-001, United States Environmental Protection Agency.

US Environmental Protection Agency (1999), 'Inventory of US Greenhouse Gas Emissions and Sinks 1990–1997', US Environmental Protection Agency.

United States Government Accounting Office (1986), 'Vehicle Emissions - EPA Program to Assist Leaded-Gasoline Producers Needs Prompt Improvement', Report to the Chairman, Subcommittee on Oversight and Investigations, Committee on Energy and Commerce, House of Representatives, GAO/RCED-86-182, United States Government Accounting Office.

Varian, H. R. (1990), 'Monitoring Agents with Other Agents', *Journal of Institutional and Theoretical Economics*, **146**, 153–174.

Victor, D., K. Raustiala and E. Skolnikoff (1998), *The Implementation and Effectiveness of International Environmental Commitments*, Cambridge, MA: MIT Press.

Vincent, J. R. and E. Strukova (1998), 'Carbon Sequestration Costs in Russian Forests', Institute for International Development, Harvard University. Draft.

Watson, R. T., M. C. Zinyowera, R. H. Moss and D. J. Dokken (1996), *Climate Change 1995: Impacts, Adaptations and Mitigation of Climate Change: Scientific-Technical Analyses. Contribution of Working Group II to the Second Assessment Report of the Intergovernmental Panel on Climate Change (IPCC)* New York: Cambridge University Press.

Weitzman, M. L. (1974), 'Prices vs. Quantities', *Review of Economic Studies*, **41**, 447–491

Werksman, J. (1996), 'Designing a Compliance System for the UN Framework Convention', in Cameron, J., J. Werksman and P. Roderick (eds), *Improving Compliance with International Environmental Law*, London: Earthscan Publications.

Werksman, J. (1999), 'Responding to Non-Compliance under the Climate Change Regime', OECD Information Paper, Paris.

Westkog, H. (1996), 'Market Power in a System of Tradable CO_2 Quotas', *The Energy Journal*, **17** (3), 85–103.

Weyant, J. P. (1999), *The Costs of the Kyoto Protocol: A multi-model evaluation*, The Energy Journal, Kyoto Special Edition.

Weyant, J. P. and J. N. Hill (1999), 'Introduction and overview', in Weyant, J. P. (ed), *The Costs of the Kyoto Protocol: A multi-model evaluation*, The Energy Journal, Kyoto Special Edition, pp. vii–xiv.

Williams, R. (1999), 'Government vs. Private Sector Roles', Presentation at the Annex I Trading Dialogue Group, Leiden.

Willems, S. (1999), 'Key features of domestic monitoring systems under the Kyoto Protocol', OECD Information Paper, Paris.

Williamson, Oliver E. (1985), *The Economic Institutions of Capitalism: Firms, Markets, Relational Contracting*, New York: The Free Press.

Yamin, F. (1996), 'The Use of Joint Implementation to Increase Compliance with the Climate Change Convention', in Cameron, J., J. Werksman and P. Roderick (eds), *Improving Compliance with International Environmental Law*, London: Earthscan Publications.

Yamin, F. and J. Lefevere (2000), 'Designing Options for Implementing an Emissions Trading Regime for Greenhouse Gases in the European Community', Report to the European Commission DG Environment,

Foundation of International and Environmental Law and Development (FIELD), London

Young, Oran R. (1994), *International Governance: Protecting the Environment in a Stateless Society*, Ithaca and London: Cornell University Press.

Young, M., P. Lee, K. Lack, D. Hemming and H. Musdilak (1998), *Greenhouse Trading: An Operational Specification for the Phased Introduction of a Nation-Wide Greenhouse Gas Emissions Trading Network for Australia*, New South Wales Department of Energy, Sydney.

Zhang, Z. X. (1998a), 'Towards a Successful International Greenhouse Emissions Trading', Faculty of Law and Faculty of Economics, University of Groningen. Draft.

Zhang, Z. X. (1998b), 'Greenhouse Gas Emissions Trading and the World Trading System', *Journal of World Trade*, **32** (5).

Zylicz, T. (1999), 'Towards tradability of pollution permits in Poland', in S. Sorrell and J. Skea (eds), *Pollution for Sale: Emissions Trading and Joint Implementation*, Cheltenham, UK: Edward Elgar, pp. 124–138.

Author Index

Subject Index